e
pa

volume 3

eric
parry architects

Artifice

Paul Delvaux,
La Ville inquiète, 1941,
private collection.

Introduction
Dalibor Vesely

"To avoid the meaninglessness of the contemporary city it is not necessary to search for some ideal order in the pre-industrial past. It is possible to start from the given reality of any existing city and to discover, in most of them, a residuum of tradition sufficient to support a consistent, imaginative and sometimes even radical reinterpretation of the status quo." – Dalibor Vesely, "Introduction" in *Architecture and Continuity* (Architectural Association, 1982).

The recent projects of Eric Parry Architects (EPA) presented in this volume are situated, with only two exceptions, in London. This defines to a great extent not only the dominating nature of the projects, but also the intention to address their location as the problem of their urbanity. What is the urbanity of London? This is a question that cannot be ignored if we want to understand the nature and the intentions behind the projects.

London has a complex and sometimes rather confusing topography, and by implication urbanity, that can be read horizontally and vertically. On the horizontal level the topography of London represents a mosaic of areas, defined originally by the duality of the City of London and the area around Westminster. The first stage of growth led to the development in the space between the City of London and Westminster (Strand and later Covent Garden) and the extension to the west and north (St James and Mayfair). The current topography of London as a whole is a result of a development that took place around existing manor houses, estates, villages or main roads. However, regardless of their origin there is a surprising sense of identity in most parts of London that does not always follow the boundary of more recent boroughs. The identity seems to be more closely linked with the memory and long-term tradition of belonging to a particular part of the city. The borough of Westminster, where most of EPA's projects are situated, is a good illustration of the ambiguous nature of identity, which is related, in a broad sense, to a particular place, but at the same time transcends it. The phenomenon of transcendence opens the second, the vertical reading of urbanity.

In that vertical reading we discover that the question and understanding of urbanity cannot be reduced to the reading of the physical body (fabric) of the city, but should be read rather as an institution, situated always in a context of culture. In conventional understanding institutions are associated with social, political or cultural phenomena, and yet we should not forget that institutions are situated always somewhere, in a particular place. The family asks for a home; local government for a town hall or some form of office space, etc. The fabric of the city has no meaning in itself. It is only the embodiment of the city as an institution that gives it meaning. This may help us to understand better the vertical depth of urbanity and answer some of the more difficult questions in recent urban development: for instance, the 'Manhattanisation' of cities in the developing world; or why even London is proud to have the tallest building in Europe; or why Germany needed to transfer the capital city back to Berlin. The power of institutional thinking has its roots in squares, gardens, parks, etc., elevated into institutions. Situations have the capacity to accumulate experience that endows them with a high level of durability in relation to which a whole sequence of other experiences do acquire meaning and as a result constitute a continuum of history rooted on the deepest level in myth, or more precisely in a mytho-poetic dimension of mythology. We may remember that modern mythology is a sister of ideology. This can help us understand the nature of such places as Trafalgar Square, where the project for St Martin-in-the-Fields is situated. It is quite obvious that no amount of investigations of individual buildings will tell us about the identity of the place, its symbolic, microcosmic representation of the British Empire and the mythology that surrounds the place and how it is re-enacted in public celebrations and demonstrations. It is only in the depth of the vertical reading of the square, seen as a typical situation or institution, that we can discover its true urbanity.

This brings us to the point where it may be appropriate to say a few words about the nature of urbanity as it is seen by EPA in their projects. Their vision coincides with the notion of coexistence manifested as sharing in contrast to consumption. The example of Trafalgar Square in its relation to Whitehall and government buildings on one side and Leicester Square and Covent Garden on the other, illustrates a contradiction as the main characteristics of the current state of urbanism. The contradiction of sharing and consumption is based on a deeper contradiction of participation and appropriation, manifested in the everyday life as a contradiction between civilised existence and its commercialisation.

Listening to music, visiting museums and exhibitions, or friends, and taking creative part in the everyday life of the city are examples of sharing. Take the same activities as means for making money and we are dealing with commerce and consumption. EPA's thinking is realistic enough to know that there is room for commerce and that we all have to consume. This is silently understood and accepted. What may not be accepted is the understanding, or rather and more often, a misunderstanding, of the relation of means and goals. Do we live to make money or make money for the sake of a better life? This is a problem that became in our time a deep dilemma clearly apparent in the projects in Savile Row and New Bond Street. Architects themselves cannot resolve the dilemma, but they face it and can create conditions that may contribute to its resolution. The creation of such conditions is the intention behind most of EPA's projects.

The intention is based on the knowledge of architectural and urban history that illustrates the tension and very often a conflict between the civic and commercial interests. The case of the Medici in Florence at the time of the Renaissance, the preference of civic values in Nuremberg in the time of Dürer in contrast with the commercial interests of the Fugger bank empire in Augsburg at the same time, or the emergence of the nouveaux riches in conflict with the French culture of the seventeenth century shows that our current dilemma has a long history. However, it is important to realise that until the late-eighteenth century cities always succeeded in the end in subordinating the commercial to the civic values and interests. This can be brought to a conclusion that the respect of civic values and the degree of participation and sharing coincides with the degree of urbanity and the civilising power of the city. Such a conclusion is possible if we do not take as a reference the current state of affairs, but a longer view of urban history.

The longer view can help to form a more relevant and realistic vision of architecture and its role in the life of the city. Eric Parry had the opportunity to form such a vision in his Diploma project at the Architectural Association (1978–1980). In that project he established for himself the main principles of urban design and the role of architecture in such design. One of the first principles was to identify and work with the difference between the nature of architecture and the city.

Architecture is by its very nature in the hands of an individual or a small group of people, whose experience, knowledge and talent define the quality of the results. A city is fundamentally different; it was, and in most cases still is, in the hands of generations of people of whom only a few were architects. We cannot understand the experience, knowledge and talent invested in the making of cities directly but only as results. This is a problem that asks for a different way of thinking, based on a deep respect for all that has been achieved in particular areas of design and can be creatively interpreted. The history of the work illustrates the nature and possibilities of such interpretation. The key to the interpretation is the creative vision of architecture and its role in the life of the city. Because it defines the nature of most of the projects the vision deserves a more detailed description.

Its main, critical element is the urban street where things are constantly changing, people are coming and moving away, shops are changing hands, old buildings are demolished and new ones are built, etc. And yet the street remains preserved very often for generations. This is the virtue and power of institutions that we have discussed earlier. Their continuity in time as a source of genuine cultural creativity is still not sufficiently appreciated.

View of the new rooftop Spa of the Four Seasons Hotel, which has an axial view north along Park Lane and with Hyde Park Corner lying behind.

left: Hélène Binet's photograph of the Holburne Museum with the reconnected axis to Great Pulteney Street and the rear galleries in the setting of Sydney Gardens.

right: René Magritte, *L'Empire des lumières*, 1947, private collection.

It is one of nearly 20 versions Magritte painted of the realm between dream and consciousness.

The identity of the street and its continuity in time has its roots in the natural conditions of its own history, and it is equally important that it cannot be treated as an isolated element, but only as part of the situational structure of the city as a whole where the street plays a mediating role. It mediates between individual buildings by creating a space they can share. The mediation continues usually in a hierarchical sequence from the street to urban segment to district or quarter and finally the city as a whole. There is a close link between the hierarchical sequence of mediation and the phenomenon of sharing. We share that which is common, what we can participate in and what is equally accessible. This defines a natural tendency towards centrality where what is most common is usually situated.

The sequence or pattern of streets defines the boundary of the perimeter enclosure, described conventionally as a block. The boundary of the perimeter divides the city into its exterior and interior. This is reflected in the spatial organisation of most European cities, where places are located in relation to their purpose either outside or inside in a differentiated sequence that represents different conditions, appropriate for shops, agencies, restaurants or cafés on the street, workshops or studios in the secondary streets and courtyards, intimate space in the gardens, etc. The development of the urban interior reached its most exemplary form in Parisian passages, which Louis Aragon describes in "Le Passage de l'Opéra" in his *Paris Peasant* (1926) as the "gateway to mystery". The movement into the horizontal depth of the city is a background that may explain some of the intricacies of the urban interior of the 23 Savile Row project.

However, cities have their interior not only on the horizontal level, but also on a vertical one. A good example is the subterranean world in St Martin-in-the-Fields, separated from the main street and the paved surface on the ground level and yet only a step away from the life on the street. A similar example of an urban interior is the Spa on the top level of the Four Seasons Hotel. Both contribute, though in different degrees, to the urbanity of London. This may not sound convincing, but we have to reconsider the nature and meaning of urbanity and what it represents today. Following our earlier discussion about the relation between the degree of sharing and the degree of urbanity, we can see the projects as representing not one, but several different degrees of urbanity that are interconnected. The most explicit example of a contribution to the partly existing and partly possible enhancement of the urbanity of a place is the case of St Martin's. The entry glass pavilion serves as a mediating link between the open space of Trafalgar Square, the axis of Charing Cross Road, and the Church Path, and turns their visible presence into a vertical communication with the foyer on the level below.

The light, scale, the material treatment and the visual communication with the world above gives the foyer, fully accessible to the public, a character of a quasi exterior. This is reinforced by the presence of the Dick Sheppard Chapel at the east end of the intervention. In the rest of the subterranean space (world) there are community rooms, one for the Chinese community, a music rehearsal room and service rooms (kitchen, storage, etc.). The density of the underground space and its main purpose, the welfare of the homeless, make the whole complex a wonderful illustration of what an urban interior can be and how much it can contribute to the public life of the urban exterior on the street level.

As a contrast, the 23 Savile Row and 50 New Bond Street buildings represent a very different kind of urbanity. In both cases the large volume of open floor space, anticipating rather unpredictable commercial use, is defined on its perimeter by elaborate, carefully designed elevations. Using different materials and spatial arrangements, the elevations bring together the virtual depth of the buildings and their external physiognomy as a contribution to the overall character of the existing streets. It is difficult to see how much the virtual depth of the buildings and their use will contribute to the life of the city and how much the buildings will participate only passively in the city's civic life, created and cultivated elsewhere.

This is a question that can be answered by a better understanding of the different levels of civic life and the corresponding degree of urbanity. An example will illustrate that better. We have described earlier the urbanity of the Spa in the Four Seasons Hotel as not convincing because it is not immediately apparent, and yet it still belongs in its essence to the tradition of public bath that was always one of the most public i.e., civic, institutions. Today the Spa is only a memory of that tradition and by implication only a memory of its urbanity. Memory, the sense of civic values, our ability to participate and share, represent a potential (latent) form of urbanity, that can, under certain conditions, become actual. The potential and the actual forms of urbanity represent a reciprocity, in which the potential can become actual, while the actual keeps alive the latent presence of the potential.

This is well demonstrated in the history and project of the Holburne Museum in Bath. Originally a casino and gateway to the pleasure garden, separated from the city, the building of the casino became a private residence and collection and later a public museum, separated this time from the garden. The ambiguous nature of the museum was the point of departure for the project. The main part of the project was the extension on the garden side and the internal transformation of the existing building. Situated as a culminating point of Great Pulteney Street the museum and its collection represent a part of the city memory, and the availability of the museum for public events makes it an integral part of city life. The most important element in the scheme is the mediating role of the extension that links the museum with the garden and brings the potential urbanity of the garden into the life of the city, i.e. into the level of actual urbanity. This is achieved by a series of intelligent moves: the public and transparent nature of the café situated on the level of the garden, and the neutral, windowless treatment of the main body of the extension.

For most of EPA's work it is characteristic to resolve the main intentions of the projects on the level of details and the materiality of the buildings, where it very often meets the independently commissioned works of art. In the case of the Holburne Museum the intention to link the museum and the garden is resolved by the appeal to material imagination. The play of imagination is activated by the ceramic fins on the surface of the extension, treated in their texture and colour as a reflection of light, animated by the movement of the trees. The movement of light oscillates between the revelation of the sublime and the material, "engulfing and appropriating all that it finds in its path, fills the slice of space, or better the slice of the world that it assigns itself by its movement, making it reverberate, breathing into it its own life" (E Minkowski). This experience points to the depth of the intentions behind the project, that can be best described as the alchemy of urbanisation.

The projects in this volume differ substantially in their contribution to the civic life of the city. This is not in most cases the failure of architects. In a situation dominated by private and commercial interests and the fragmented nature of our cities, the creation of the places where the sense of civic values, creative participation and sharing can be established is very limited. And yet the civic values and the possibilities of participation and sharing are to all of us potentially available as part of our latent world mediated by history, tradition and culture. The reality of the latent world coincides with the EPA vision of architecture and its role in the life of the city, discussed earlier. It is the power of the vision that helps the office to move away from the pessimistic view of the current actual state of architecture and our cities to the appreciation of the potential urbanity based on the richness of the latent world. This is, I believe, what keeps the optimism and enthusiasm of the office alive.

Material metamorphosis, detail of Joel Shapiro's cast bronze sculpture suspended over the entrance to 23 Savile Row.

No loading
at any time
ORDOVAS
ORDOVAS

Culture, Construction, Character, Continuity
Edwin Heathcote

Corner view of Savile Row and New Burlington Place with view into the principal gallery of Hauser & Wirth.

London was historically a city of three centres. There was the trading, beating heart of the City of London, the square mile of the Roman walled city. There was the world of Westminster, with its strange cocktail of Parliament and parks and its genteel quarters of consumption and clubs, Mayfair and St James's. And there was the seamier southern side of the city, Southwark, the historic escape from the City's restrictions and codes, a place of release and abandon. Characters and moods have been juggled and rejigged; Southwark was taken over for a couple of centuries by warehouses and factories, becoming a place of work rather than entertainment, whilst the theatres emigrated up West. The guilds and markets largely abandoned the City for all but ceremonial purposes, leaving it to the hard world of finance. But, with the return of big culture to the South Bank after the Second World War and the boost given to it by the rebuilding of the Globe and the extraordinary resurrection of Tate Modern as a cathedral to the power of art rather than electricity, the three archetypal humours which have historically constituted London have remained remarkably consistent.

Finance, culture and consumption are divided, not equally, but recognisably between the constituents. This particular moment in architecture is seeing a reinforcement of those identities in intriguing ways. The West End is being slowly tarted up as the Crown Estate attempts to turn the imperial Edwardian Baroque of Regent Street into a grander version of itself capable of attracting the heavy rents of the global brands. Meanwhile Mayfair's dense grid of streets is being slowly homogenised as many of the traditional businesses, which had made it such a diverse and eccentrically satisfying place, are being replaced by a blend of hedge funds and global labels. Southwark has changed almost beyond recognition from the web of soot-stained, warehouse-lined alleys, solid industrial blocks and the brick cliffs of social housing into a pedestrianised playground of cafés and culture. It has raised its flag in the shape of the Shard, Renzo Piano's vast spire (which the architect rather disingenuously compared to a sail on a boat of the Thames in one of Canaletto's versions of the city). Southwark's marker had been the chimney of the converted Bankside power station; now it has the Shard, a tower of luxury hotels and apartments and premium rent offices–a symbol of the spread of the City.

But it is the City itself which has changed most dramatically. Its tight, complex web of Roman and medieval roads, alleys and lanes that survived so extraordinarily intact has been extruded upwards to create a strange landscape which has neither the internal logic of the grid nor the spiky electrocardiogram of Christopher Wren's skyline. Rather, its jagged, incomprehensible and constantly changing profile recalls the financial system of 'light touch regulation' that sparked the economic crisis which has formed the background to its now much-surveyed and suspected financial activity.

Model façade study for the Rothschild headquarters building in St Swithin's Lane, City of London. Proposed stone podium with ceramic weave to the tower.

model: Cast plaster over wire and timber veneer.

Despite significant efforts to create a public realm and a culture of consumption beyond office hours the City remains a distinct quarter; and its alienating towers, overweening security and the awful, bland inexpression of its endless glass façades have not realised the real urbanity we might have desired. The architecture of a city can communicate something about the attitudes and mores far more articulately than we might otherwise be able to through other media. The city says something concrete and legible about the age in which it is built, or at least in which its current condition was conceived—there is always a distance between the two in the slow world of construction. The City's disregard for an entire layer of its history—the strata of post-war reconstruction—has been revealing. Those few decades have been almost totally erased from the City yet there were plenty of serviceable, decent Modernist structures that could, with a little intelligence, have been repurposed, maintaining something of the generosity of an architecture which attempted to create the commercial infrastructure for a contemporary city whilst also leaving some space, plazas, setback slabs, slender towers. Its erasure indicates a callous disregard for the values of that era, even if the architecture and urbanism itself may have passed from fashion, it will, I think, be seen in the future as a mistake—particularly as what we are replacing these buildings with is rarely significantly better, usually just denser, newer, more lettable, more profitable.

Intriguingly OMA's New Court headquarters for the Rothschild Bank has been to some extent a homage to that era as well as a brilliant realisation of the City's Mies tower that never was, a strikingly clever piece of that seemingly oxymoronic notion—Modernist contextualism. Yet the way its conference room sits in a separate box glaring down at the Bank of England below tells us something symbolic about the way banks tower above our national institutions. The building, otherwise subtle and sophisticated, makes it quite clear who is running the show. The other problem that plagues London is expense. Westminster's property prices have exploded to the point at which only the international super-wealthy can afford to buy, its heart has become a place of mostly vacant status houses and, simultaneously, the City's traditional presumption against residential development (residents tend to complain about incessant and growing construction—and nothing can be allowed to get in the way if a bank wants to expand) has made it a curiously artificial place, a simulacrum of a city. The City remains, despite its density of history and its intensity of architectures, a central business district. Yet, despite these reservations, London remains an extraordinarily dynamic engine, a complex place capable of absorbing and digesting change on a remarkable scale and turning the force of that rapid transformation into a nutrient on which it not only survives but thrives. Whatever the architectural and structural change, the three centres have maintained a certain psychogeography, enough of the traces of history and use to preserve at least a spirit of the particular—the place. These three historic foci of the London landscape also, usefully, form the cores around which the most significant recent work of Eric Parry Architects has revolved. I hope that in exploring some of these interventions in their spatial, urban and perhaps even sociological and political contexts we may be able to extrapolate some ideas which form the basis of the practice's praxis and of Eric Parry's profound interest in and empathy and engagement with place.

The Southwark Gateway was amongst the smallest of all of these but, partly due to its timing (at the beginning of the transformation of the area into a cultural as well as a fledgling business centre) but also partly due to its prominent position on the messy southern side of London Bridge, has become a critical intervention in the complex, cluttered cityscape. I don't intend to cover this project at any length—as it has already been written about in *Eric Parry Architects: Volume 1* of this series—but it is worth revisiting as I think it has prefigured some other developments in the immediate area as well as predicting and foreshadowing some other concerns which will become clear in the projects more pertinent to us here.

First, and most visible of these, is the spiky, Expressionist form of the urban marker which creates the most visible identity of the intervention. The single, slanting-but-more-or-less-vertical spike cannot help but presage the vast form of Renzo Piano's Shard, which has since burst out of the skyline behind it. Conceived and executed before the turn of the millennium that gave the area such renewed impetus, this small but intriguing programme of new public space now seems to foreshadow much of what has taken place around it. The original environs were a shocking mess of concrete and municipal neglect, a traffic-planning collision of ramps and scraggy grass, tunnels and undercrofts, busy incomprehensible crossings and air pollution; a perfect illustration of the problems encountered by a well-meaning modernity in the replanning of a city to cater for cars and not people. Eric Parry Architects' interventions embraced the strange nature of this patch of dysfunctional city as a place of railways—both buried and elevated, of deep archaeology, of a kind of London urban chaos unthinkable in the centre of, say, Paris or Copenhagen. In straddling the subterranean, the sculptural, the urbane and the neglected public realm, the project began, in the humblest of terms, to address the issues which would crop up again in projects including St Martin-in-the-Fields and the Leathersellers' Hall, where the confluence of a vertically layered city, an unreadable public realm and the incessant flows of foot traffic create particular conditions which could potentially animate each other but more usually agitate against one another. It is a kind of stitching together of the sectional city.

I came to Eric Parry's oeuvre through a book which still sits above my desk (looking well-thumbed and a little tatty), an AA publication entitled *Architecture and Continuity*, published in 1982. It features the work of AA students in exploring urban themes around an unglamorous but archetypally London section of railway and former industrial land in Kentish Town. Parry's contributions are a series of exquisitely executed pencil drawings which evoke a complex sectional city, a vertical realm of real rooms and dark volumes excavated from within the heart of the urban fabric. They are firmly dated with their emphasis on the necropolis brief—they were a big thing back then—but I was transfixed by these drawings. I studied during the mid-1980s when the emphasis was on theory, on façade and on deconstruction, an increasing abstraction of actual space, and these kinds of carefully rendered sections were no longer particularly fashionable. Yet they pointed me towards an articulate manner of expressing the dense and intense 'cityness' of a particular architecture which interested me. Although the schemes themselves might seem rather fanciful in a Borgesian or Rossi-esque manner (an urban forum, a necropolis and so on), it seems to me that the concerns illustrated in Parry's delicate drawings are still those that drive his practice in the contemporary city. In severe contrast to a generation of contemporaries (whose work is now highly visible around Southwark and in the City), Parry has not succumbed to the easy temptation of the icon or of the façade as a superficial mask to conceal a generic commercial interior. This corner of London, between bridge and Cathedral, Borough Market and the unsatisfactory but intriguing layer of post-war modernity, presents a compelling model for intervention in London as an act of surgical but also archaeological skill, a blend of the organic nature of the living city and the museographical act of excavating into its fabric.

A few steps away, over the once-inhabited London Bridge and into the City, we find the nexus of Eric Parry Architects' newer works. From Aldermanbury and Finsbury Squares in the north (both profiled in detail in *Volume 1* and *Volume 2*) and Paternoster Square in the south to 60 Threadneedle Street and the proposals for Gresham Street in the heart of the City, there is a significant body of work here which rewards attention, as it questions the prevailing approach to the City that treats it as a site for self-conscious towers and monuments, where architecture is more concerned with the creation of a logo than it is about the creation of a place.

Perhaps the most interesting occurrence in and around Eric Parry Architects' buildings in recent times has been the strange concentration of the City's developing sites of protest. Whilst there is obviously nothing intentional here, the extraordinary coincidence of their building at Paternoster Square (designed as a speculative development) being designated the City's new stock exchange and of the firm's 60 Threadneedle Street being built on the site of the now demolished original stock exchange creates one particular history of a dialogue between two sites of trading at the centre of the discussions about London's reliance on the vagaries of finance. But perhaps more interesting even than that accidental history is the manner in which anti-capitalist protestors and those inspired by the Occupy Wall Street movement have chosen to inhabit the sites of the practice's key interventions.

In October 2011 protestors attempted to set up a camp outside the London Stock Exchange in Paternoster Square, part of a global movement of protest against big finance. They were not able to because it transpired that the public square at the heart of the scheme was not public at all but actually belonged to the Mitsubishi Estate Co. This was a revealing piece of news which said much about the condition of civic space in the contemporary city. Major developments are given planning permission in part because of agreements to provide public spaces—planning gains—in return for increased floor area or height. When it transpires that those spaces are not public at all, the whole system of trade-offs is brought into question. I remember vividly chatting to a quietly incandescent Parry who that morning had been wandering through a development in London's Docklands and had been stopped from taking a photo by a uniformed security guard who told him this was not public land. A day earlier I had also been asked to stop photographing buildings (in Southwark) and was only a few days ago told to stop making a sound recording on a completely public street. It is the kind of sinister encounter which is slowly but ineluctably altering the democratic nature of the shared city.

The story of Paternoster Square in particular—with its dense history of publishing, of destruction, of Modernist rebuilding and of interventions from the Prince of Wales and its subsequent classicalisation—deserves a book by itself, but it is nevertheless a compelling representation of the nature of modern development, its compromises and its half-truths. These kinds of developments are sold to the city and its citizens as having public space at their heart. These squares and streets are, we are told, a public gain. But when they are tested, as they were by the Occupy London protestors, they are found to fail in their civic role.

View of the corner of 60 Threadneedle Street from the new eastern passage.

Prunella Clough, *In Half Light*, 1998. Late work by the much-admired artist, niece of Eileen Gray and conjurer of the everyday.

They turn out to be not public at all but extensions of the corporate interior realm. They are outdoor office lobbies patrolled by security guards and policed by a publicly funded police force whose real job, as ever, is to protect private property above public rights. Thus, the building that was the target for the protestors, Eric Parry Architects' speculative offices, which had been taken on by the London Stock Exchange, was found to be inaccessible and the protestors moved across the road to the nearest accessible accommodating open space, which happened to be the precincts of St Paul's Cathedral. For the next four months, until an injunction was granted against them, the City was treated to the unusual and counterintuitive sight of protestors against the power and influence of global finance camping out not in the City but outside the Cathedral. In a way, the odd site chimed with the ill-defined targets of the protest, which was less against a particular institution and more concerned with providing a visible symbol of disaffection with the system itself. Those few months provided a stunning spectacle, the juxtaposition of the ragged tent city and its emerging institutions with the huge mass of the City's most famous landmark. They also constituted a fine illustration of the inadequacy of public space as a space open to appropriation—the Cathedral (or at least its precincts) opened up—as in the old Nolli plan of Rome—as the city's default public space of participation.

Curiously, London's other site of outdoor occupation was (it still was at the time of writing—by now it is long gone) Finsbury Square. Here the protestors met with more success, the curious central bowling green creating a perfect place for encampment—more akin to New York's Zucotti Park (which, it transpired was also a private space though the owners let the protestors stay), a fringe site outside the northern edge of the City. Overlooking it all is Eric Parry Architects' 30 Finsbury Square, sitting stonily silent. I suppose there is not much beyond coincidence in this history of occupation and protest (certainly I can't find anything specific in Parry's designs which encourages it) but there is a sense in which the recent crisis in capitalism and the protests which have greeted it have made it impossible to pretend that there can be such a thing as a neutral building, a purely speculative piece of depoliticised real estate. In fact quite the opposite, every act of construction in the City is a political act in some small way and we should not easily forget it. The political nature of the building might only be in how its elevation addresses the street or the public arena in front of it—but far from being a superficial act this is perhaps one of the most profound facets of an architecture of civic engagement. If I say that 30 Finsbury Square is a building which is all about a façade—it seems to apply a kind of minimal engagement with surface, an idea of façadism which would be totally false. In fact, what this particular building did was to introduce a depth into the façade (combined with a visible structural strength rebutting the idea of an applied skin) which creates a zone between the public and the private and a level of subtlety or ambiguity in the distinction between the two. The rise of the icon in the City architecture has led to a particular architecture of shape. These glass-clad forms sheath their shapes as their smoothness emphasises a reflective banality just as it does a faux transparency.

The interface between outside and in, between public and private, is invariably left to a glazed screen, and that glass does not create porosity but rather an alienating sense of exclusion. Eric Parry Architects' architecture in the City strives against this easy classification, creating instead a more playful and sophisticated differentiation between the zones, an architecture in which the section through the elevation is one of complexity, of light and shadow. 60 Threadneedle Street and 5 Aldermanbury Square share the same sense of engagement with the street, the pillars or columns, the glass as it winds its way through the elevations on Threadneedle Street, the curving, projecting fins, the stainless steel-clad, Chicago-inflected Aldermanbury and the little plaza created by setting the building back; each creates a little civic breathing space.

The conditions of the City of London are extremely particular. The combination of raw economic energy and a kind of disregard for civic space, the sheer value of real estate, the lack of a residential population and infrastructure, and a long history which has left traces through every layer of its construction makes a very unusual environment for building. Eric Parry Architects have managed to make a substantial contribution to that fabric, and two forthcoming projects are reinforcing that history of intervention. Most characteristic is the Leathersellers' Hall, situated in the long urban room of St Helen's Place, a kind of Uffizzi-like classical corridor, which generates a compelling, theatrical perspective.

In the West End too, Eric Parry Architects' architecture has both reflected and prefigured the subtly changing character of Mayfair and St James's. Substantial developments including 50 New Bond Street and 23 Savile Row have made a real impact on Mayfair's streetscape, but their contextual language, their ability to absorb the characters of their surroundings whilst still proposing something new and striking, is unusual and commendable.

50 Bond Street picks up on the exuberant Edwardiana of the area, much of it developed in a moment in which London developed a freestyle architecture that played with Queen Anne, with Art Nouveau, Arts and Crafts and with the bombast of municipal grandiosity. The glazed green façade and the bowed windows evoke the delicate displays of the arcades which are such a notable architectural feature of the surrounding streets. They also suggest a subtle interplay happening within the depth of the façade, in which glass is used for display—pushed out beyond the plane of the elevation and into the realm of the street just as bow windows once were—as if the building could barely contain its commerce and was bulging out. In Savile Row the blend of gallery space and premium-grade commercial offices exemplifies two significant strands of Mayfair's commercial character, art and hedge funds, each impinging on the world of the other as the money made in markets fuels the market which has seen London rise as the centre of the art trade. At Savile Row Eric Parry Architects have built on the language of post-war conservative Modernism, the London version of post-Deco solidity. Yet the building allows Joel Shapiro's wonderful work to introduce a note of caution, a visual instability and tension as the huge bronze pieces are suspended precariously above the entrance. These worlds too, despite their wealth, suffer from the insecurities of an inherently unstable financial system.

There are reasons to be cautious about the directions in London's development, but more than any changes in its physical fabric it is perhaps the growing disparity between the wealthy and the rest which gives us most concern in the contemporary city. Mayfair was once bounded by seedier quarters, Soho and Shepherd Market, and by areas defined by production or the rag trade, like Fitzrovia. Now it is becoming a monoculture of consumption for the global super-rich. The City meanwhile may be trying to diversify, to attract back something of the trade and the retail which once made it such a vibrant place, but the shops it is attracting only seem to amplify the sense of a culture of cloned consumption, the chain stores familiar from every high street in the country. Southwark might be appearing to stand out with its artisanal market and its mix of makers, designers and studios, but the Shard is a grim omen of real-estate inflation, the first stake in the ground setting out a new era of property speculation even amidst the longest recession the City has ever seen.

Architecture can and is illustrating these shifts, but Eric Parry's work continues to reflect on the established nature of the particular. He himself is keen on the word 'simultaneity'—the idea that uses, histories and appropriations in the city can create striking and surprising juxtapositions just as they can, oddly, create moments of extraordinary beauty and unexpected harmony as the city begins to gel into something that makes real sense. If you take a Parry building out of its context you could almost begin to rebuild an idea of its physical surrounding in a forensic manner, building up a picture of a place which might not be accurate but would certainly be intriguing, a metafiction of place. These are buildings that feel appropriate—even as they may sometimes be genuinely surprising. In the deep green glazed ceramics of 50 Bond Street you can detect a whiff of the dandified shop displays and the Edwardian exuberance of a silk waistcoat or cravat. In the structural stonework of Finsbury Square you can divine the seriously solid centre of the insurance industry, an industry built on trust. In Threadneedle Street you can get a sense of the dynamic sweep of the markets refracted through an echo of the curving walls of the Bank of England. In the glass pavilions outside St Martin-in-the-Fields you get an intimation of the illumination of a subterranean landscape of deep history and a contemporary reflection on the baroque of Gibbs's church. This is an *architecture parlante*, an inventive oeuvre which speaks of its moment and of its history. It is a difficult thing to achieve, and few architects can do it well.

When it is done, as Parry has been doing it, it creates an architecture of enhancement of the small moments in a city in which we encounter something that is simultaneously surprising and familiar, new layers communicating with the layers that have come before it, the layers that stand beside it and the people who walk past them or use them every day. I remember a student in a crit I was in one day telling the assembled audience that his building "set up a dialogue with the city". "And what", the dry old tutor asked "did the city say?" It stuck with me as a mental picture, and I think Eric Parry's office has managed to form an answer. It has created an architecture which has subtly and generously enriched London's streetscape. The city, I would think, doesn't say much in reply, but just continues on, quietly satisfied.

Installation view, Venice Biennale 2012. The Biennale theme was Common Ground. In our case, architecture as host to art, with the two projects exhibited, St Martin-in-the-Fields and the gateway to St James's, One Eagle Place, Piccadilly.

City of Westminster

In this volume, with the exception of the Holburne Museum in Bath, and Iringan Hijau in Kuala Lumpur, all the projects are set in the topography of either the City of London or the City of Westminster—two interdependent, but Janus-headed, parts of the same city.

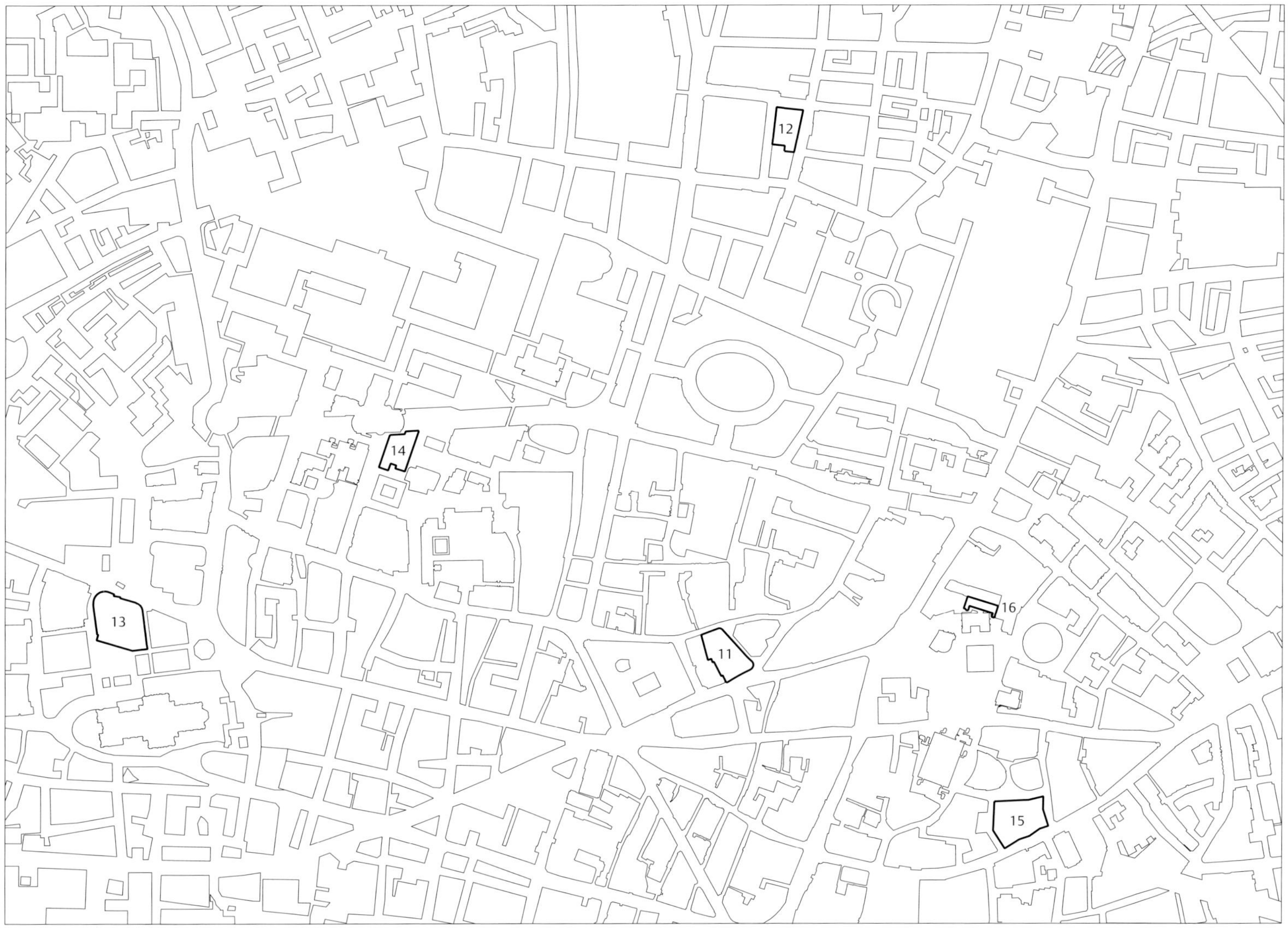

1 St Martin-in-the-Fields
2 23 Savile Row
3 50 New Bond Street
4 Timothy Taylor Gallery
5 26 Albemarle Street
6 Four Seasons Hotel Spa
7 Selfridges Entrance
8 St James's Square
9 One Eagle Place and 15 and 20 Jermyn Street
10 Sebastian + Barquet
11 60 Threadneedle Street
12 30 Finsbury Square
13 London Stock Exchange
14 5 Aldermanbury Square
15 120 Fenchurch Street
16 Leathersellers', St Helen's Place

City of London

e
pa

volume 3

Contents

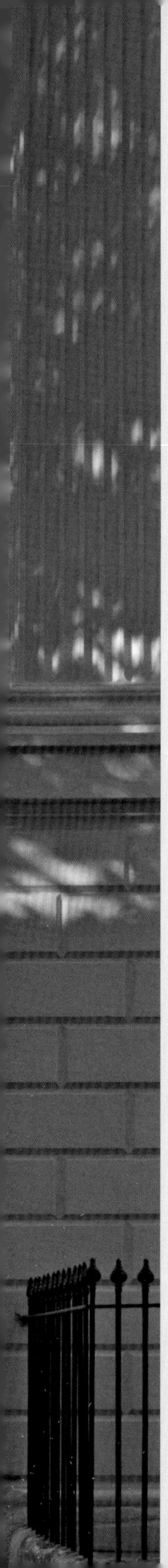

St Martin-in-the-Fields

Cities have their interior not only on the horizontal level, but also on a vertical one. A good example is the subterranean world of St Martin-in-the-Fields, separated from the main street and the paved surface on the ground level, and yet only a step away from the life on the street.

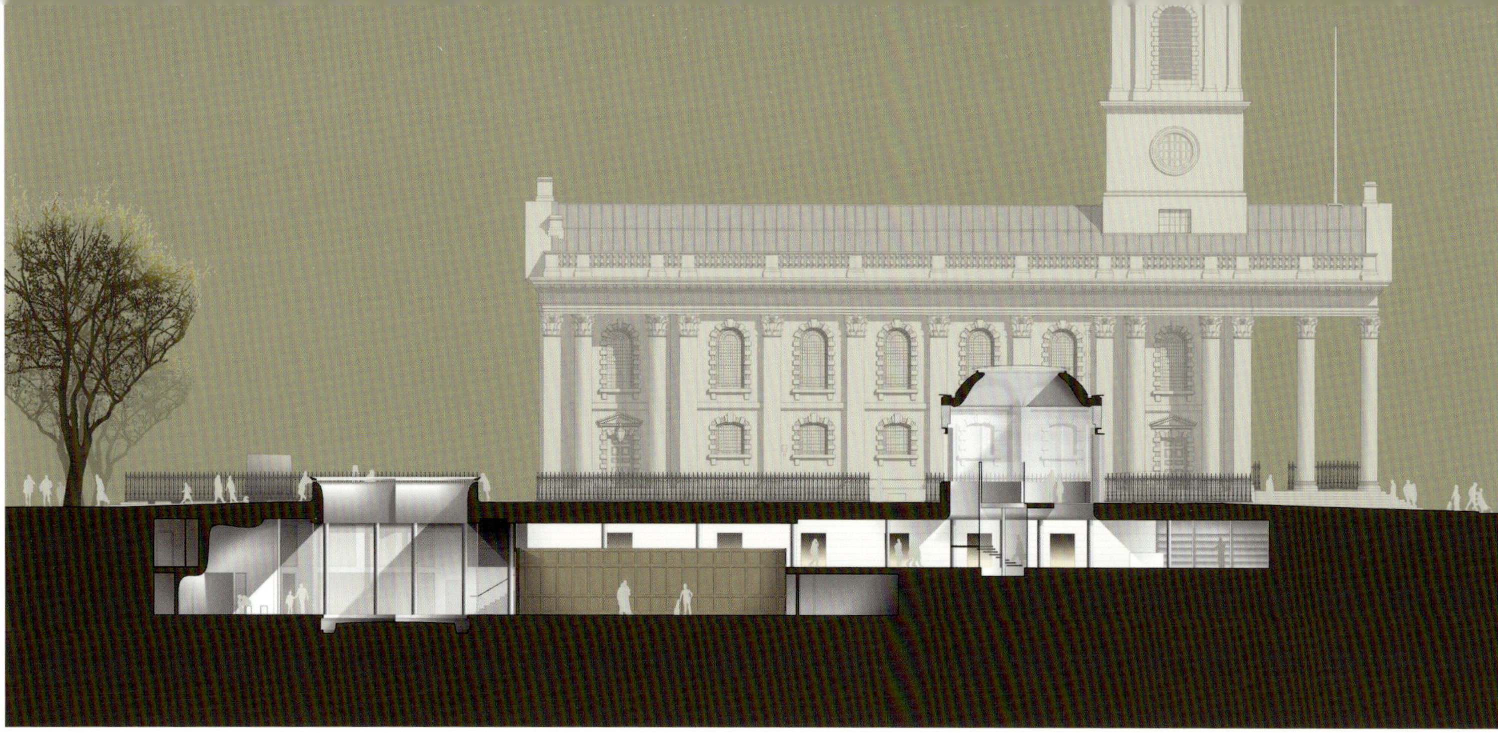

left: East–west section of the newly formed public realm below the reconfigured Church Path. From the east (left): Dick Sheppard Chapel; lightwell; church hall; pavilion; shop/exhibition.

opposite:

above left: Plan, gallery level.
1. clergy office
2. vicar's study
3. office reception
4. IT training room
5. hub/training area
6. teaching room
7. art room
8. IT office
9. consultation room
10. clergy flat

below left: Plan, ground level.
1. Austen Williams Room
2. Vestry Hall
3. day room
4. reception
5. pavilion
6. Church Path
7. lightwell
8. new gates and stair
9. vestibule with new lift and stair to crypt
10. redefined churchyard
11. portico
12. ramped access to church

above right: Plan, level of the crypt.
1. care activity
2. servery and dining
3. medical room
4. laundry
5. refuse
6. exhibition and display
7. tickets
8. shop
9. gallery
10. café
11. kitchen
12. music office
13. music changing rooms
14. meeting rooms

below right: Plan, level of the Dick Sheppard Chapel.
1. plant room
2. parish kitchen
3. store
4. Church Hall
5. cloister
6. lightwell
7. chapel
8. Ho Ming Wah Centre
9. office
10. music rehearsal room

This is a project which exemplifies the density and complexity of context in Central London perhaps better than any other site ever could. Here, at the Church of St Martin-in-the-Fields, there is a confluence of streams, historical, social, religious, architectural, commercial and memorial; a palimpsest of layers, erasures and constructed planes creating a place which stands at the pivot of a number of distinct and discrete London quarters and which mediates between the different kinds of city which surround it.

It is also not only a symbolic space for the city (between Westminster and the royal palaces), it is a place of protest and dissent, a place where the voice of the city has been heard on political issues from Apartheid and nuclear disarmament to anti-war protests. It is a site connecting the riverside of what was once the site of the city's grandest palaces and the classical pomp of the buildings which cocoon the city's clubs, places of influence and intrigue. And it is a site which extends its influence way beyond London itself. It has cast its influence far abroad, most notably in the United States, where James Gibbs's beautiful church became a template for colonial church building.

Standing between Trafalgar Square and the Strand and between the city of commerce and the city of leisure, the parish church of the Queen and of 10 Downing Street occupies a prominent position in the imagination and orientation of the city. It is a place of worship and charity, an urban and civic marker, and a building which defines a complex series of public spaces not only around it but also beneath it.

Situated outside the Roman walls of the City, St Martin's stands at the centre of the Anglo Saxon city, which was built as the successor to the, by now ruined, Square Mile. This once-liminal zone beyond the city walls became the Aldwych—or the Old Wick or Market—and it seems to have been continuously used as a site of worship of real significance to the city; a conclusion which was reinforced in the extensive excavations required for the construction of this largely subterranean intervention.

The particular character of St Martin's as an institution is not so much architectural as social. The fourth-century St Martin, for whom the church is named, tore his cloak in half to share it with a beggar and is, appropriately, the patron saint of reformed drinkers. During the First World War trainloads of soldiers returning from the Western Front disembarked at Charing Cross Station and found themselves lost in London. Often shell-shocked, traumatised, physically and mentally scarred by their experience and alienated in the city, many found themselves in St Martin's. There they were given shelter by the incumbent, HRL 'Dick' Sheppard, a minister who had himself served

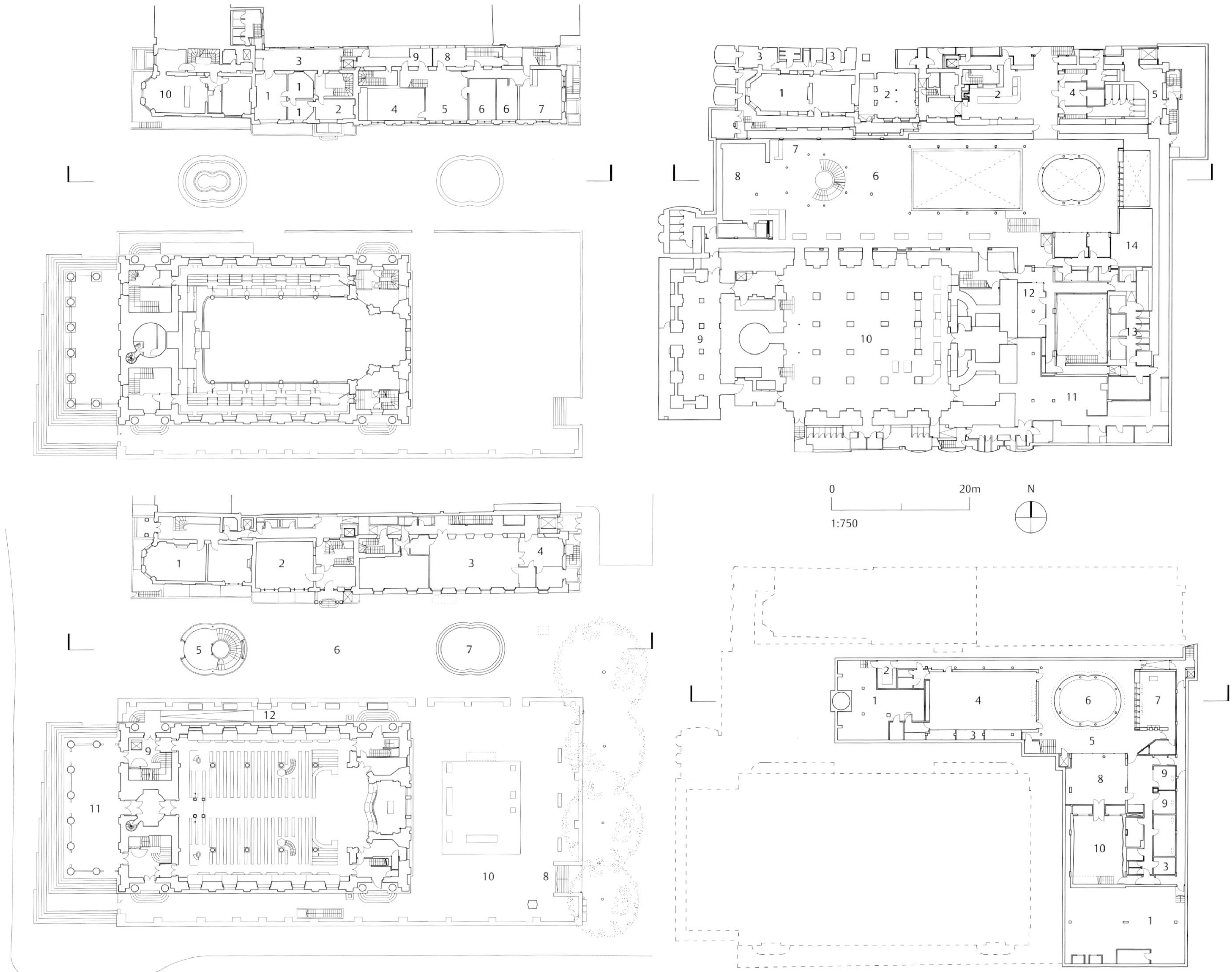
0
20m
1:750
N

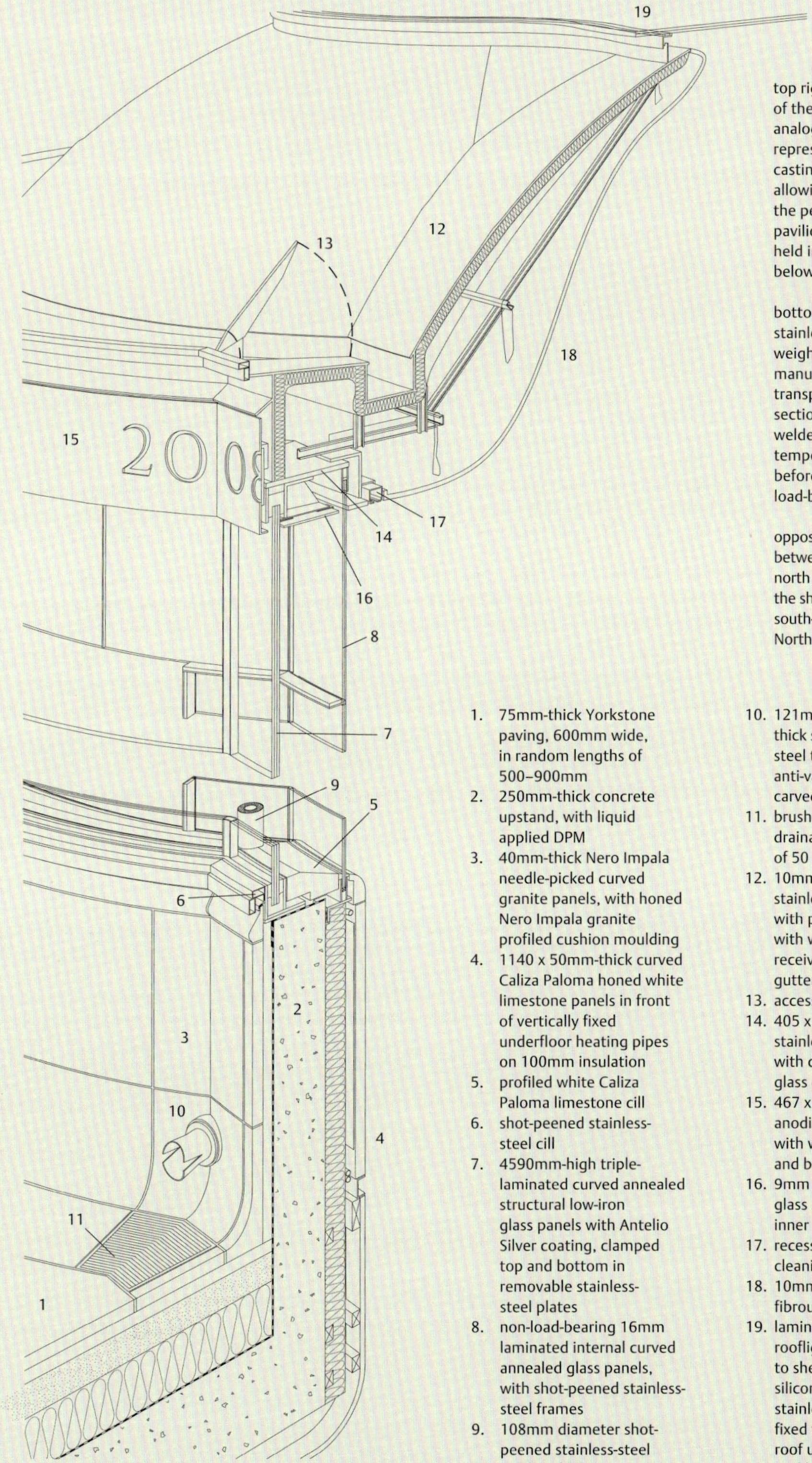

top right: The glass walls of the pavilion echo the analogy of the crystal as a representation of the soul—casting no shadow—whilst allowing the plaster, soffit and the penumbral image of the pavilion's geometry to be held in the mind's eye below the ground.

bottom right: The shot-peened stainless-steel pavilion roof weighing 8.5 tonnes was manufactured in Switzerland, transported to site in two sections where they were then welded together, lifted onto a temporary prop as illustrated before being lowered onto the load-bearing glass walls.

opposite: Pavilion placed between the shadow of Gibbs's north Portland stone wall and the sharp light of Nash's south-facing painted stucco North Range.

1. 75mm-thick Yorkstone paving, 600mm wide, in random lengths of 500–900mm
2. 250mm-thick concrete upstand, with liquid applied DPM
3. 40mm-thick Nero Impala needle-picked curved granite panels, with honed Nero Impala granite profiled cushion moulding
4. 1140 x 50mm-thick curved Caliza Paloma honed white limestone panels in front of vertically fixed underfloor heating pipes on 100mm insulation
5. profiled white Caliza Paloma limestone cill
6. shot-peened stainless-steel cill
7. 4590mm-high triple-laminated curved annealed structural low-iron glass panels with Antelio Silver coating, clamped top and bottom in removable stainless-steel plates
8. non-load-bearing 16mm laminated internal curved annealed glass panels, with shot-peened stainless-steel frames
9. 108mm diameter shot-peened stainless-steel insulated RWP
10. 121mm diameter x 4mm-thick shot-peened stainless-steel tube, with internal anti-vandal rod, fixed to carved granite spout
11. brushed stainless-steel drainage grille made up of 50 x 5mm fins
12. 10mm curved shot-peened stainless-steel plate roof with profiled 10mm ribs, with welded upstand to receive rooflight, integral gutter and fascia
13. access to rain-water outlet
14. 405 x 20mm welded stainless-steel head-plate with curved plates for glass clamping
15. 467 x 8mm-thick curved anodised aluminium fascia with water-cut lettering and backing plates
16. 9mm laminated dark grey glass soffit panels between inner and outer glazing
17. recessed galvanised steel cleaning rail
18. 10mm-thick profiled fibrous plaster ceiling
19. laminated low-iron glass rooflight cold-slumped to shed water, with silicone bonded curved stainless-steel angle fixed to hit-and-miss roof upstand for trickle ventilation

ST MARTIN IN THE FIELDS

far left: The new pavilion joins the dialogue between Nash and Gibbs in the reconfigured Church Path.

left: The negative equivalent to the pavilion, the light-well void is manifest in the solid granite balustrade and the floating stainless-steel rail with the words of Andrew Motion's poem in cast raised letters by Tom Perkins.

opposite: The third perspective from the subterranean cloister around which most of the new spaces are gathered.

as a military chaplain in a field hospital in France and personally experienced the trauma of war. This was the beginning of the church as a place of shelter and succour for the homeless and the dispossessed.

The church's extensive crypts and its extraordinary warren of underground vaults and spaces were pressed into service as one of the city's most remarkable institutions, in which the homeless were helped, fed and seen to by doctors, in which they could doze in chairs or learn to use computers, all this beside the perennially popular 'café in the crypt', a genteel place which is far less Gothic than it sounds. The mix of uses could be breathtaking, the confluence of laundry and music rehearsal, of social work and socialising, memorial slabs and institutional furniture, the strange sympathy between the itinerant tourists and the deracinated homeless. The mood was captured in a striking series of photos by Chris Steele Perkins which highlight a fundamental humanity framed by the odd blend of institutional, representational and ad hoc architectures.

The church itself is a beautiful building, a delicate piece of a peculiarly English Baroque which, drawing on Wren and Hawksmoor with its spire and portico, also saw Gibbs attempt to employ the lessons he learnt whilst working for Carlo Fontana in Rome.

It didn't quite come off—his original circular designs were abandoned and the building is more conventional than might have been the case. But even so, its slender spire must have created a real spectacle emerging from the slums of what was then still a resolutely poor part of London bordering on wealthy enclaves, surrounded by rookeries, and plagued by homelessness, disease and cramped conditions.

The church was completed in 1726, stitched tightly into the medieval network of narrow streets and alleys. In the early nineteenth century, with Nash's urban improvements and the half-realised plan for a grand axis between Regent's Park and Trafalgar Square, its context was tidied up—the rookeries and the last of the lanes made way for a large churchyard which was cleared around it.

Eric Parry Architects' huge project to rationalise and reorganise the incomprehensible warren of spaces around the church was, for the first few years of the new millennium, one of Central London's biggest yet least visible projects. The site's total footprint is, astonishingly, the same size as that of nearby Leicester Square. The project manifests itself at street level through a pair of glass pavilions which indicate the presence of the subterranean realm. Initially conceived as sculptural cubes, one as a positive above ground, the other as a negative, a framed hole in the ground, these have morphed into something

opposite: Looking east, the plane tree canopies in Adelaide Street reflect the quietude of the subterranean spaces.

left: The east–west axis terminates in the new Dick Sheppard Chapel. Dick Sheppard was the vicar of St Martin-in-the-Fields between 1914 and 1926. His tenure saw the opening of the crypt for the benefit of soldiers coming and going from Charing Cross to the battlefields of the First World War. This act of charity has extended to the work of the Connection at St Martin-in-the-Fields, now housed in Nash's school building and extending under the entire length of the North Range. Each year the congregation and homeless numbering more than a hundred make a pilgrimage to the burial place of Dick Sheppard in the cloister of Canterbury Cathedral, where after his tenure as vicar he became the Dean.

left: For the first time there is now a music rehearsal space with changing facilities and offices. The double-height space is set beneath the dais in the churchyard, lit by pavement lights.

right: Nash's mortuary room beneath the Vestry Hall, utilising cast-iron posts to maximise space and ease the movement of the heavy lead-lined coffins, is now a dining room and part of the day-centre of the Connection at St Martin-in-the-Fields.

far right: The Art Room, housed in part in a space occupied by a stair, has large round-headed windows to the north and south. It is a place where a secure world can be conjured away from the insecurity of the street.

very different; curving glass structures on a figure-of-eight plan. The positive of these is an entry pavilion, a delicate, ethereal structure which evokes the form of a *tempietto*—notably that of Bramante's exquisite Tempietto of San Pietro in Montorio in Rome (Gibbs's own Radcliffe Camera in Oxford is also cited as an influence). Like Bramante's building, the pavilion is designed as an object to sit in a constricted urban space, an intervention which changes the flow of pedestrian traffic but which also makes an urban space which has traditionally been one of the city's vague, underused walkways, a real and specific place. The urban space itself has been transformed. Church Path (linking St Martin's Place and Adelaide Street) was widened by moving the original churchyard railings closer to the church and creating a more generous public space, more akin now to a small piazza than an alley and made less of a thoroughfare, less transitory, by the insertion of the pavilion. The other new structure is the inverse of the entry pavilion, a negative version manifested as a lightwell surrounded by a low wall. Around its parapet is inscribed a specially commissioned poem by Andrew Motion.

These two pavilions act as lanterns for a huge new space below, a subterranean square which forms the nexus of the new intervention. This space bridges the sacred and the profane just as it does the world of the sky and the realm of the earth. The lightwell forms a window to the world above and the newly restored St Martin's spire impinges on the view of the sky—one of the key moments Parry picked up in an early sketch. The other pavilion houses a stair which winds around a glazed lift shaft down into the lobby space.

This new public corridor between the church and the secular buildings houses the spaces for the charity but it also creates a new underground piazza which links together a chapel (dedicated to Dick Sheppard), the remodelled café in the crypt, community meeting rooms (including spaces for the Ho Ming Wah Chinese community centre) and a music rehearsal room—St Martin's has a popular programme of music throughout the year. The architectural expression of the chapel is modest, reminiscent of a kind of Modernist Nordic sacred space. There is a hint of Erik Bryggman's Resurrection Chapel in Turku, 1941, with its asymmetrical walls, one with a wall which opens onto the landscape. At the Dick Sheppard Chapel, Eric Parry Architects have similarly supported one side on a row of fins which give a glimpse into the everyday life of the subterranean concourse. It is light, bright and almost invariably busy, an expression of the idea of this below-grade

world as a reflection of the city above and of this as a chapel in a busy urban location—albeit one buried in the archaeology of the site. The chapel features Parry's own elegantly pared-down furniture, notably the sparse, specially designed Vigilia benches and a simple stone altar. A tapestry by Gerhard Richter, on display at the time of writing, makes an extraordinary impact. The music rehearsal room is buried even deeper in the site, crowned with a fully-glazed clerestory which becomes a window allowing people to look down into the timber-lined space.

The church itself appears to have been barely touched—always, of course, the perfect accolade in a historic building. In fact a huge amount of work has gone into it. The most visible change has clearly been the new east window by Shirazeh Houshiary and Pip Horne. This extraordinary work sees the leading in the Palladian window distorted by an oval centred, but canted, beneath the central arch. It evokes a vortex and subtly suggests the form of a crucifix with a sacred heart at its centre. The lightly etched glass is transparent except for the central oval, which is a translucent milky white. It creates a hypnotic effect at dusk from outside when the great vaulted ceiling of the church is visible and the oval appears to float in the middle of the view. Beneath the window a Victorian dais was replaced with a subtly bowing raised stone floor—a form that was suggested both in Gibbs's original intent and in a painting of the church by Hogarth. Other changes have been made to accommodate the church's status as one of Central London's most popular venues for classical and choral as well as sacred music. The pulpit was moved into the centre of the church and the pews were rearranged and some redesigned to clear a space for musicians at the eastern end in front of the altar. The altar, also by Houshiary, has similarly become an object of real beauty and symbolic depth.

What appears as a single, dense block of travertine actually reveals itself in darker conditions to have a top which is merely a veneer of stone—it subtly glows, gently illuminated from within. The altar appears to float above the sanctuary floor. In fact it stands on a recessed plinth of dark oak (referring to the dark timber of the pews and furniture), giving the impression of being suspended. The single block of travertine is intended to suggest a sarcophagus (the traditional symbolism of an altar being a tripartite blend of tomb, table and reliquary) and the glow implies a moment of transformation and echoes the light of the window above.

It is the new work that is most noticeable, but a huge amount of restoration has gone into the church, from the intricate ceiling to the pews. New pews have been designed and made to create a more intimate space for small services but also to be easily removable for performance layout, and the chancel steps have been remade in stone in an image closer to Gibbs's original intentions. The elliptically vaulted ceiling (designed by Gibbs for a sympathetic music acoustic) has been restored in white stucco and the decorative elements in the sanctuary ceiling have been re-gilded; the pilaster capitals and dentils, garlands, winged putti and a radiant sun create a heavenly realm, a visualisation of the etymology of ceiling as *ciel*, a physical and symbolic representation of the sky. This is contrasted with the dark, earthy tones of the timber pews and panelling, and the stone floor which together create a stratum of an earthly and a heavenly realm with the restored windows and their hand-blown clear glass illuminating the interstitial space of real life and the everyday between earth and heaven.

Parry talks often of the adjacencies and simultaneities of urban construction, the way unexpected things happen next to each other and the manner in which functions rub up against each other. It is, in a way, the essence of the city, the confluences of chance, coincidence and coexistence. It is difficult to think of any London building which more clearly illustrates the collision of such a startling, urbane and humane set of uses and historical layers. Nash rubs up against Gibbs and creates the friction which has allowed Parry to remodel and rethink this extraordinary fragment of city.

above: The crypt of James Gibbs's church is an important part of the parish economy and is used as a gallery, restaurant and occasional space for jazz performance, cabaret and poetry recitals. Its use has been enlarged with the removal of the shop, ticketing and kitchen, which previously shared the single space. The ledger stones of the floor were lifted and put back with air ducts placed between the bases of the stone piers in order to allow the simple architecture to remain uncluttered by ductwork.

left: West end of the nave looking south from under the gallery. The restored interior included the redecoration of the Bagutti and Atari soffit stucco-work in white; capitals, bases and secondary doorframes in a warm white; timber panelling lightly cleaned and oiled; new Purbeck flooring to the central aisle and handblown clear glass to replace the 1950s studio glass. The whole space was re-serviced and re-lit.

opposite left: From paint scrapes it was possible to establish that the original decoration of the sanctuary was an oil-based Portland stone colour and that this included the only area of gilding in the church.

The redecoration as originally intended and the re-ordering of the sanctuary, with the removal of the Victorian checkerboard dais, has re-established Gibbs's vision. The new east window by the artists Shirazeh Houshiary and Pip Horne was the result of a competition organised by Vivien Lovell on behalf of the Art Advisory Panel. The continuous movement of cames is achieved by the use of stainless steel and the glass is a digital reproduction of the artists' paintings, moving from a relative opacity in the central oval which dissipates through the whole. The glass was manufactured by Franz Mayer, of Munich.

right: The rite of consecration was celebrated by Rowan Williams, then Archbishop of Canterbury, and Richard Chartres, Bishop of London, and the Vicar Nicholas Holtam.

PRINT
hair & beautystore

Savile Row

The development of the urban interior reached its most exemplary form in Parisian passages, which Louis Aragon describes in “Le Passage de l’Opéra” in his *Paris Peasant* (1926) as the “gateway to mystery”. The movement into the horizontal depth of the city is a background that may explain some of the intricacies of the urban interior of 23 Savile Row.

1819

1951

from 1990

2011

0 50m N

1:2500

1. Regent Street (formerly Swallow Street*)
2. New Burlington Street
3. Conduit Street
4. Savile Row

This part of Mayfair is dominated by a very interesting, rather curious and also rather unique form of conservative Modernism which coexists very comfortably with the indigenous Georgian domestic scale of the streets. Opposite the site of this commercial development is the chunky stripped Deco of Savile Row police station and another blocky 1930s office building, whilst Michael Rosenauer's superb Time Life Building occupies a corner nearby. The original occupant of this site was Fortress House, a late-Deco leftover built too late for its style after the war. Although there was some controversy in its destruction, Fortress House was a curious building. Situated in type somewhere between The In and Out Club and a posh garage forecourt, the old building's slightly clunky and oddly proportioned mass was set back from the street, which broke the continuity of one of London's most consistently compelling streets. The banded ribbon windows of these modern structures and their shopfronts is making the street as attractive to galleries as it has been to tailors, with an odd parallel occurring between the idea of making and display in both suits and art that makes for a constantly changing street corridor which is very much about appearance and aesthetics. The big speculative office though is also about the changing character of a Mayfair which has become the heart of the city's hedge-fund industry.

The new building melds the existing contextual languages of Savile Row and of the broader Mayfair scale to create a sober, urbane architecture that belongs to this conservative world rather than to the glassy realm of the speculative office, which is in fact what this building, despite its appearance, is. Just as the Modernists toned down their minimal language when they arrived here post-war, to create an architecture of stone sobriety, so Eric Parry has created an architectural language positioned comfortably between the modern and the conservative classical.

In an echo of the former incarnation of the site, the new building is arranged as a pair of wings enclosing a recessed central section. This memory of the forecourt is defined by a highly theatrical sculpture by Joel Shapiro which is suspended, seemingly precariously, above it. The tripartite elevation is matched by a classical elevation of base, shaft and attic expressed as a band of dark stone enveloping the retail units, light Portland stone for the main office floors and a recessed attic storey in a lighter, glazed language. Most of Parry's walls, from the early work at Pembroke College to the expanses of the Olympic Village, are sculpted subtractively from a series of layers, leaving an intimation of a once-flush façade which has been carved into, revealing the form within. The walls at Savile Row feature stepped continuous

opposite (left to right): Plan of the site based on Richard Horwood's map of London, 1794–1819. The north end of Savile Row was connected to Conduit Street by a small passage, passing through the boundary of two London estates, which accounts for the mismatching urban grid to north and south.

Plan of the site based on the Ordnance Survey map of 1951, showing the headquarters building for the Central Electricity Board built on bomb-damaged sites.

Plan based on the Ordnance Survey map of 1990. The site known as Fortress House was the home of English Heritage from 1971 to 2006.

Plan of the site with completed building in 2011.

above right: Pre-existing view of Savile Row, looking southeast, from the north side of Conduit Street, with Fortress House at the centre of the image.

above, far right: Pre-existing view of New Burlington Street, looking southwest. The austere 42m elevation of Fortress House dominates the streetscape.

string courses above the windows, which accentuates the plane of the horizontality of the structure—despite its relatively tall scale in this tight street. At the same time a layer of pilasters is recessed so that the vertical articulation is just as clear but less prominent. This Portland stone façade is partially self-supporting and its architectonic language is consistent with its structure, an effort most clearly legible in the trabeated retail layer in dark stone. These envelop the retail units in the two flanking wings. The street is on a gradient and Parry has contained the shop windows within the trabeated recesses as freely expressed bays. These faintly echo the bow windows of Georgian London; the idea that a shop display is somehow a window into a different realm, separated from the mundane world of the building which contains it. This also allows the integrity of the windows to be maintained despite the gradient so that the slope is taken up in the dark recess below the windows. That the shop units were taken over by a gallery has clearly delighted the architects, as it not only opens the building up to the public but allows clear views into the huge spaces behind them. The deep perspective of the ceiling strip lighting seems to reinforce the idea of a separate realm addressing the street, a stagey glimpse into an interior which exists independently. That both spaces have been taken by the same gallery is yet more pleasing, creating a symmetry of use and a continuity of intent.

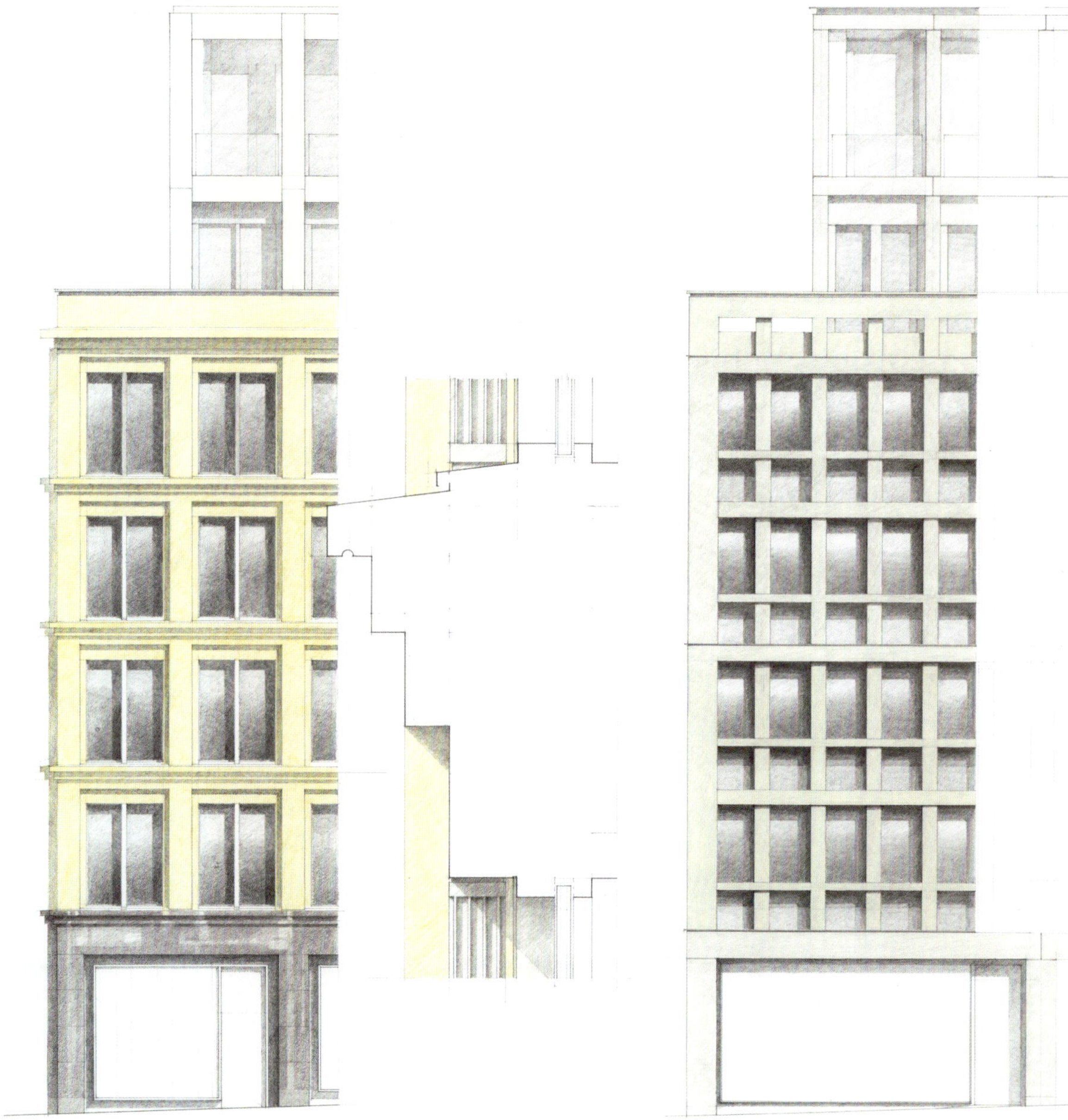

far left: The Westminster City Council planning department dictated the use of stone in this conservation area. The drawing illustrates two early alternatives drawn at a scale of 1:50, the first incorporating string courses, the first time a projected element has been used in the work of the practice. The preferred alternative was the development of a 'weave of stone' with the subtle ordering of single- and double-storey elements and setbacks. The former was chosen and the detail, drawn at a scale of 1:50, at this early stage formed the principle of 3m centred openings with a metal central mullion.

left: Typical preparatory sketch for the finished drawing.

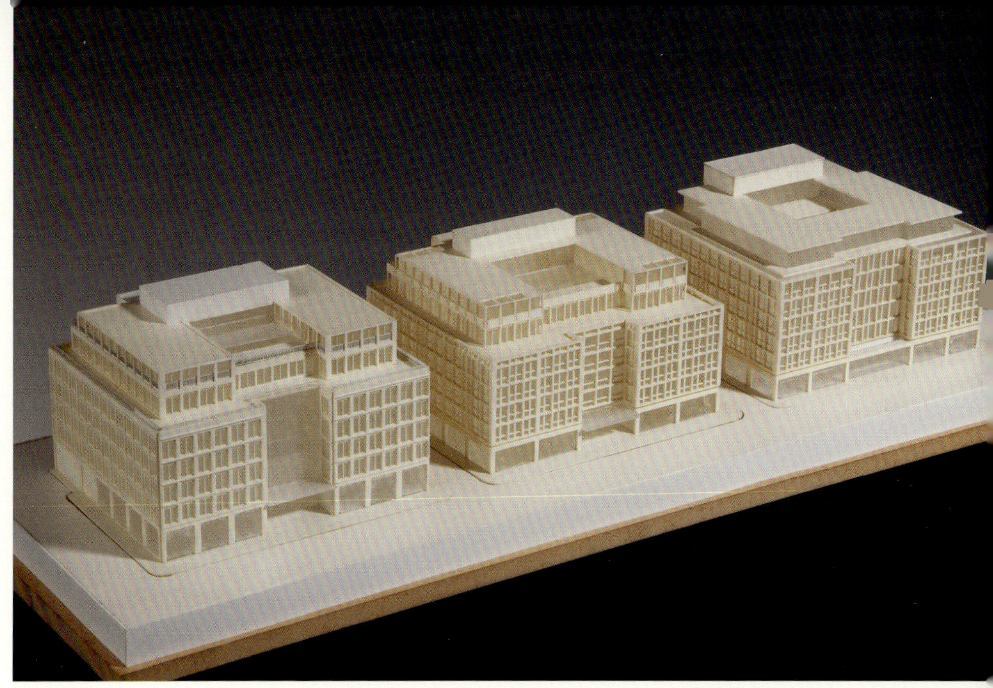

above right: Models illustrating the different forms of stonework and emphasis or suppression of the central bay and roof massing at the scale 1:400, prior to the development of Joel Shapiro's sculpture.

The gap between the two solid flanking pavilions (and the galleries they contain) presents a kind of open vitrine for Shapiro's sculpture. It becomes a huge slice of art scything into Mayfair, a counter to the hedge funds and financiers who inevitably take up this kind of top-end office space.

The glazed atrium behind and the glass revolving doors dissolve away to leave the bronze sculpture floating. It is in fact suspended on cables in a subtle and complex piece of engineering. The genesis of the work was apparently inspired at least in part by the profoundly unsettling image of people falling from the Twin Towers after the 9/11 attacks, suspended in photographs permanently in a terrible mid-air limbo. Something of the uncertainty that 9/11 unleashed on the Western world remains clearly legible—even without the background. There is an existential angst in the dislocation of the elements (oddly suggesting a human figure despite their abstract placing) and their unnatural suspension in a space which punctures the public realm, standing slightly proud of the elevation and becoming a cipher for the entrance below when approached from Conduit Street.

top left: Plan of ground floor. The site falls 1.8m across the 50m width of the Savile Row elevation. A balance is struck at the office entry between the flanking pavilions. Both wings have been taken by Hauser & Wirth, the taller north wing providing a single main gallery space of the scale of a major museum, whilst that to the south has been divided between exhibition and showing rooms.

top middle: Plan of a typical floor. The rigorous simplicity of the plan illustrates how much is achieved in the design of the external wall, which absorbs the structural frame, whilst allowing enough depth and layering to animate the external surfaces with shadow and reflection (see pages 52 and 53). The structuring of the external corners, the 15m span and adequate frame stiffness to allow fine masonry without lateral movement joints in the 42m-long east and west elevations were a notable design team achievement in the face of normal commercial development pressures.

top right: Plan of top floor. The setbacks to the upper levels create generous terraces overlooking Mayfair and its complex cultural and physical topography. The ascending tonality, dark base, Portland body and aluminium upper levels reinforce the tripartite order.

bottom left: Elevation, Savile Row.

bottom middle: Elevation, New Burlington Street.

bottom right: Section through the reception, atrium and core.

1. reception
2. atrium
3. retail
4. office
5. WCs
6. accessible WC
7. loading bay
8. vehicle lift (to basement car park)
9. terrace

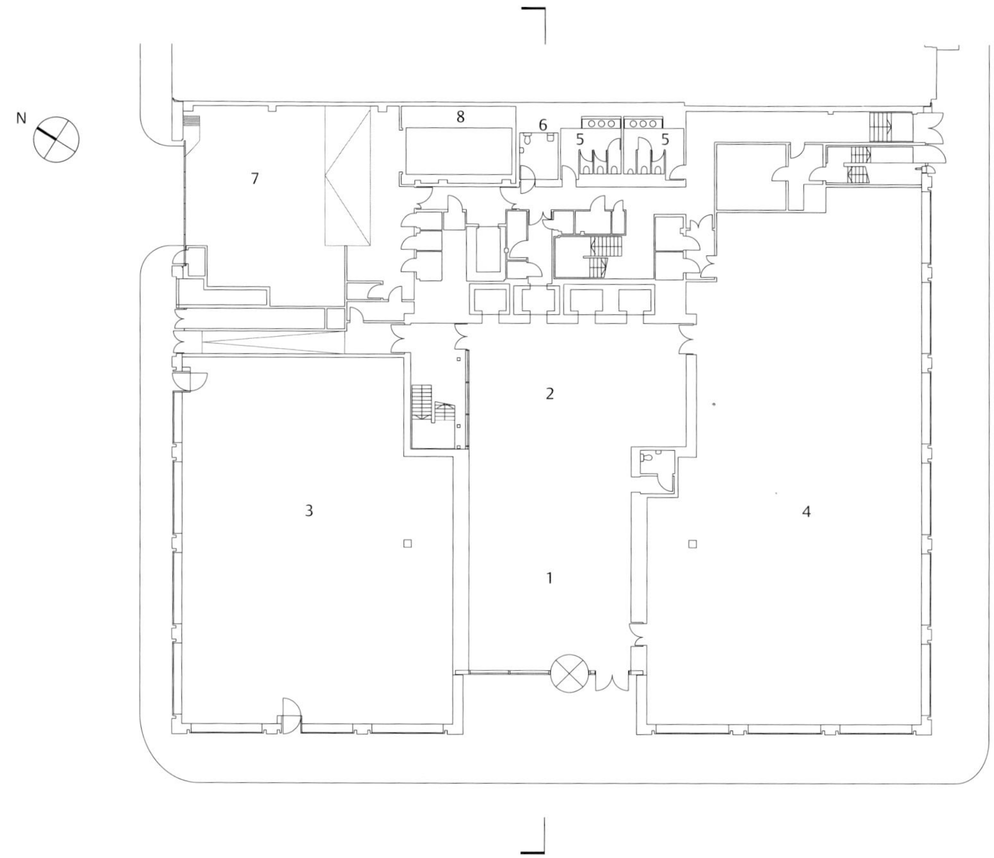

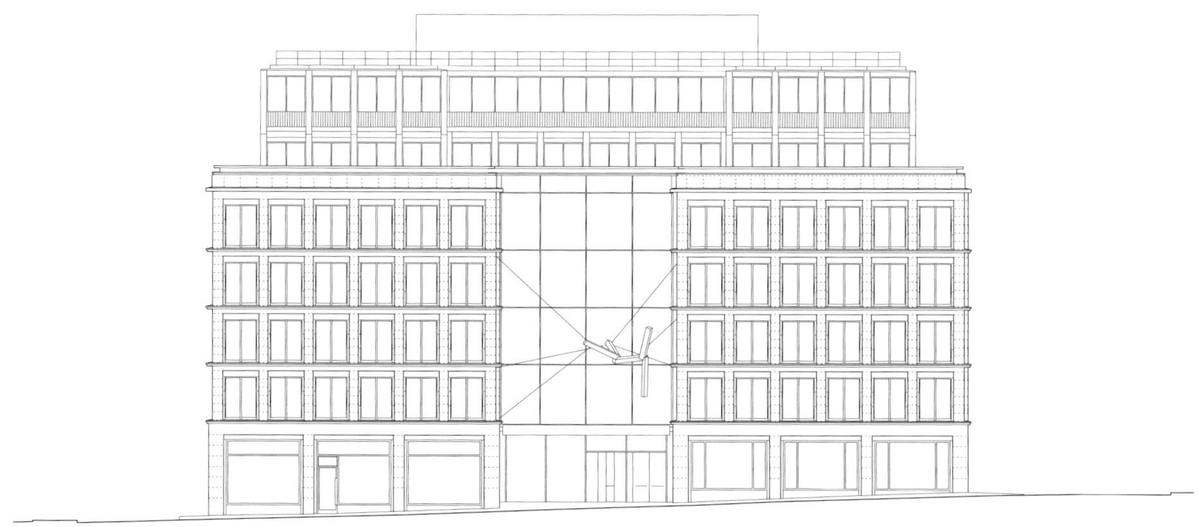

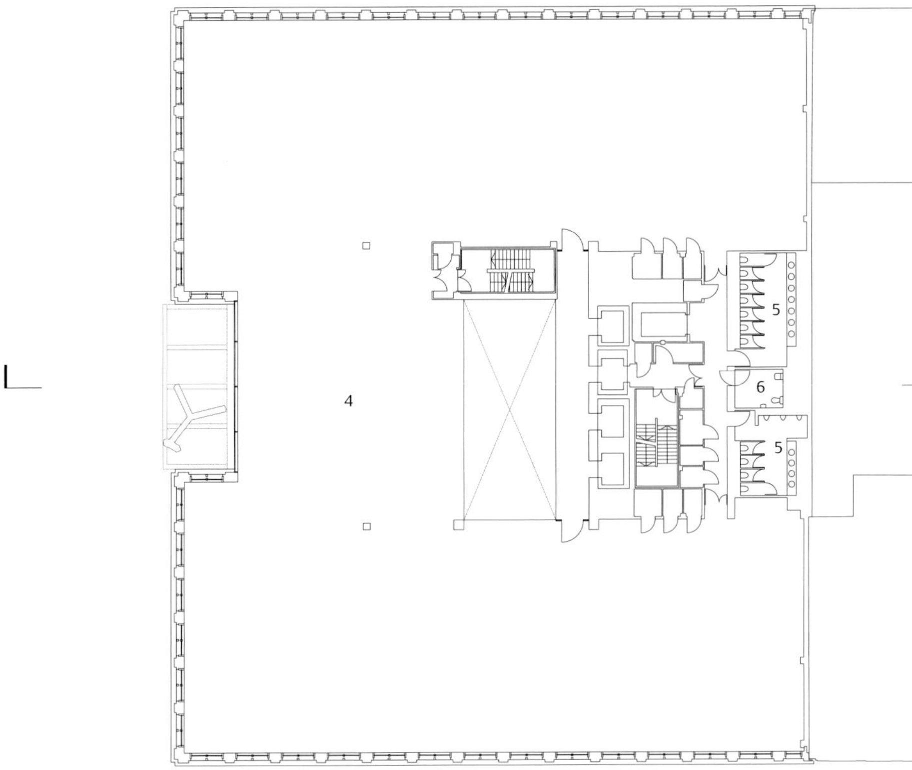

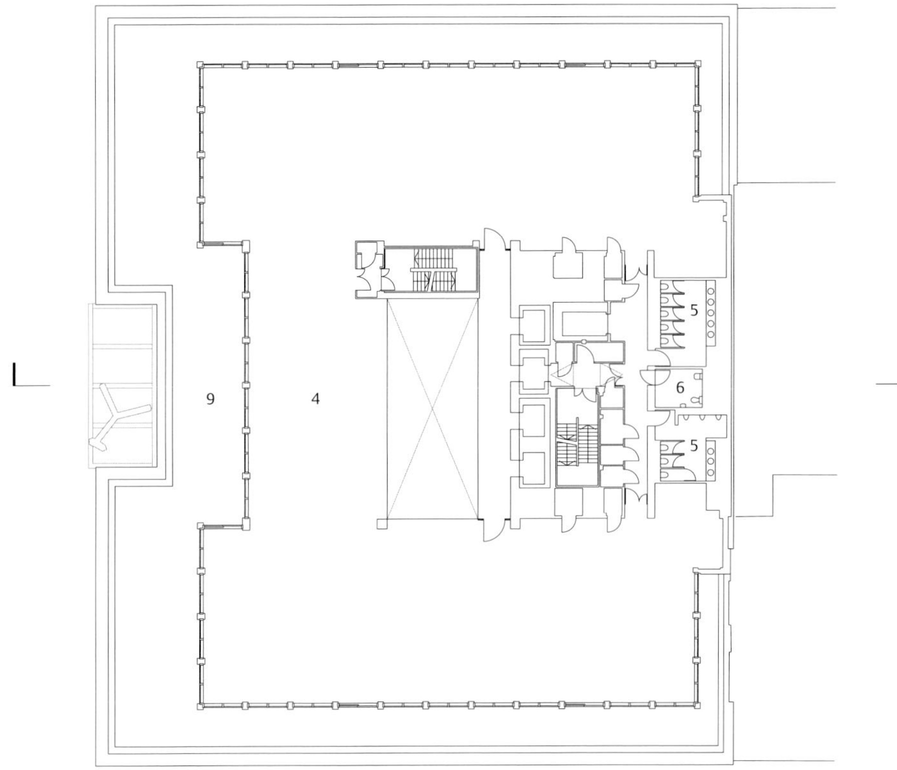

N

0 10m

1:500

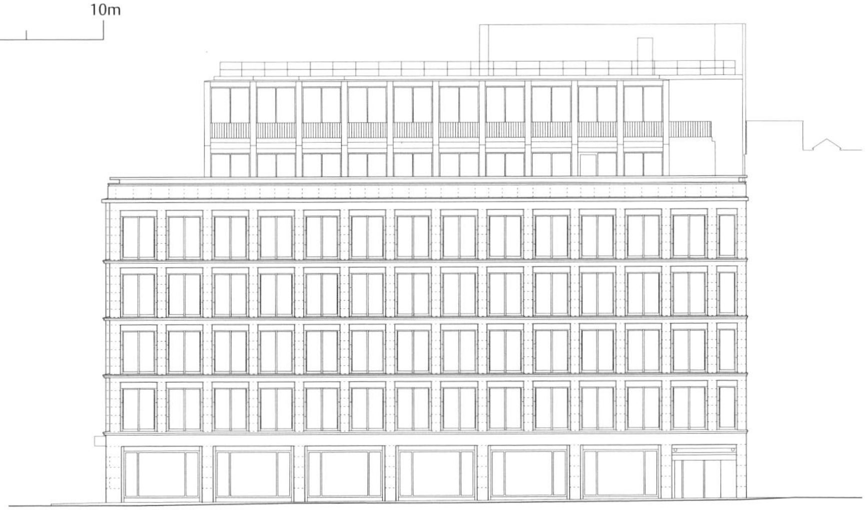

left: Detail view of façade. The layering of stone and shadow with the principal lintels below the projecting string course constructed of 3m-long units.

right: Joints and Portland stone elements are illustrated in the cutaway drawing.

cutaway drawing

1. 140mm Portland stone whitbed lintel
2. 250mm-deep Portland stone whitbed cill
3. 130mm reinforced concrete structural slab
4. typical primary structural column (305 x 305 x 198mm UC)
5. typical primary structural beam (457 x 152 x 52mm UB)
6. 150mm raised access floor
7. suspended accessible ceiling with inset light fittings
8. perimeter recessed blind box
9. powder-coated aluminium window frame; thermally broken
10. office double-glazed laminated safety glass
11. 70mm-thick rigid insulation
12. natural anodised extruded aluminium pier
13. precast 'grey back' secondary panel fixed to floor slab with restraint fixing; primary external façade restrained to secondary support panels
14. DPM
15. 3mm bed joints dry packed
16. open joints
17. pressed metal cill, powder coated
18. 220mm honed granite lintel / pier
19. black anodised aluminium cladding panels
20. high-quality paint finish to extruded aluminium window frame

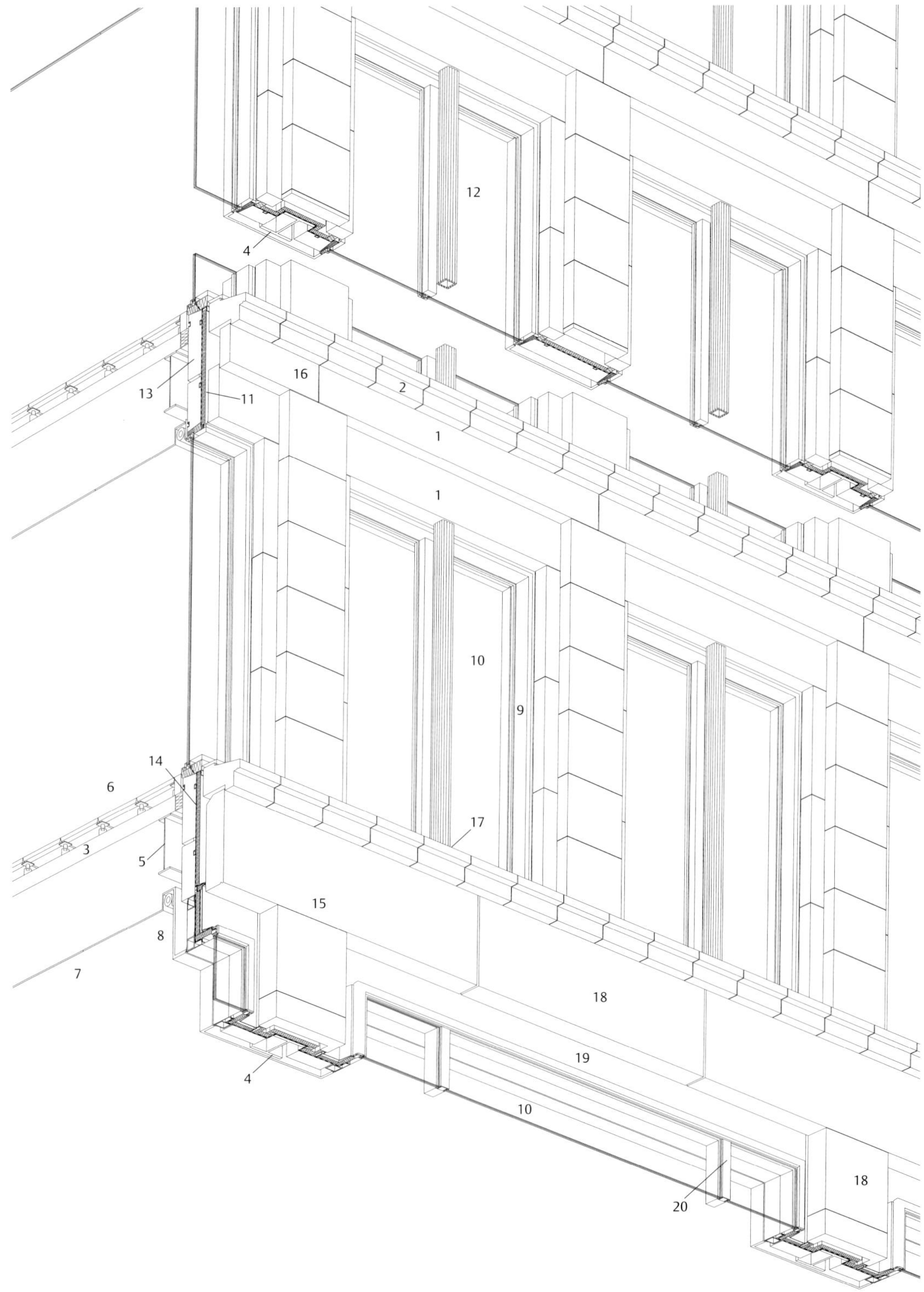

far left: The dimensions of the sculpture required the pre-assembly of the two sections for transportation; photograph of the sculpture *Verge* (2008) assembled at the Tallix foundry in Beacon, New York.

left: Early iteration and maquette in the Shapiro studio in New York. The choice of artist for this commission was that of the architect.

In all, the process from the first site visit prior to demolition of the existing building to installation of the finished artwork took six years of dialogue between architect, artist and project team.

Up close the sculpture takes on an entirely different character. When seen from within the building the striations caused by casting the five metal members are clearly seen, like the timber grain left visible in concrete forms. The massive pieces appear to be tautologically made of rusting timber; it is a curious effect which gives them a carefully crafted look and chimes with their meticulous placing in the air and the engineering required to tie them back to the building.

In this deceptively complex layering we can see the vestigial remains of Parry's original conception of the façade as one of 'woven stone', a version of Gottfried Semper's notion of the façade as a representation of the tent fabric dwelling. The ideas are clearly and intriguingly expressed in Parry's exquisitely rendered pencil studies for the building. Apparently this idea fell foul of Westminster's planners, who preferred a more conventional—and more classical—solution and my impression is that Parry remains disappointed by what he considers a lost opportunity. Having briefly worked in the old Fortress House (when it was the London headquarters of English Heritage) I can attest that it was never a successful building—although its quirky exterior had some stolid and reliable charm. Now, with Hauser & Wirth opening up the huge spaces below to the public as a commercial gallery space and with Shapiro's sculpture thrust into the public realm, it has become a building which—despite its increased footprint on the site—is far more porous and both makes and engages with the streetscape in a far more successful fashion than the old building ever did. This is partly due to the articulation of detail as well. The new building injects an urbane solidity and scale making it a gateway to the more domestic scale, of the Georgian architecture which makes up the Mayfair streetscape. It reminds me of the work of Hans Kollhoff in Berlin; serious in scale and intent, it seems to bypass questions of style in the sheer certainty and facility in the handling of a traditional architectural language. There are no classical columns here, no capitals and appliqué pediments; instead a cocktail of Chicago School Modernity and Prussian sobriety combines with that flavour of Mayfair Modernism to create a truly wonderful piece of streetscape which will, I think, come to be more admired as the years pass by.

The finished artwork, 1.8 tonnes of cast bronze, suspended by six cables from the building structure, is a celebration of the artist's freedom beyond the complex urban negotiation of the architecture of the building.

left: The setback floors of the attic of the building, almost unseen from the street, are surrounded by generous terracing overlooking the urban grid of Mayfair.

opposite: View of 23 Savile Row. Dark Indian granite base with a 6m modulation; Portland stone pavilions above; entrance canopy with the sculpture, breaking the orthogonal order of the whole.

23 Savile Row

far left: The inclination of the street northwards resulted in the potential for an internal ceiling height of 5m. It was the hope that this would attract a gallerist and, post-completion, Hauser & Wirth's occupation has fulfilled that aspiration.

left: Detail from the street of Paul McCarthy's installation *The King, the Island, the Train, the House, the Ship*, November 2011.

right: Detail of the granite order of the ground floor. 4m lintel over stacked pier; anodised shadow gap and high-gloss window frames.

New Bond Street

In both 23 Savile Row and 50 New Bond Street the large volume of open floor space, anticipating rather unpredictable commercial use, is defined on its perimeter by elaborate, carefully designed elevations. Using different materials and spatial arrangements, the elevations bring together the virtual depth of the buildings and the external physiognomy as a contribution to the overall character of the existing streets.

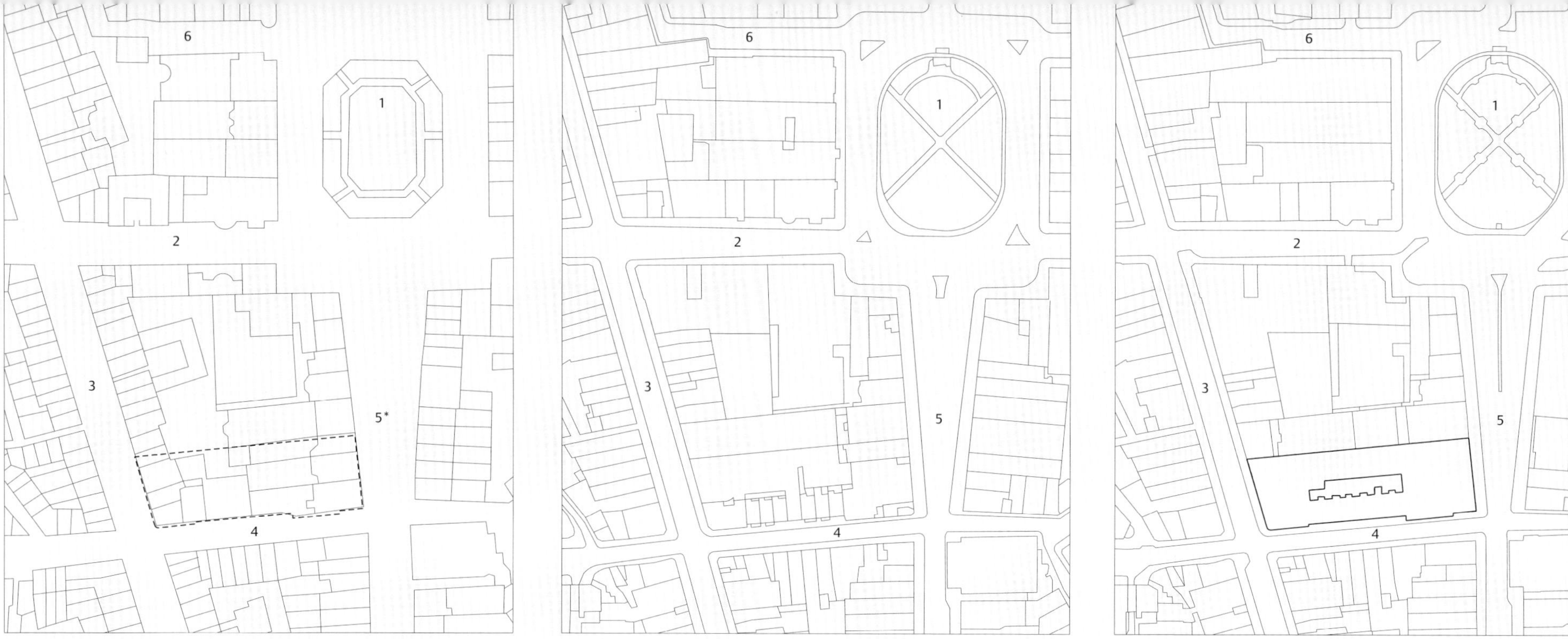

1819 1951 2011

0 50m N
1:2500

The Pinet Building on Bond Street appears a little alien, a Rococo blend of chic Paris and industrial SoHo inserted into the conventional Georgian cityscape. Its delicately cast bronze windows chime with the craftsmanship of the shoes inside. Its window turns the corner in an elegant curve—something London buildings rarely do—and its impeccable horizontal delineation of retail, commercial and more domestic accommodation is expressed in different architectural languages in the most resolutely functional of styles. Parry recalls it from shopping trips as a child, and they seem to have made a deep impression. Perhaps because the unusual detail of those windows and the sumptuous bronze spandrels are at child-height, a layer just above the pavement which is rarely considered in British building traditions.

The redevelopment for Scottish Widows entailed an architectural coddling of the Pinet corner building and the creation of a series of new elevations around it whilst attempting to maintain the particular and wildly differing characters of Bond Street, Maddox Street and George Street. It is a complex stitching of hugely disparate elements together into a coherent block which nevertheless recognises the distinct character of the streets and the façades around the block. The urban condition here is intriguing because it blends a London landscape of Queen Anne and Georgian brick buildings with an encroaching modernity, and a retail culture which was once based on thriving independent luxury goods companies but is increasingly being transformed into a street of ubiquitous global brands. The local landscape is also rapidly transforming from a place of craft (the tailors, couturiers, chocolatiers and jewellers, etc.) to a nexus of hedge-fund management, international finance and the particular culture of consumption that comes along with it.

The new building on Bond Street replaces a work by Michael Rosenauer whose Time Life Building is one of the defining structures in the area, setting a tone of conservative, stone-clad Modernism which marked this part of the West End out as very different to the rest of the city. It was a Modernism which acknowledged the distinctive successes and inherent urbanity of these eighteenth-century streets, a modernity of decorum. This was not one of Rosenauer's better buildings, however, and it had been significantly altered from his original designs.

The new building—in all its multiple elevations—expresses the changing character of Mayfair through a variety of different approaches addressing the uses and architectural feel of the variegated city. Most visible and most distinctive is 50 New Bond Street. Here the façade is defined by a combination of mould-green faience fins and elegantly stripped-down bow windows. The curves of the corners of the windows refer quite

above: The three stages in the development of the site.

left: A plan based on Richard Horwood's map of London of 1819, illustrating the development from the original layout of the Hanoverian square and adjoining streets, following on from the succession of George I in 1714.

middle: Development of the site including Chappels Piano Works, the Pinet Building and the development of Maddox Street.

right: Plan of the site with completed buildings in 2011.

1. Hanover Square
2. Brook Street
3. New Bond Street
4. Maddox Street
5. St George Street (formerly George Street*)
6. Tenterden Street

above left: View of pre-existing buildings on the corner of New Bond Street and Maddox Street.

above right: View of pre-existing buildings from the corner of Maddox Street and St George Street looking west. The last remaining Hanoverian townhouses on St George Street had been gutted by a fire in the early 1970s and an ugly extension created on Maddox Street, predominantly housing toilets and a staircase, interrupted the pavement and the view towards Grosvenor Square, providing the opportunity to create a better return for the historic building and to cantilever the new building over a re-established area.

clearly to the exquisite corner of the Pinet Building—notably the first floor, which follows a Central European model of very clearly expressing the three symbolic bands of urban structure—retail, commerce and residential—in a vertical layer cake.

The faience elements are faceted in a way which recalls the complex geometries of Czech Cubist architecture but the material itself, and particularly its green tinge, evokes an Edwardian urbanism designed to resist the ravages of the polluted city of a century ago. Those late freestyle buildings embraced terracotta and faience as robust and resistant materials which allowed easy modelling and playfulness whilst implying (and employing) a solidity of form and function. Most famous now is HP Berlage's 1916 Holland House, but it is just as important to remember the backs of Bond Street buildings, the glazed brick lightwells and tile-clad stairwells of Edwardian fabric. This kind of tactile, wipe-clean material was fundamental to the emergence of a proto-Modernism in London. It also to me suggests something of the luxury of material around which Bond Street and its environs are built. There is something between tweed (in its colour) and silk (in its sheen), a crafted, hand-made material stitched into the street. The bow windows respond to the Pinet Building's delicate detailing, its aedicular architecture in which every window is framed by fine polished stone columns and intricate garlands.

The Pinet store might be dedicated to shoes but its architecture is frilly French knickers. In those suggestions of a femininity the Pinet store does what most contemporary architecture fails to do; it introduces a character to the street expressed in the depth of the façade so that the elevation becomes a plane for communicating something about an idea. In the bow windows Parry does something similar, using the depth of the elevation to begin to engage with the public realm, to gently cantilever into the street. Bond Street is not the kind of street where you stop and look at buildings, but rather one in which you might linger at a shop window. In this way the architecture is appreciated either whilst the pedestrian is in motion, walking down the street and perceiving the façade obliquely, or it remains almost unseen, a presence hovering above the layer of plate glass windows which are the real *raison d'être* of the city's most expensive shopping location. In this way the elevation is relatively rigorous when seen straight on. There are the shadows cast by the bow windows and the gentle undulations of the cranked fins but it appears as a wall into which windows are set in a traditional fashion. It is only when the building is seen from an angle—as it invariably is—that the real animation comes into its own. The curving corners of the windows pick up glints from the sun or the street lights, the shadows they cast appear to be deeper and the green faience appears to disappear into the green tinge of the glass so that the whole façade seems to be of glass, as transparent as the first floor of Pinet.

0
10m
1:500

right: Preliminary façade study. At an early stage of the project there was a wider frontage to New Bond Street being considered and the proposal included a major and minor oriel bay. With the final width at 19m, the same principle for the undulating ceramic film was adopted for six bays of repeating size.

opposite top: Elevation to New Bond Street with (to the north) Fenwicks department store, and showing the new elevation adjacent to and incorporating the Pinet Building at the corner of Maddox Street. The dashed line indicates the limit of the intervention extending from the corner with Maddox Street.

opposite middle: The elevation to Maddox Street. The central Regency terrace has been re-established as residential over small retail units at ground. The new cantilevered section is shown with a reduced width to allow the double window bay on the return of the St George Street elevation onto Maddox Street.

opposite bottom: Elevation to St George Street.

Both in order to achieve the economic viability of this complex project and to mask the upper levels of the new office building a sensitive negotiation has successfully concluded with the planning officer Robert Ayton to raise by an attic storey the two four-bay Hanoverian townhouses. The dashed line indicates the limit of the intervention extending from the corner with Maddox Street.

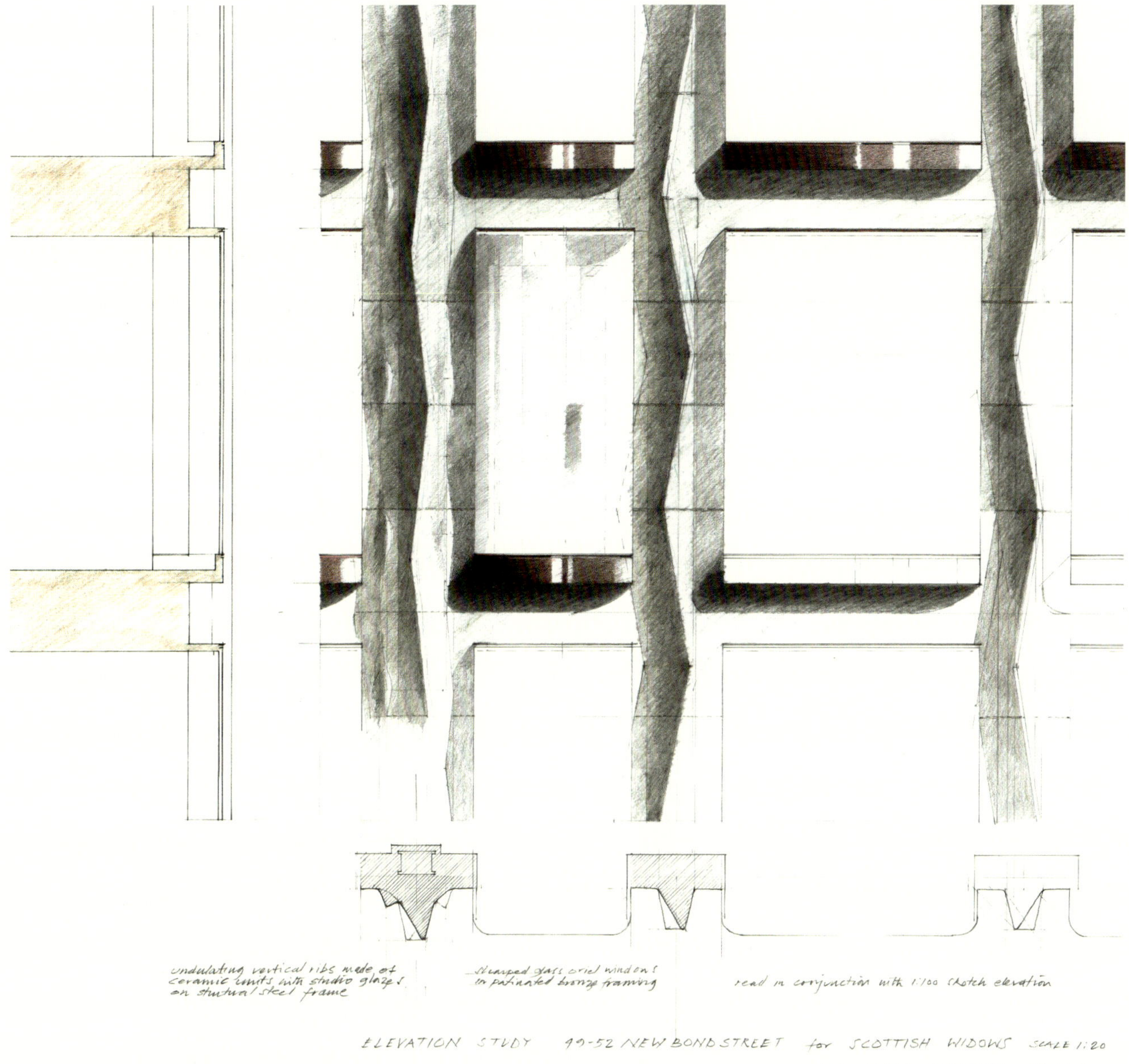

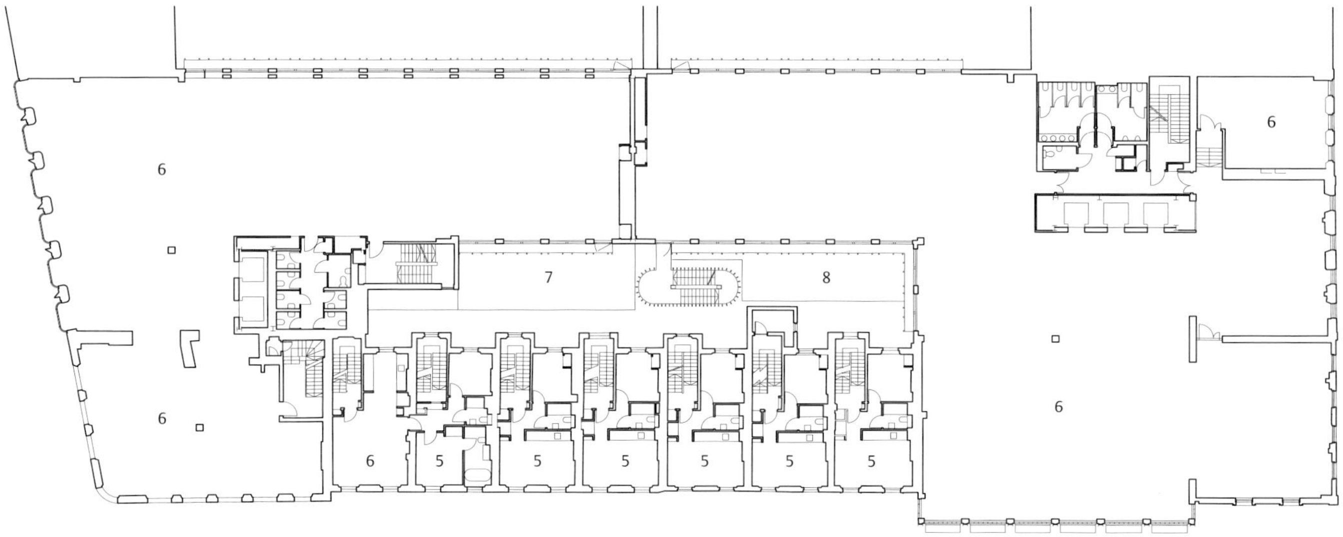

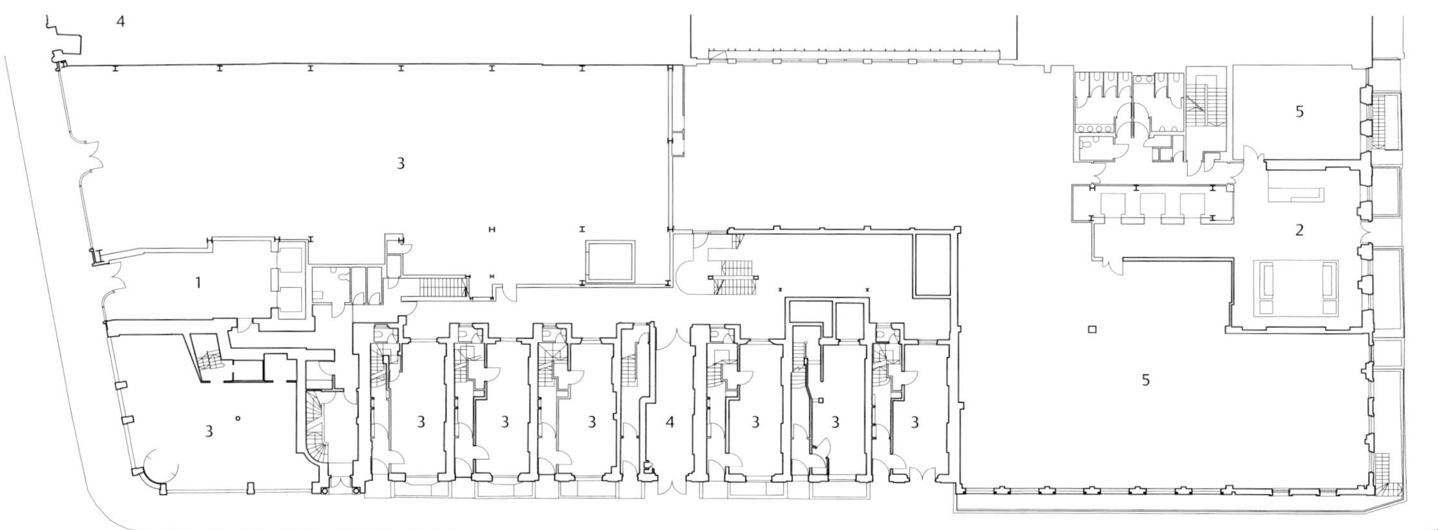

top: Longitudinal east–west section illustrating the sectional differences between the two office buildings and the lightness of the architectural language to the central courtyard spaces. The interior of the urban block has been optimised and replaces a wasteland of flat roofing and poor-quality space.

bottom: Top floor. From the complex composition of parts, surprisingly clear office space is created, reinforced by the slender wall sections created by the use of solid billets of steel of a sectional dimension of 10 x 30cm. The building steps back to provide a notable area of green roof and bio-diversified environments.

opposite top: Typical floor plan. Both the brief and the different sectional heights derived from the adjoining existing buildings, conspired to create two office buildings, one entered from New Bond Street, the other from St George Street. The surrounding streets are acoustically and environmentally aggressive whilst the interior of the block is surprisingly quiet and peaceful, which led to the opportunity of a mixed-mode system of heating and ventilation with openable windows to the block interior. Reflecting the density of the urban grain, residential units sit between the flanking offices.

opposite bottom: Ground floor plan with the valuable new retail space on New Bond Street and the new office entrance snugly fitting between this and the original party wall of the listed Pinet building. The variety of retail spaces is added to by the smaller ground floor units to Maddox Street, punctuated by the service bay entrance to the entire site at its mid-point. From the St George Street entrance a generously proportioned reception space is created, giving access to the compact new core.

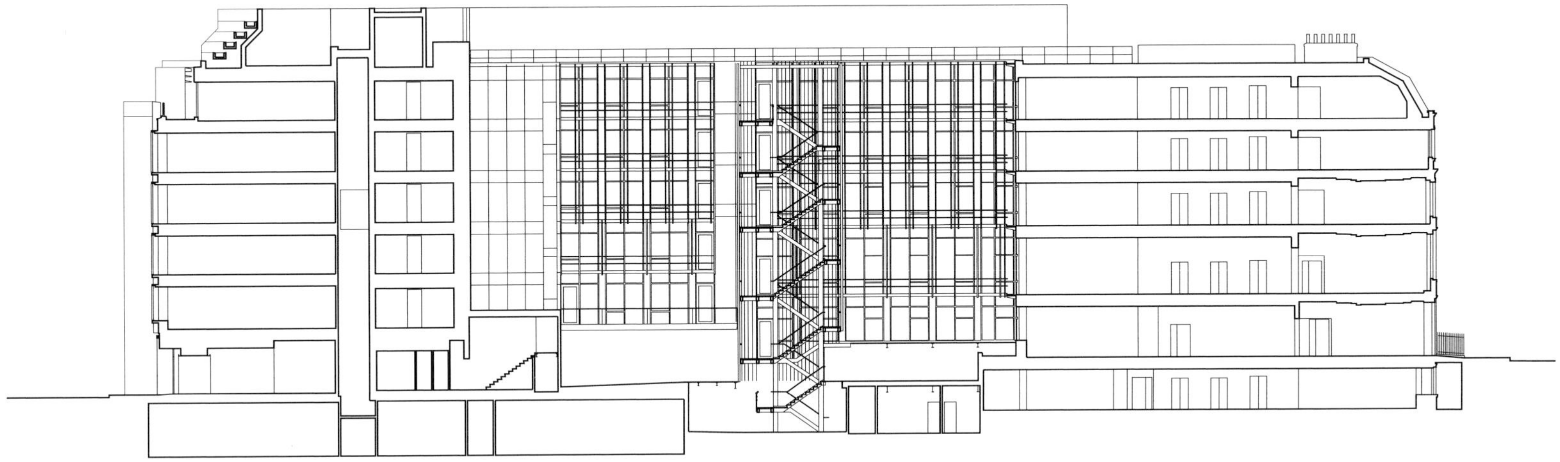

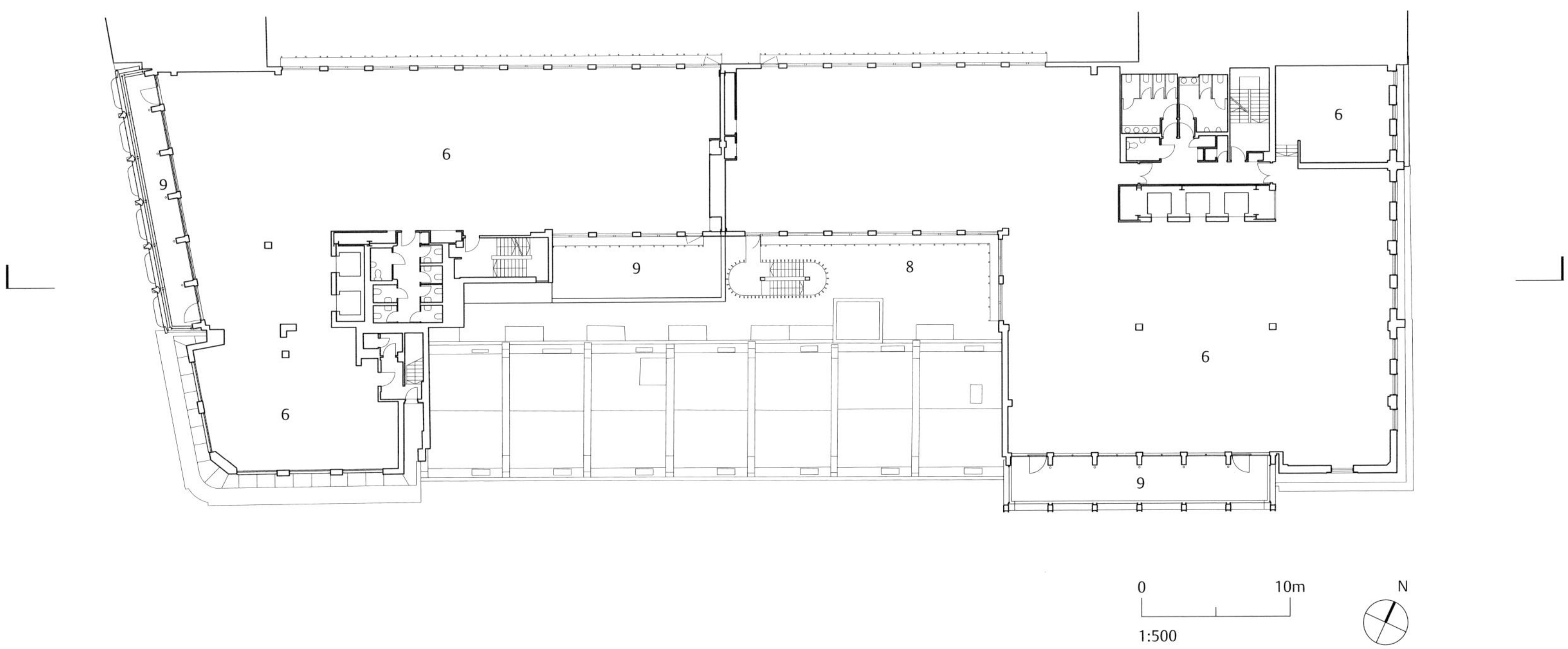

1. reception (New Bond Street)
2. reception (St George Street)
3. retail
4. service entry
5. apartment
6. office
7. lightwell
8. courtyard
9. terrace

left: Details of the completed façade for New Bond Street in evening light, illustrating the quality of glaze and sculptural form of the cast ceramic fins.

cutaway drawing

1. 40mm-thick faience (glazed terracotta) cladding, supported by a system of bespoke stainless-steel brackets fixed back to the unitised cladding via stainless-steel Halfen channels
2. column units are stacked on dead-load support brackets at each floor and tied with restraint brackets at each subsequent joint
3. with the exception of key movement joints, all joints are bedded on and pointed with dark grey lime mortar
4. aluminium unitised cladding system, contains 160mm mineral wool insulation and framework of galvanised steel reinforcement to transfer loads from the external faience cladding to the primary structure
5. bay windows have been formed as an integral part of the unitised cladding system; dead loads associated with the projecting bays are picked up by a frame of steel RHS within the floors; opaque areas are filled with mineral wool insulation
6. flat double-glazed unit (8/16/4/6) and curved double-glazed units (4/4/16/4/6), argon-filled cavity, low emissivity coating and matching high-performance solar control coatings
7. external aluminium window profiles and panels are finished with a satin dark brown metallic hyper-durable organic powder coat to maintain a high level of resistance to UV degradation; internal profiles are finished with a matt white polyester powder coat
8. fin to mullion, formed by 50 x 15mm extruded aluminium profile fixed back to proprietary mullion via aluminium spigots
9. soffit panels to bay windows are finished with a high-gloss black polyester powder coat
10. aluminium gutter formed along rear edge of bay window roof, directs rainwater run-off to sides
11. low-energy LED lights form façade lighting installation by artist Martin Richman
12. primary steel structure, protected with intumescent paint
13. 130mm-deep in-situ steel hollow rib deck and reinforced concrete composite floor slab
14. 100mm-deep raised floor to provide flexible service void
15. suspended ceiling conceals 570mm-deep void containing steel beams and building services
16. curved fibrous plaster lining to column
17. fire and smoke seal between slab edge and back of unitised cladding

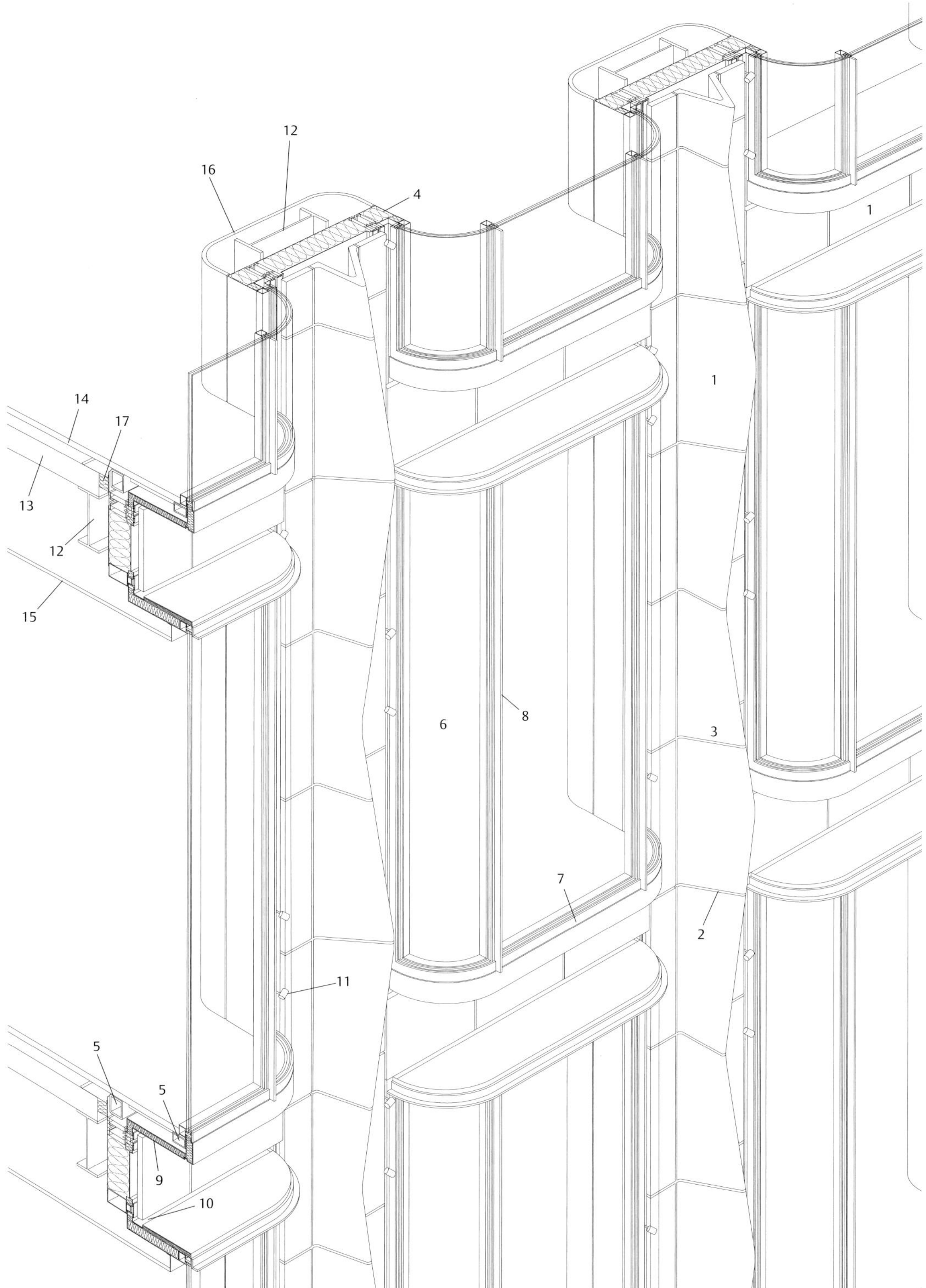

From casting to fixing; three stages in faience. Our dialogue with Shaw's of Darwen began with the glazing of the polychrome wall for Wimbledon School of Art (see *Volume 2*).

top: The body of the faience unit is cast into a mould, made about 5% larger than finished dimensions, released air-dried and hand-finished before leaving the glazing slip applied.

middle: The layered glaze and particularly the top stippled coating is dependent on the applicators' arm movement as well as the chemistry of the glaze and the kiln regime. A dry lay of the entire façade to ensure consistency within a control range takes place in the factory.

bottom: Fixing the faience units on site, where allowing for deviation and tolerance, which depending on unit size is greater than masonry, the procedure is close to contemporary thin-bed masonry fixing practices.

opposite: View of the corner of New Bond Street and Maddox Street of the completed project. Two new façades represent the reforming of the entire section of the urban block with a ground plan dimension of 85 x 30m. It is a collage of five sections responding to the three orientations; the artifice and craft of New Bond Street; the Hanoverian grid and its architectural echoes in St George Street and the supporting mix of retail and restaurants in Maddox Street.

F. PINET
F. PINET
F. PINET
F. PINET

perspectival section

1. 300 x 300 x 100mm ribbed glass blocks with translucent fibreglass interlayer formed into panels using a proprietary glass block wall system, consisting of a silver anodised aluminium frame, stainless-steel bed reinforcement, plastic locator clips, and clear silicone mastic sealant
2. unitised aluminium glazing unit comprises window and glass block spandrel panel
3. unitised aluminium column unit encapsulates primary steel RHS, includes 40mm high-performance rigid insulation
4. primary steel structure, protected with intumescent paint
5. column cladding formed from 300 x 70mm extruded aluminium channel and two 180 x 15mm extruded aluminium RHS in up to 4.5m lengths
6. insulated window head and reveal
7. insulated window cill with 70mm projection formed from folded 3mm aluminium sheet
8. double-glazed unit (6/16/4/6), argon-filled cavity, low-emissivity coating and high-performance solar control coating
9. dummy mullion formed by 50 x 15mm extruded aluminium profile, fixed at window head and cill
10. *brise-soleil* formed from 3mm folded aluminium sheet, fixed back to window head by three brackets formed from 8mm-thick aluminium flats
11. external aluminium profiles are finished with a satin dark brown metallic hyper-durable organic powder coat to maintain a high level of resistance to UV degradation; internal profiles are finished with a matt white polyester powder coat
12. opaque spandrel panel, contains 100mm mineral wool insulation
13. fire and smoke seal between slab edge and back of unitised cladding
14. stack joint
15. 130mm-deep in-situ steel hollow rib deck and reinforced concrete composite floor slab
16. 100mm-deep raised floor to provide flexible service void
17. suspended ceiling conceals 570mm-deep void containing steel beams and building services
18. recess for roller blinds formed in plasterboard
19. internal plasterboard lining to columns
20. Venetian glass (tesserae) mosaic installation by artist Antoni Malinowski
21. aluminium support frame to mosaic soffit
22. 70mm high-performance rigid insulation
23. 140mm blockwork cavity wall
24. proprietary stainless-steel cavity wall lintel
25. painted render with string line features
26. satin white polyester powder-coated aluminium frame to ground and lower ground floor windows
27. ventilation grille

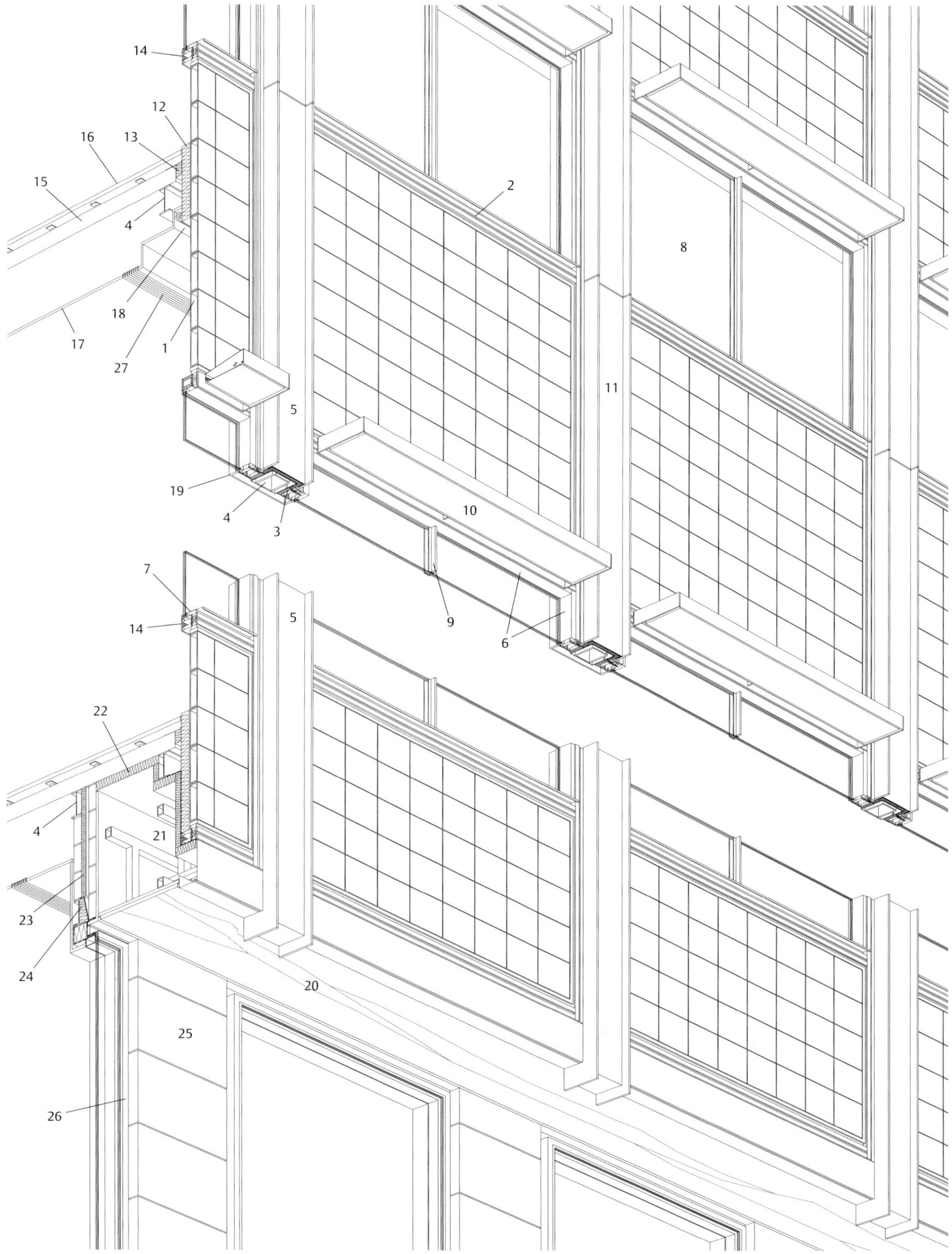

The benefit to the streetscape of replacing the existing streetbound bulk with a cantilevered bay was easily agreed. Less easy with the planning authority was the logic of a steel and glass tectonic. In contrast with the flush white aesthetic of a parkland pavilion (see Office Building W3, Stockley Park in *Volume 1*), the dark metal finish, recessive planes, protruding solar shelves and glass block panels are less strident in the urban collage and reflect the working world of the mews as opposed to the showcase of New Bond Street. The soffit was then an obvious canvas for an art commission and a competition was held to choose an artist.

left: Construction detail of the Maddox Street façade.

right: View of the façade after completion.

Around the corner in Maddox Street, Parry has replaced the existing grim 1970s building with a contemporary commercial elevation expressed as a volume cantilevered over the street, which returns some of the public realm relative to its former state. The elevation appears as a single black steel-framed bay being squeezed by the neighbouring brick and stone elevations. Its complexity is made by a sculptural composition of *brise-soleils* and black steel I-beams which shoot up above the building line in a supra-Miesian expression of their structural function. Glass block spandrels below and above the office windows allow the architect to avoid the deadening flatness associated with contemporary commercial architecture but admit just as much light—whilst still managing to create a discreet modernist ribbon window from which to look at the city.

The verticality and height of the circulation spaces is emphasised through a language of attenuated timber columns which encase the stairs and the floors to the atrium. The wood also softens the interior in a surprising twist not indicated by the Chicago-inflected elevation. The most surprising move however is the painted soffit beneath the overhanging upper floors, a work by the artist Antoni Malinowski, a colourful rip through the fabric of the cantilever as if exposing a psychedelic spectrum.

It has a cheering effect on the street, though surprisingly few people I observed even notice it which is—perhaps, precisely its charm.

Then the building turns the corner once more into St George Street, where the scale of the buildings picks up on the neighbouring Hanover Square. These are classic Queen Anne with tall, attenuated windows crowned by shallow arches and contained in bands of stone. Here the architects have added a new storey above the cornice line, which appears as an attic and helps mediate between the square and the commercial building behind (as well, of course, as making the project more commercially viable).

This is a substantial urban intervention which does something that has, in many ways, become architecturally unfashionable. It acknowledges its context. What makes it so interesting is that it has not one single context, or even two to make it Janus-faced, but three strikingly different façades responding to the rapidly changing streetscape of Mayfair. I think 50 Bond Street in particular will stand robustly alongside the extraordinary and beautiful Edwardian façades which define the street, from the florid decorative excess of Bond Street Arcade to the delicate iron and glass filigree façade of Aspreys.

opposite, left and right: The language of the courtyard to the urban block interior is almost sylvan in contrast to the street. The glazing with openable sections is cleaned from access walkways. Shading, both solar and social, given the proximity of different uses, is created by the larch patterns that overclad the metal skeleton.

right: This twilight view westwards from Maddox Street towards Grosvenor Square was obliterated by the previous building. Antoni Malinowski's beautiful artwork celebrates light reflected by glass through the ancient art of Venetian glass and colour.

Belgravia Residence

The vertical movement through the building centres on a stair which springs from a basement excavation beneath the mews house and a one-storey drop in street level from front to back. The mews house at the rear becomes the private, intimate part of the dwelling accommodating bedrooms and the more private activity of the domestic everyday.

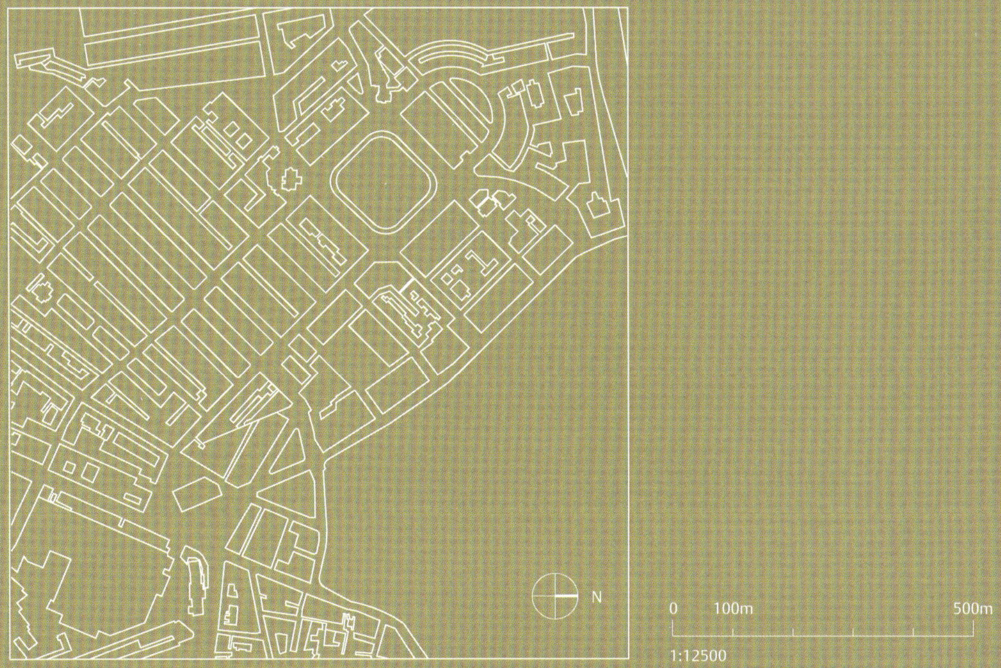

left: Urban plan of Belgravia (after Thomas Cundy's plan of 1821).

opposite: Typical configuration in plan and section of the Belgravia terraced houses and mews. The street is 'made up' by the excavated site spoil and consequently the mews is at the original datum of the land.

opposite right: Axonometric longitudinal section of the laterally organised apartment.

This house reveals an interesting and unusual section which seems to reverse the normal relationship of house to mews, of scale and size pivoting around a courtyard garden. Belgravia Residence represents the classic London landscape of the substantial Cubitt houses which define the character of so much of the heart of the city's prime real estate. The white stucco fronts with their porticoes and the seemingly endless grid of rigorously repetitive aediculed windows are delicately separated from the street by filigree black iron railings (the border made manifest in the contrast in colour, black to white, out to in, public to private) and, of course, by that very British architectural motif, the oddly named 'area' which creates both a symbolic moat between street and interior as well as making a subterranean realm for staff to operate unseen and to engrain a class structure deeply into the foundations of the architecture.

The usual hierarchy of those houses is that of grand public front and service architecture to the rear, a diminution of architecture from the emulation of the terrace palace to the workmanlike brick boxes behind. In this unusual project the client has decided to keep only the ground and basement of Belgravia Residence and to create a horizontal house stretching through the section of the entire block, from street to mews. The effect is that the larger block of accommodation is at the rear of the property whilst only a horizontal sliver of space penetrates into the fine front of the building. The vertical movement through the building centres on a stair which springs from a basement excavation beneath the mews house and a one-storey drop in street level from front to back. The mews house, at the rear becomes the private, intimate part of the dwelling accommodating bedrooms and the more private activity of the domestic everyday.

The grand living room remains at the front of the house, a big, representational space for the family's substantial art collection. It is bookended on one side by the street and on the other by a small patio which cuts deep into the heart of the house. Planted with bamboo and with one wall covered in green (the landscape was designed by Christopher Bradley Hole), the courtyard is designed very much as another room in the sectional progression.

The little library room acts as a buffer between the public front and the more private nature of the mews and leads onto the staircase to the rear of the house, which is a very different proposition from the traditional Cubitt stair. With its stone treads and a dark, sinuous handrail snaking up around, the stair acts not only to draw one up the house but to draw light down into its depths.

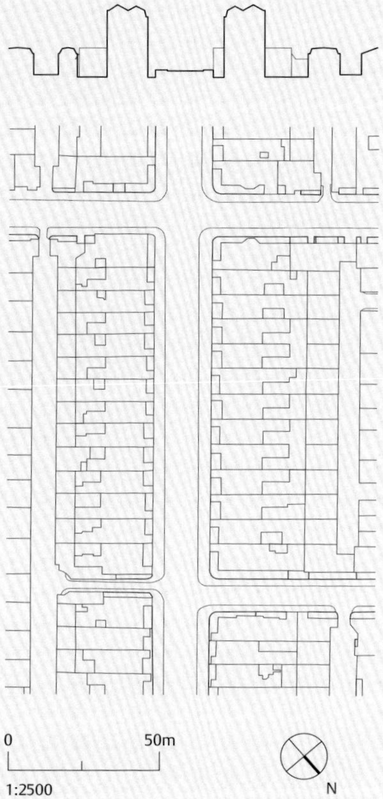

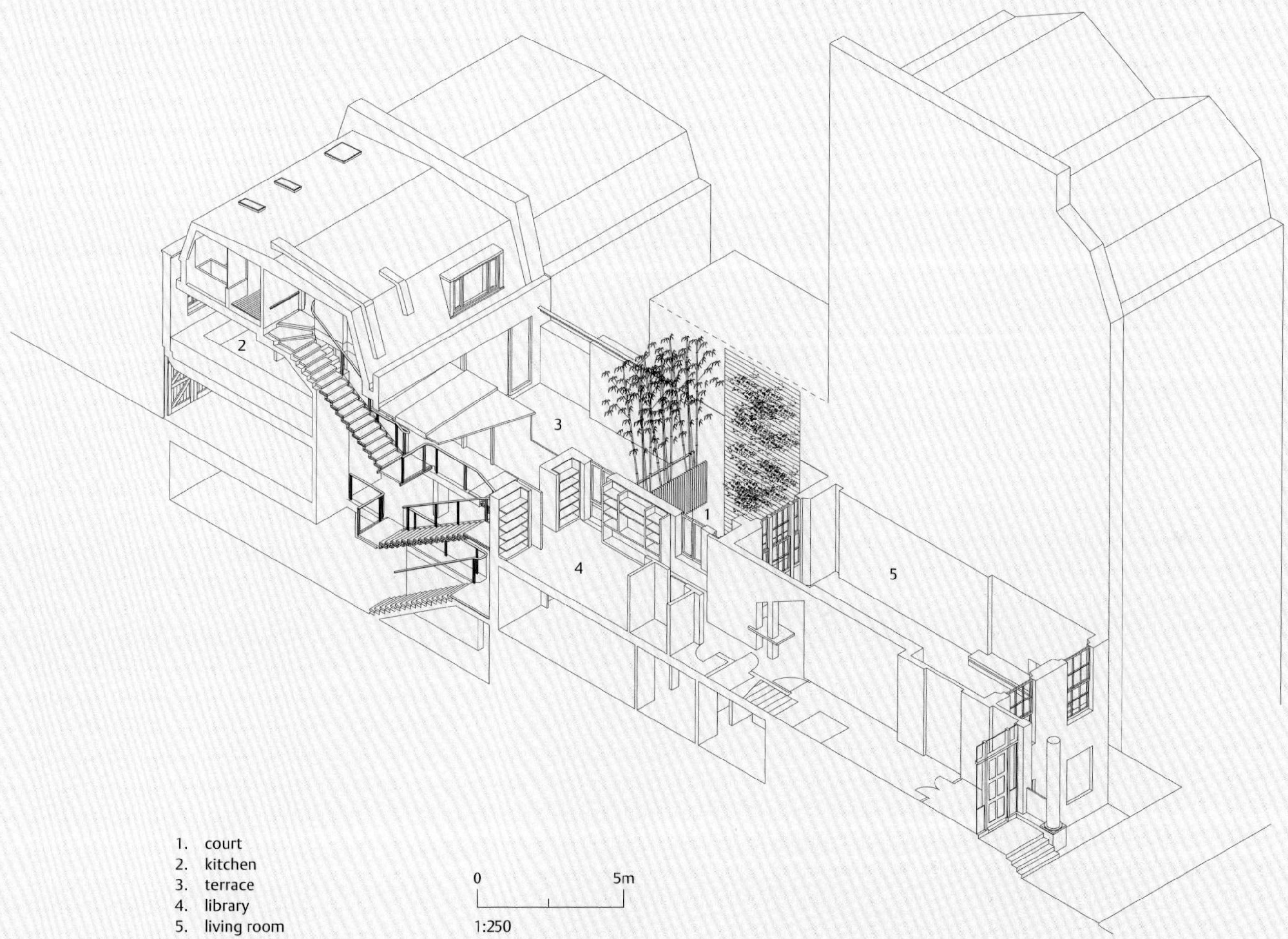

1. court
2. kitchen
3. terrace
4. library
5. living room

0 5m
1:250

1. master bedroom
2. walk-in closet
3. dining room
4. kitchen
5. terrace
6. library
7. living room
8. garage
9. hall
10. bedroom
11. utility room
12. study
13. court
14. media room
15. plant room
16. gym
17. store

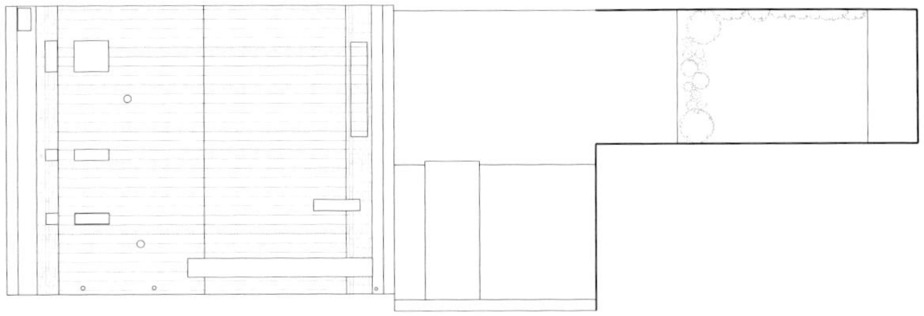

roof plan

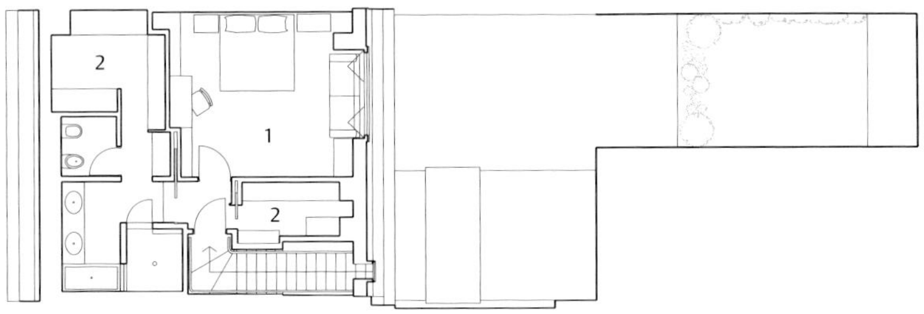

plan of the first floor

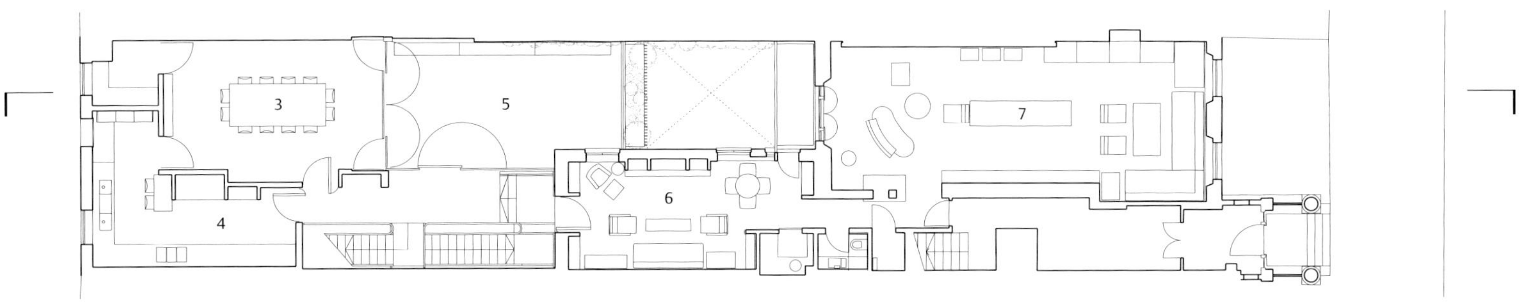

plan of the upper ground floor (street)

plan of the ground floor (mews)

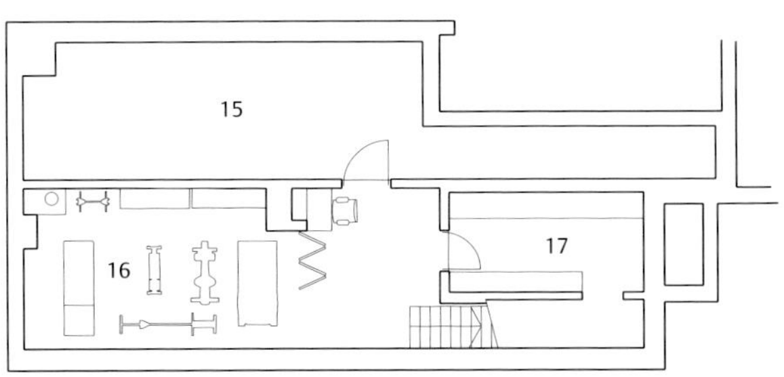

plan of the basement

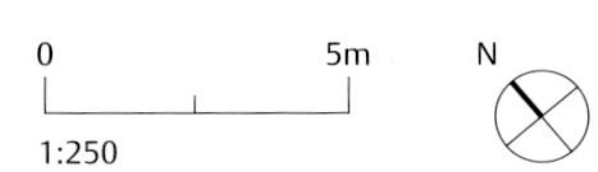

right: Design model of the stair and connected spaces. This model is the third iteration from the initial studio model used to resolve details. When completed it was on site as a reference to help coordinate the many trades involved, from concrete to acoustic panels.

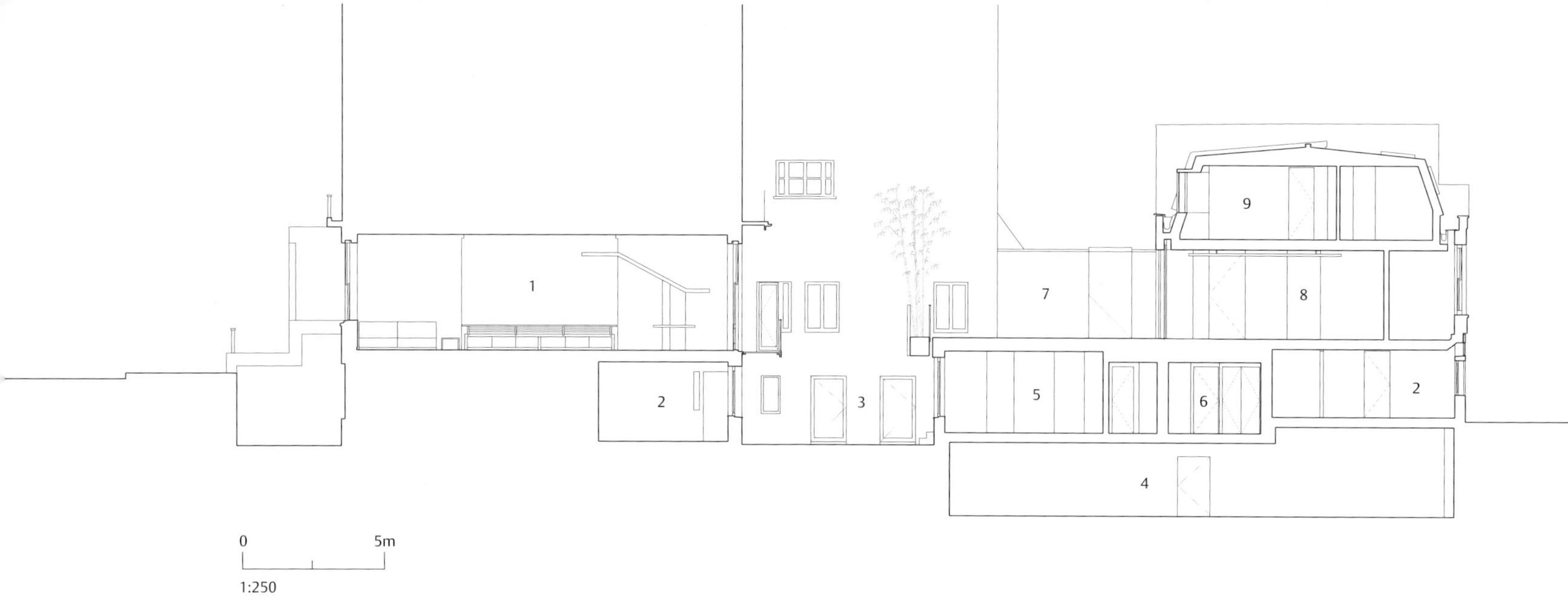

longitudinal section looking southwest

1. living room
2. bedroom
3. court
4. plant room
5. study
6. utility room
7. terrace
8. dining room
9. master bedroom

There are no risers between the treads, and the light from above casts a filmic light on the plain plastered walls, an analogue of the shade created by the row of bamboo and the vertically striped screens outside. With an attenuated strip of natural top light above, the lightness of the stairs makes this space feel like a breath of crisp Modernist air at the heart of the home. It is also the element around which the juggled-around plan functions, allowing the new spatial arrangement to be understood. The plan is complex—accommodating a lot of functions—but also arranged in a very slim, long shape. The openness of the stair dispels this sensation of an attenuated plan and also obviates the need for anything approaching a corridor which would have made the plan almost unworkable. In one reading of the house you could argue there are two parallel systems of organisation—the courtyard patio and the stair—both creating a well of light and space, both articulated and emphasised by vertical elements—the bamboo and the stairs.

The slatted nature of the riserless treads also chimes with a series of horizontal elements which appear throughout the house; the dining room ceiling with its slatted timber canopy; the bookshelves that line the library and so on. These are picked up again in the stairwell by expressed concrete lintels, marble surfaces across the waists of concrete structures which act as hall tables, and the ubiquitous built-in furniture always present throughout, creating seating, sideboards, shelving and surfaces for display and function.

There are also barely visible yet somehow very perceptible architectural touches which create a constantly surprising sense of lightness in the interior. One of the most visible is the articulation of the edge of the concrete ground floor slab, which is chamfered to make it appear less monolithic.

What is particularly striking about this intervention is the way the typical, grand Cubitt dwelling has been left more or less intact above and around this new house. The new building slots through the original Victorian house but it also creates an intriguing reversal of the hierarchy of served and servant. The appropriation of mews, basement and yard—spaces seen as the sole domain of the servant classes—creates a very interesting snapshot of the changes in the readings of the fabric of the city. Just as in many other EPA projects, the intervention acts to rationalise a building through its section but also to reconnect it with the darker realm of the earth. The particular materials which appear in the below-ground levels—the marbles, the fair-faced concrete and the black steel—each speak of the ground, of materials extracted and then reinterred in the making of a subterranean space. The plan and the section each look complex, yet from within this is an extremely easy building to understand—it leads you through by the hand and it exemplifies and vindicates the thinking about architecture through the section which is so typical of Eric Parry Architects' work.

right: View from the dining room to the central courtyard. Behind the station point is a James Turrell wall light sculpture. The central glazed panel with side doors emphasises the importance of the axis between town house and mews.

left: The library is set between the new glazed roofed stairwell and the body of the main house. The full horizontal dimension approached 40m from street to mews, syncopated by natural light and courtyard spaces.

right: The concrete structure is conceived as spreading from a central stem. The raw finely crafted concrete lends a calm gravitas at the apartment centre.

The stair, which floats free of the walls in the lightwell, is embedded into the structure of the mews, the insertion echoed by the long cutting of the skylight above.

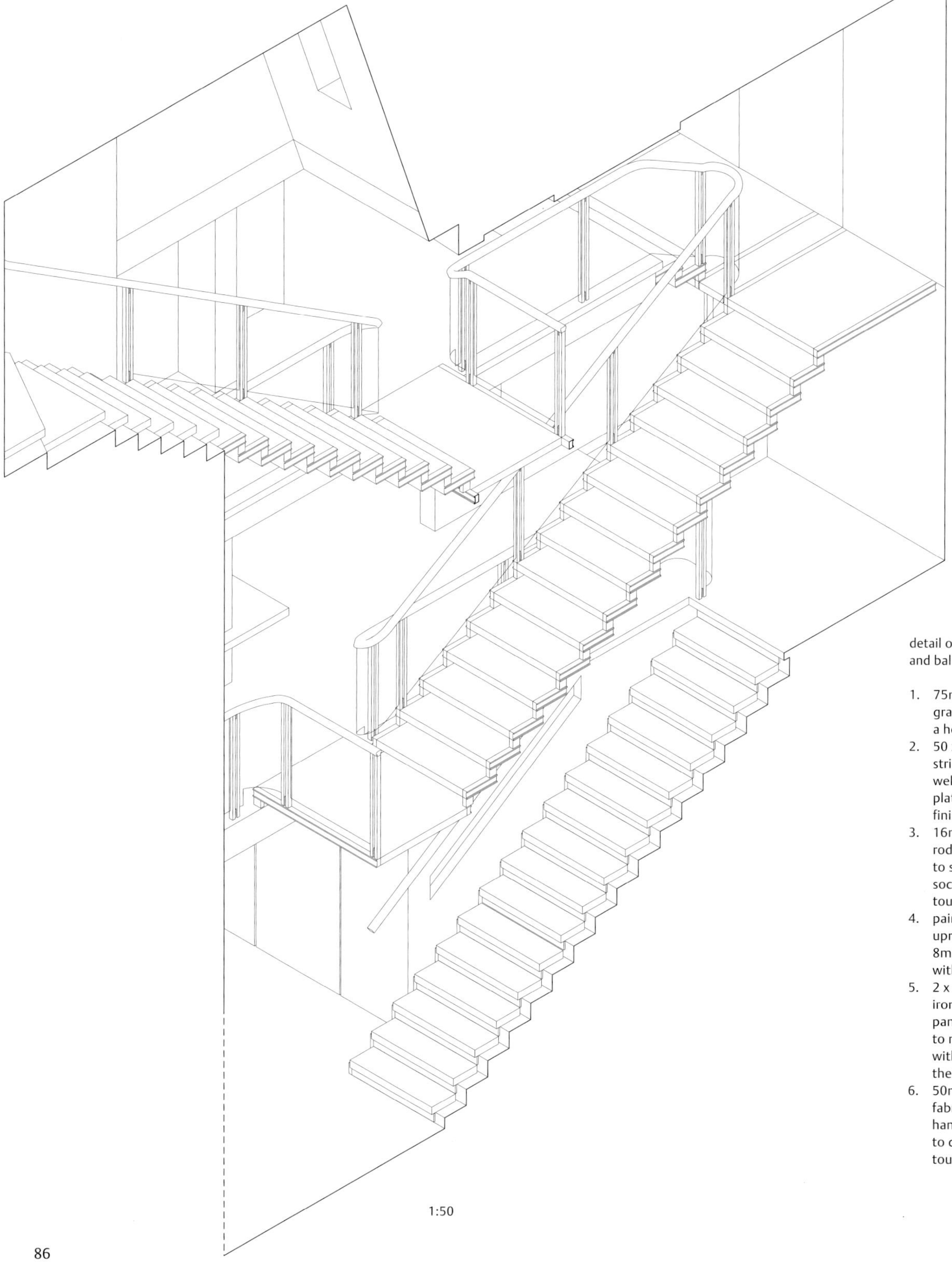

detail of handrail
and balustrade

1. 75mm-thick natural pale granite stone treads with a honed finish
2. 50 x 75mm profiled stringer fabricated from welded solid mild-steel plate, with a tourmaline finish
3. 16mm mild-steel tensioned rod (3 per tread) fixed to stringer with countersunk socket-headed screws with tourmaline finish
4. paired channel balustrade uprights fabricated from 8mm-thick mild-steel plate, with tourmaline finish
5. 2 x 10mm laminated low-iron glass balustrade panels, adhesive-fixed to mild-steel uprights, with radiused segments at the change in direction
6. 50mm-wide profiled fabricated mild-steel handrail secret-fixed to channel, all with tourmaline finish

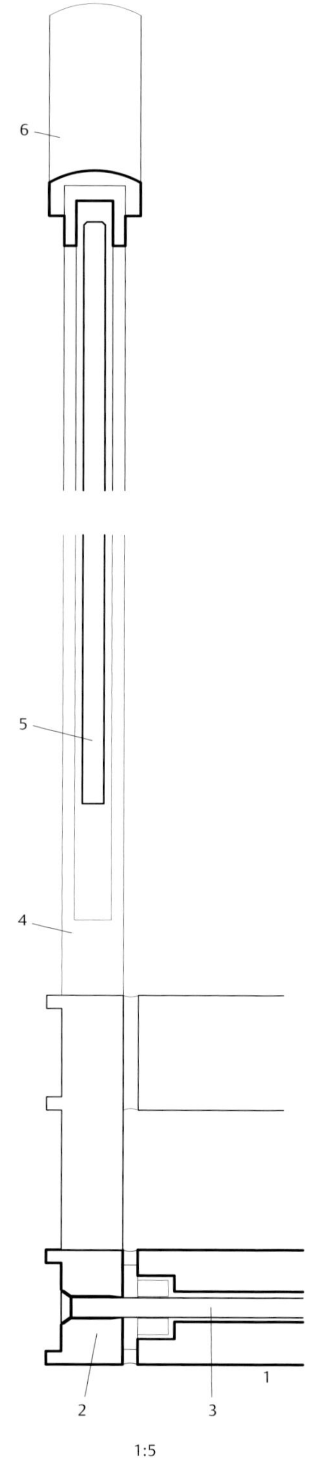

The solid steel stringers supporting the granite treads span from wall to landing. Michael Hadi, our structural engineer, accurately predicted a liveliness stiffened by the glass panels. Of note, the wreathed curved glass panels at changes of direction.

left: The terrace at the centre of the plan is bound by a west-facing party wall on one side and the main stair landing enclosure on the other. The composition consists of a transparent glass wall, translucent roof unit, solid bronze roof and door section, and a smaller glass neck (out of picture).

right: The elevation to the mews is intended to recapture the original pragmatic austerity of these buildings and ran counter to the rules of 'gentrification' prescribed by Westminster—bay windows, porches and flower boxes.

Timothy Taylor Gallery

The gallery itself is framed by pure white walls and a ceiling punctuated by four top lights which attempt to evoke a neutral northern top light. The original heavily decorated columns were stripped right back to reveal spindly steels, elongated poles which enhance the semi-industrial language.

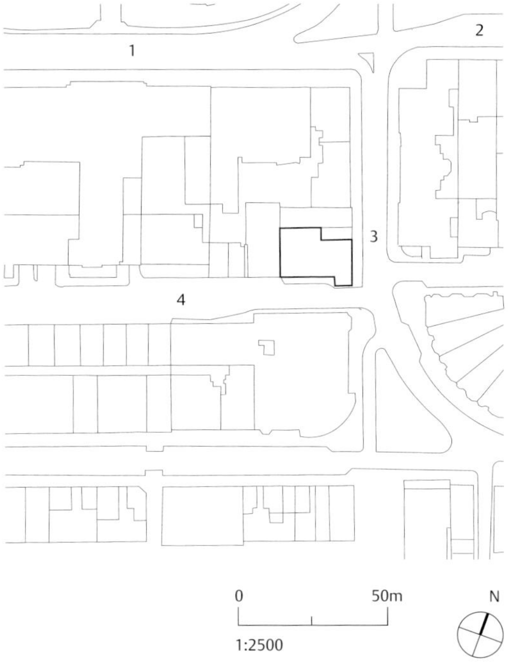

site location plan

1. Grosvenor Square
2. Grosvenor Street
3. Carlos Place
4. Adams Row

There's something pleasingly contemporary about a bank being transformed into an art gallery. The physical presence of money in the city is expressed not through the solid, stolid neo-Georgian puddings of banks straining every sinew to look respectable, trustworthy and civic. Instead the city's commercial thrust appears to come through art. When urban centres attempt to regenerate, it is artists and galleries they attempt to attract, not bank branches. Art has taken on a new meaning as an economic entity; trade through culture.

This, however, is not exactly an area in need of regeneration. In fact it is very difficult to think of any piece of any city in the world less in demand of regeneration. The swish streets converging on Mayfair's Carlos Place, the neighbouring Grosvenor Square and the Connaught Hotel are redolent of a certain kind of well-being, a place in which the international super-wealthy feel comfortable and have their needs attended to. Yet here it is, a small corner of London with a plaza and fountain designed by Tadao Ando as a focus of some of the most prestigious retail in Europe. Having said that, it is also a small enclave which has very successfully managed to retain a particular identity. These few streets retain the very distinctive feel of an Edwardian city with its blend of stone and terracotta. The shopfronts are delicate and elegant, glassy and open beneath freestyle mansion blocks. But Timothy Taylor's gallery is resolutely not one of those. The arched windows to the old banking hall were made to appear more akin to the domestic architecture which was once prevalent in an earlier manifestation of this part of Mayfair. They do not reach down to the pavement and have a further level of implied visual security in the wrought-iron railings on their stone cills. The idea was that passers-by would glimpse the ornate plaster ceilings of the banking hall, but not the customers themselves. Those windows have now been blocked out and the ceiling blanked off. But the attenuated neo-Mannerist arches have not been completely blinded. They have been subtly back lit so that in the dark, and perhaps most noticeably in the twilight hours when openings and private views take place, they give a ghostly white glow, redolent of the minimal white walls of the interior, a subtle suggestion of modernity.

This means the gallery doesn't have a conventional front, a shop window, but it does allow the creation inside of a surprising white box, not exactly entirely neutral but unencumbered by windows or views. The space is white, bright and clean. The poured concrete floor brings a touch of the industrial to this extremely non-industrial enclave, but it also roots the gallery's presence in the city, weighing it down as a permanent presence and creating a kind of continuity with the paving of the city outside so that this feels like a less privileged space than the swanky boutiques that surround it. There is a small lobby which acts as an acclimatisation space; a threshold between the wealthy contented buzz of the street and the quiet, white intensity of the gallery. The gallery itself is framed by pure white walls and a ceiling punctuated by four top lights which attempt to evoke a neutral northern top light.

left: The original bank entrance has become an urban foil to its gallery incarnation.

opposite: The opening show was on the recent work of Alex Katz. His large landscape paintings, like windows onto a heightened reality, illustrate the ceiling light panels' mimetic capacity to echo natural light. Around the perimeter of each panel is a light track to allow additional lights. The three solid cast-iron columns were the cores to the decorative plasterwork of the Edwardian banking hall.

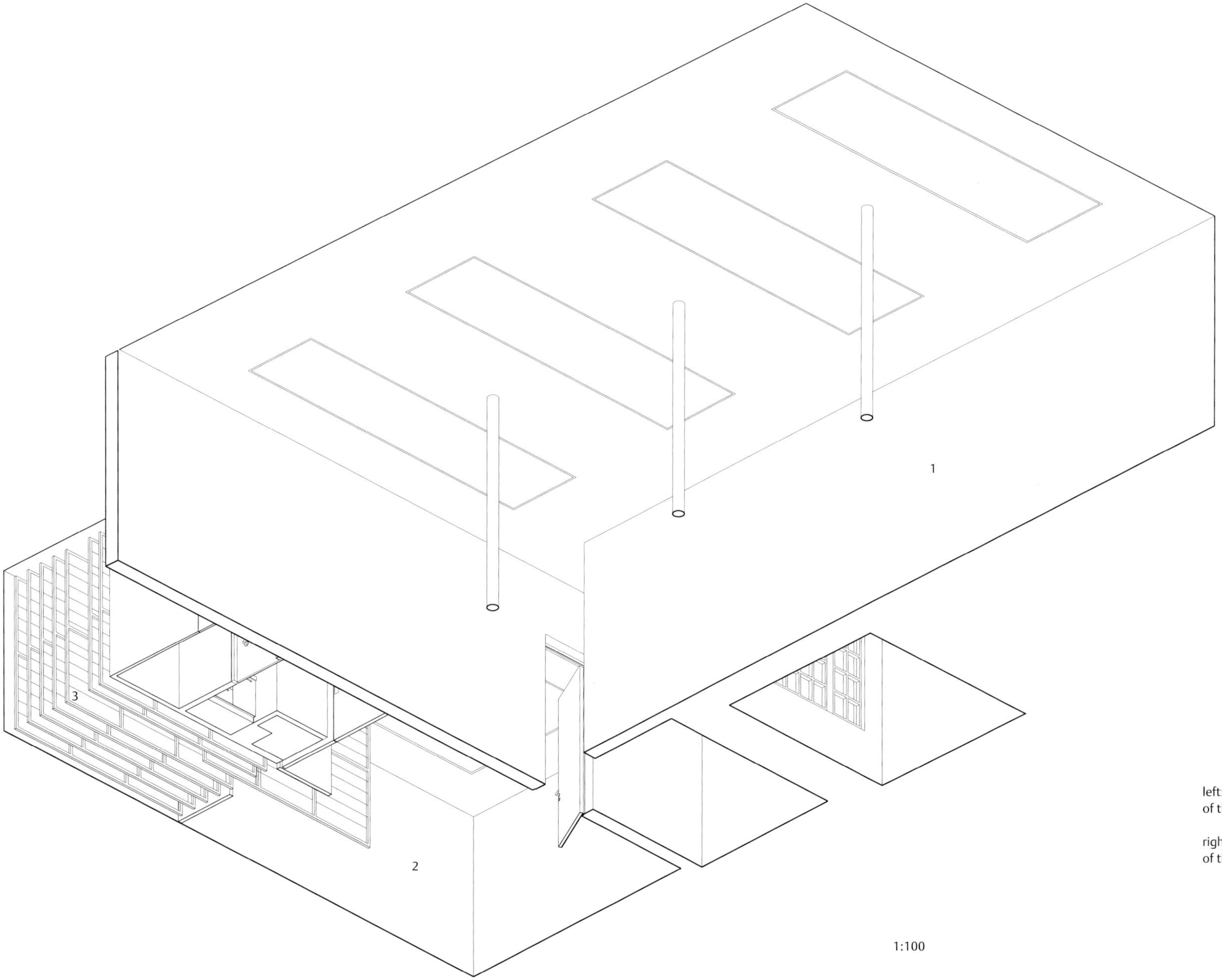

left: Isometric (worm's-eye) view of the ground floor of the gallery.

right: Isometric (bird's-eye) view of the basement.

1:100

1. gallery
2. viewing room
3. picture store

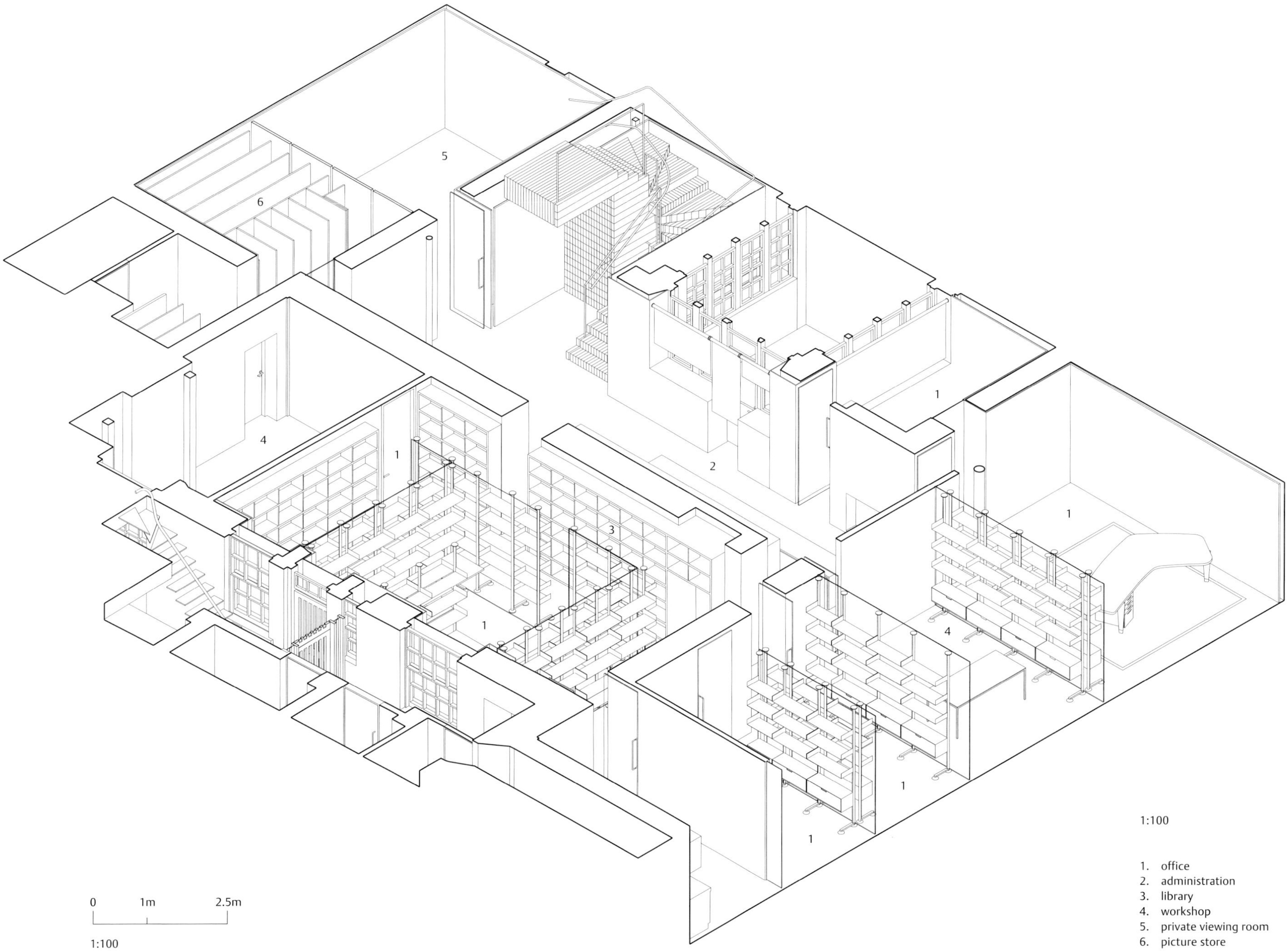

1:100

1. office
2. administration
3. library
4. workshop
5. private viewing room
6. picture store

The original heavily decorated columns were stripped right back to reveal spindly steels, elongated poles which enhance the semi-industrial language.

It is interesting to compare this space to another converted bank branch of a similar period nearby. Hauser & Wirth's Piccadilly gallery occupies a Lutyens bank, which was far more heavily listed through the renown of its architect (though not necessarily because of the quality of the building). There, the dark panelled and galleried banking hall has been retained with its original character. It is an intriguing space but one suited only to a particular kind of theatrical installation. The gallery has used it well, each installation responding to the particular character of the cubic, timber-clad, almost cuboid interior. Timothy Taylor's gallery however is geared far more to canvases, and these work beautifully on the white walls of the Mayfair space. The crispness of the rooms and that flat, cool light allows them to shine, with nothing in the interior distracting from them.

This is the second gallery Parry has built for Taylor; the first, designed in 2003, was a complex interior in the little art nexus of Dering Street in the galleries formerly occupied by Anthony D'Offay. Here the central architectural move had been the insertion of a precast concrete stair to bring two disparate spaces together. In Carlos Place, there is far more room, and what there is is far more easily accessible.

But here too a staircase has been employed to bind the two volumes of upstairs and downstairs together. Here the challenge was to reconcile the industrial weight of the concrete floor on the ground-floor gallery level with a more deliberately domestic feel of the offices and private viewing rooms below. To do this, Parry used a solid timber stair, stacked like Jenga blocks, with each tread a distinct chunk of timber. The obvious visual mass of the stair allows the transition from concrete to the timber floors below in an elegant, winding gesture of descent, the wood expressing a kind of natural root to the building. The subterranean private viewing rooms with their sliding racks of canvases provoke a sense of enclosure and security, an idea of being alone with a painting, of spending an intense moment, getting personal with the art. The offices around are top-lit where possible and the floor is surprisingly light, with partitions of glass and bookshelves acting as space dividers so there is a sense of the continuity of space and an openness.

This is a deceptively simple scheme which uses to its advantage the incongruity of the contemporary vogue for stripped industrial arts space and the bourgeois fabric of its shell and the surrounding streets. The translucent windows glow at night and the interior glows during the day. A stolid Edwardian expression of middle-class money has been turned into a subtle container for art as a cipher for how the manifestations of capital and status have changed.

above left: At the most remote part of the basement the gallerist's office is connected by the glass walls of the cellular offices.

above right: The stacked timber stair connects the timber basement floor to the industrial neutrality of the screeded ground floor gallery showing room.

opposite: The bank's top-lit customer meeting room has become the main showing room, with picture racking that can be closed off.

Four Seasons Hotel Spa

The spa is about a retreat from the world and, if the underground site of the Mandarin lent itself perfectly to the exclusion of the cityscape, the interest at the Four Seasons is in the way the glimpses of the city are managed as a backdrop and a realm which comes into view once the various processes of scrubbing and cleansing, massaging and bathing are completed.

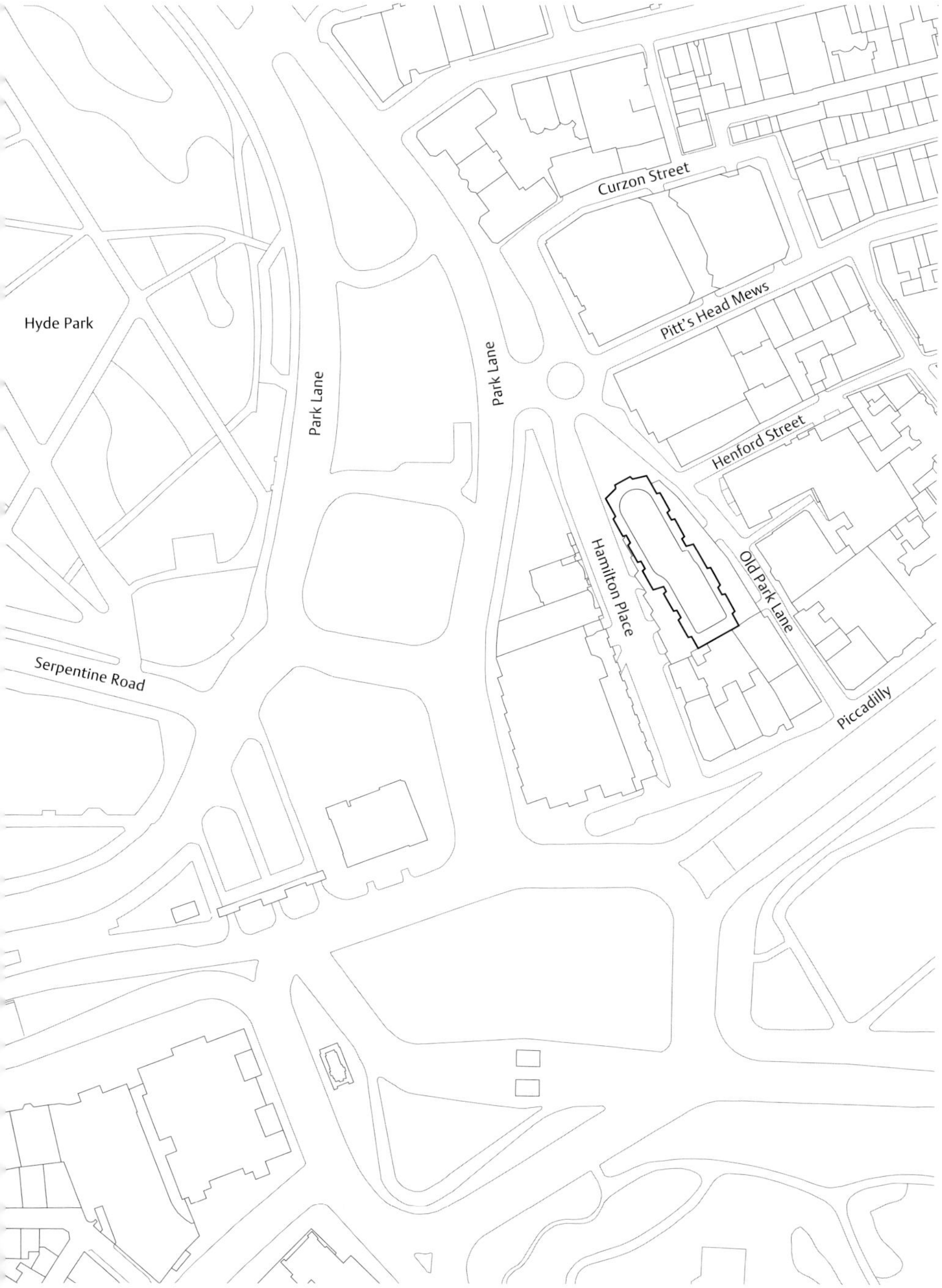

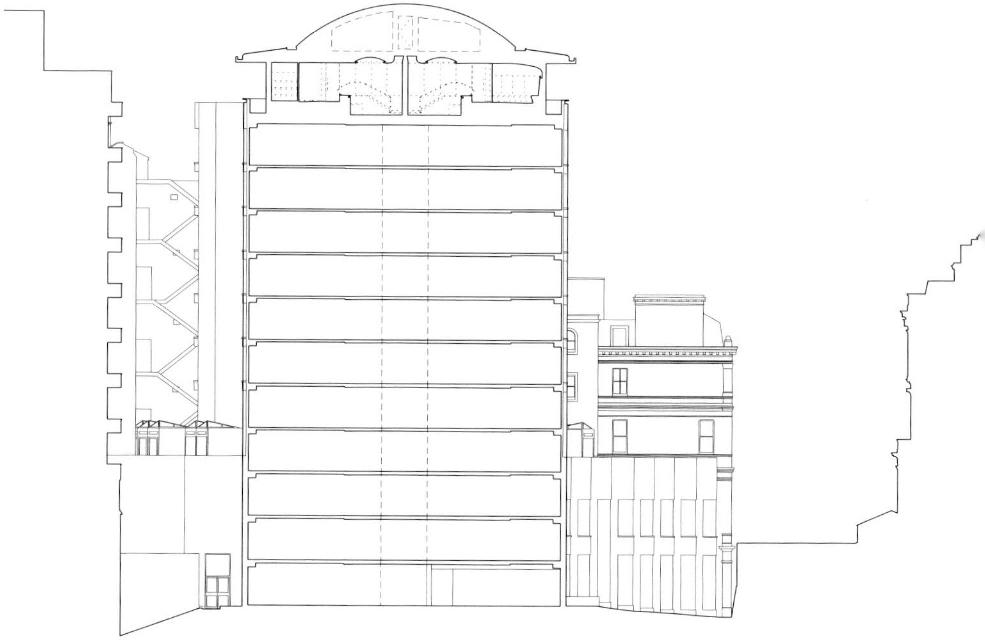

0 2m 10m
1:500

0 10m 50m
1:3000

N

far left: Site location at the axis of Park Lane.

left: Section showing the additional two levels.

above: Initial sketch to support the argument that the building would benefit from a positive addition to act like the brim of a hat.

right: The unseen quality of the zinc roof which absorbs elegantly a multitude of plant and servicing requirements.

The spa has become an emblematic space in contemporary culture. Its particular cocktail of luxury, relaxation, consumption and quiet has made it a hybrid of modern aspiration. It blends a sense of sacred space (in a culture which rarely uses actual sacred space for contemplation), exoticism (the idea of a spa is somehow eastern or ancient—not quite of our own time or place) and expense (a cocooning in a space of luxury). Oddly it is also a space of decadence which has become defined by its minimalism rather than by any overt luxury.

The Four Seasons Spa sits atop the hotel in London's Park Lane, the shallow vault of its roof creating a tenth-floor crown for the rather inexpressive Modernism of the 1970 building. The hotel is part of the vast cliff of structure which faces Hyde Park, an odd wall of building (which was once itself fronted by a wall dividing it from the park) as buffer between Mayfair's genteel and expensive streets and the open green space. The hotel itself always looked (as did many of the buildings of the era) curiously unfinished, lacking a base or attic storey. A new bronze-coloured parapet wraps around the top of the original structure, faithfully following its plan form, and then the roof appears to float above a glass wall.

EPA completed the successful subterranean spa at the Mandarin Oriental in London but, in a way, that setting (although nearby) was the diametric opposite of this structure. The Mandarin spa was below ground; Parry refers to it as a "cave" and its feel was of a dark, intense space which acknowledged the pressure of the buildings bearing down upon it yet which carved out a space for quiet luxury from the fabric of the city itself.

The Spa is about a retreat from the world and, if the underground site of the Mandarin lent itself perfectly to the exclusion of the cityscape, the interest at the Four Seasons is in the way the glimpses of the city are managed as a backdrop and a realm which hoves into view once the various processes of scrubbing and cleansing, massaging and bathing are completed.

The Spa is organised around a journey, a pseudo-spiritual idea of a ritual route. The sequence of spaces begins with the background of the city visible and then becomes increasingly intimate and cocooned. The visitor then emerges as if cleansed and prepared for the city once more as the city is revealed again. Views and light are controlled through a series of translucent layers including a graded ceramic frit on the glass and Merit Claussen's exquisitely diaphanous veils, woven in a double-weave technique, using a propriety nylon yarn for longevity. The rich, deep lacquering of the surfaces, the deep, overhanging eaves outside the windows, the dark stones and timbers and the horsehair wall coverings congeal into an impression of a tropical temple with a deliberate hint of Bali. Along the ritual route are a series of intimate spaces including treatment rooms, in which the ceilings are relieved by delicately concave domes seemingly carved into the surface, and

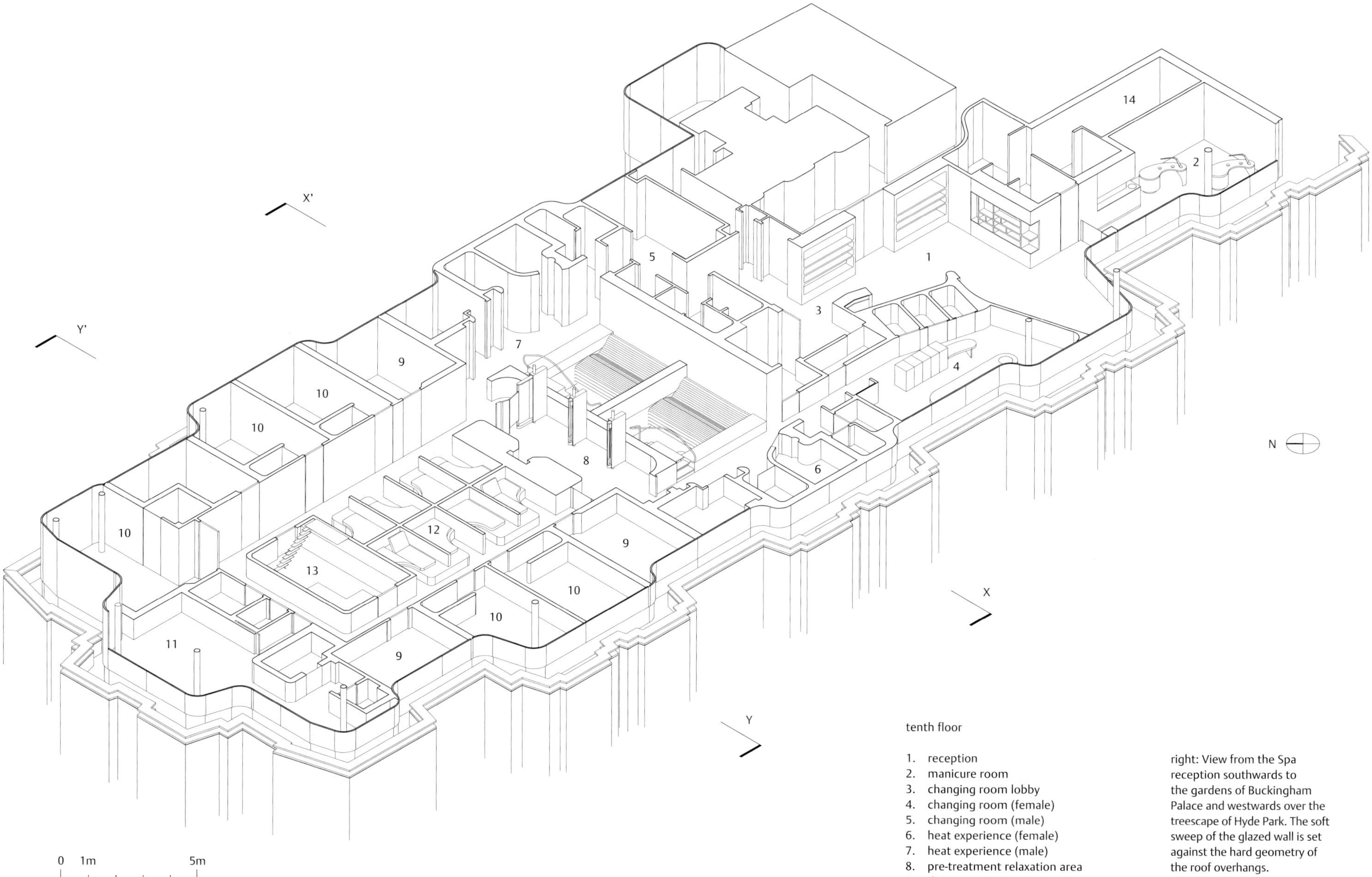

tenth floor

1. reception
2. manicure room
3. changing room lobby
4. changing room (female)
5. changing room (male)
6. heat experience (female)
7. heat experience (male)
8. pre-treatment relaxation area
9. dry treatment room
10. wet treatment room
11. VIP treatment room
12. post-treatment relaxation area
13. back of house
14. administration

right: View from the Spa reception southwards to the gardens of Buckingham Palace and westwards over the treescape of Hyde Park. The soft sweep of the glazed wall is set against the hard geometry of the roof overhangs.

far left: Stephen Cox's Egyptian alabaster sculpture, echoing the quality of skin with a crust from which water emerges to moisten and emphasise the stratigraphy of the marvellous stone.

left: The female changing rooms connected to the sky by a view at clerestory level but given privacy by the translucence below.

right: Detail of the granite-lined steam rooms where the meticulous geological alignment of the flows across stones is interrupted by the backlit disc and the side light that separates bench from floor.

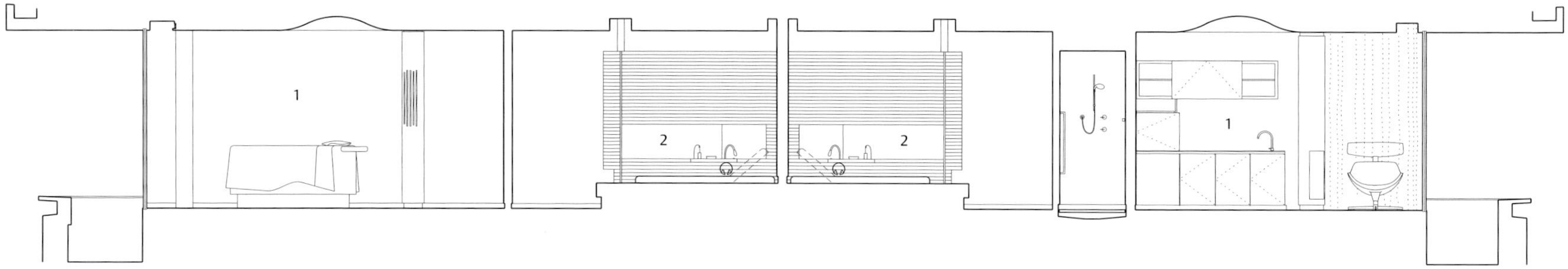

section YY'

1. treatment room
2. post-treatment relaxation room

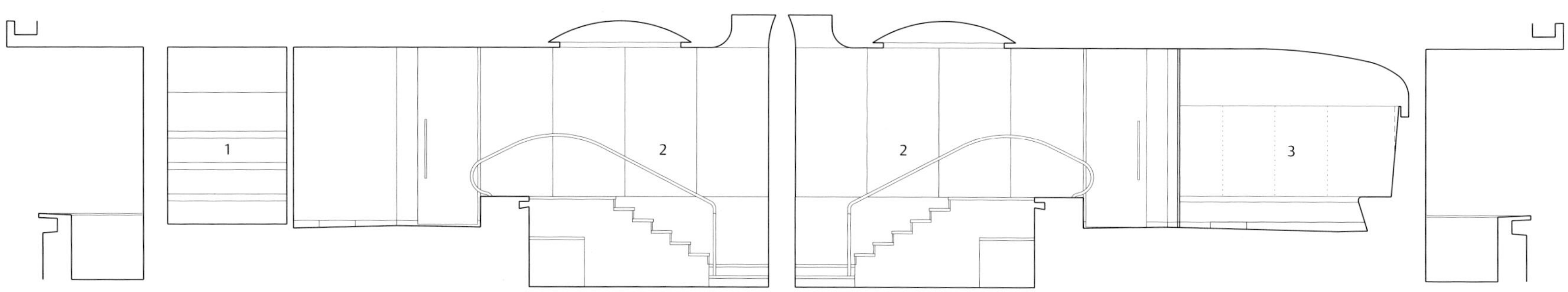

section XX'

1. sauna
2. water therapy
3. steam room

0 2m

1:100

left: View of the pre-treatment waiting space; to the right, a fire place is flanked by Stephen Cox's wall installation of the senses; to the left, pull-out screens can create private niches within the common area.

right: Night view of the female changing room (see page 104) and the reflective soffit of the overhang.

massage booths defined by dark veils and warm, organic timber furniture. The surfaces are deliberately tactile, privileging the neglected sense of touch over the overused sense of vision.

There is also a hard-edged, minimal pool which gives a moment of immersion in the fabric of the architecture. Here too a dome is inserted into the ceiling whilst a sliver of natural light illuminates the rear wall, casting intriguing shadows on the surfaces and glistening reflections across the water. The presence of the simple stairs is announced by a subtle concealed strip of light beneath the treads as they overshoot the risers, a golden yellow colour contrasting with the bluish glow of the natural light on the opposite wall creating a gentle play of golden and silvery tones on the water.

Throughout the spa a series of sculptures by Stephen Cox play with abstract representations of nature (in varying degrees of abstraction, some of which take on geological as well as natural form). The other thing that is omnipresent throughout the spa is water. Whether as steam and condensation in the spa, a thin wall of water in the shower, the still surface of the pool disrupted by the immersion of a body or just trickling down the side of one of Stephen Cox's pale stone sculptures, it is everywhere. The evening I visited it was also trickling down the windows outside, fostering a very London sense of security in the interior, of protection from the clouds outside.

The twin-bedded treatment space at the prow of the building with its landscape surrounding epitomises the original design intention to create an aerial place of reverie.

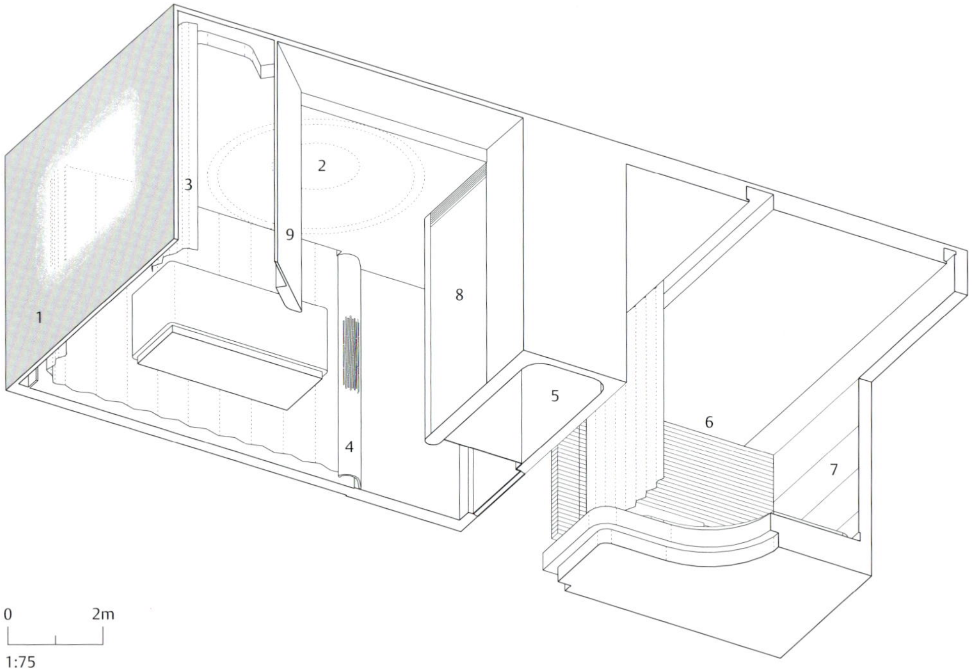

axonometric view

1. 47mm-thick double-glazed unit with argon-filled 16mm cavity and white frit pattern generated by computer scripting
2. 1600mm-diameter sculpted relief in fibrous plaster with paint finish
3. bespoke fabric curtain with three-dimensional structure and two-tone yarn
4. oak timber column with built-in lantern lined with Rigid Acrylic Warlon Sheet – Shoji
5. shower room in continuous heat-formed white solid surface with 180mm radius corners
6. dark timber veneer screen with 5mm horizontal joints, 20mm fixed and sliding polished polyester lacquer panel, 40mm profiled polyester lacquer side table with built-in audio and reclining bed control unit
7. 500mm-high horizontal horse hair panels on MDF boards with wadding
8. 20mm-thick polished polyester lacquer panels hung on concealed aluminium Z-bar
9. brown/grey polished polyester lacquer column with built-in low-level niche and concealed lighting

top, far left: Complementing the closed top porch of the Spa, the interior of the treatment rooms transforms into the cocooned interior surrounded by the purpose-designed double-woven and pleated textiles.

left: The ceilings of the treatment rooms have risings in the fibrous plaster that are analogous to a body's curvaceousness.

bottom left: Isometric view of treatment room and post-treatment room.

right: Post-treatment 'stalls' are given a spaciousness by the beds' side extension, arm-rest controls and acoustic rear panels.

Threadneedle Street

60 Threadneedle Street is a few moments' walk from the Bank of England, at the busy, bustling junction with Broad Street. It sits on the site of City's old stock exchange, which is a curious coincidence as Parry's contribution to the Paternoster Square development adjacent to St Paul's Cathedral now houses the new stock exchange. The sinuous walls of the Threadneedle Street building, the curving corners and the building's brooding, dark presence in the streetscape are very obviously heavily influenced by Soane's Bank. But this is a building for a City in a very different financial age.

Historical site location plans (from left to right): plan based on Richard Horwood's map of 1794–1819; plan based on the Ordnance Survey map of 1916; plan based on the Ordnance Survey map of 1998; plan based on the Ordnance Survey map of 2011, with the location of the new building for 60 Threadneedle Street, post-completion.

1. Sir John Soane, Bank of England (1788–1833)
2. Nicholas Hawksmoor, St Mary Woolnoth (completed 1716)
3. George Dance the Elder, Mansion House (1739–1752)

4* Edward Jarman, Royal Exchange (second building campaign)

4. Sir William Tite, Royal Exchange (third building campaign)
5. James Stirling, Number One Poultry office and retail building
6. 60 Threadneedle Street

Sir John Soane's Bank of England is an exercise in walls. The building's street presence (as opposed to its rich interior) was an attempt to evoke a particular idea of security and strength. The walls are made to appear massive through a blend of rustication, niches, cut-outs and the famous Tivoli Corner. These apparently massive walls curve around the corners, like those of a castle—as if to be able to better deflect missiles or cannonballs. But all those features in fact also help to tie this extraordinary mass into the fabric of the city streets. The essentially decorative devices employed to emphasise the impenetrability of the wall also create a richly articulated, though completely blind, mass. It is something akin to the fortified base of a Florentine Renaissance palazzo, which simultaneously speaks of urbanity and the generosity of a genuinely civic structure (with in-built benches) and serious financial might.

60 Threadneedle Street is a few moments' walk from the Bank of England, at the bustling junction with Broad Street. It sits on the site of the City's old stock exchange, which is a curious coincidence as Parry's contribution to the Paternoster Square development adjacent to St Paul's Cathedral now houses the new stock exchange.

The sinuous walls of the Threadneedle Street building, the curving corners and the building's brooding, dark presence in the streetscape

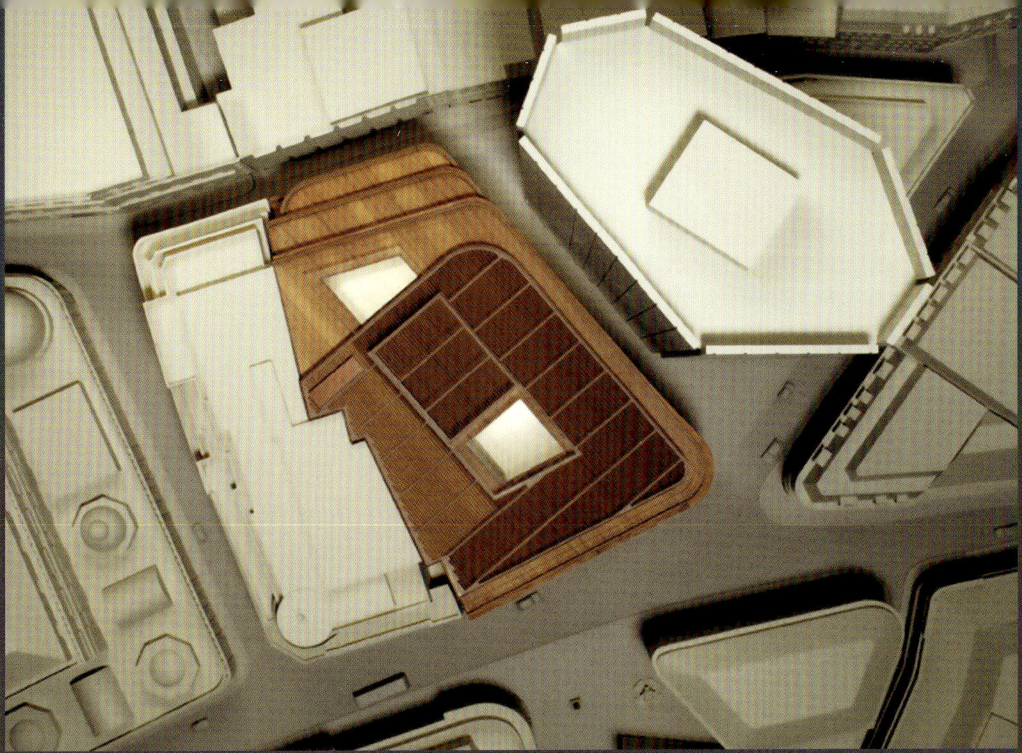

is very obviously heavily influenced by Soane's Bank. But this is a building for a City in a very different financial age. Soane's walls, like those of the Florentine palazzo, were a visual cipher for the presence of power and the physical existence of the money inside. Finance is now more ethereal; it exists in cyber rather than real space, and contemporary financial buildings are about the mysterious and obfuscating processes of trading, of derivatives, swaps and futures rather than the stolid idea of banking.

So it seems appropriate that despite its striking black presence its façade curves more akin to a sheet of paper or black silk than a solid stone wall. With its horizontal banding it recalls Erich Mendelsohn's 1927 Petersdorff Department Store in Wroclaw. In the gentle curve segueing into a sharp curving corner we can almost see the sweep of Mendelsohn's rapid, Expressionist pen strokes. Mendelsohn's ideas about generating an urban architecture of light in which the polarities of a building are reversed between its daytime and night-time images appear here too—the windows becoming sleek bands of light after nightfall; but in fact Parry attributes its façade to the influence of sculptor Tony Smith and his minimal black-painted steel pieces, which create such a memorable image against either landscape or the white walls of a gallery. To me there is also a suggestion of something slightly sinister in that darkness.

A model at scale 1:500 illustrates the separate nature of the urban volumes generated by number 60 as a distinct building. The roof illustrates the plan form organised around the two atria, stepping back with four receding planes to mediate to the tighter, smaller scale of Throgmorton Street.

The elevational model photograph illustrates the horizontal emphasis of the solar shelves; the double-order base and the predominantly glazed façades to the deep-plan office floor behind (typically 15m to the atrium).

opposite: Looking upwards on Threadneedle Street the 6m sections of the solar shelves have a sculptural weight as they sweep gently towards the corners of the building; below them the 3m post and beam (which acts a as further shadow caster) 1.5m of the 1.5m office module of the glazed façade.

right: View of Threadneedle Street looking west towards the Bank of England. The height of Soane's perimeter Portland stone wall was the guide to the double-height order of the base of number 60, with a 6m bay width.

The blend of an offered transparency framed between curvaceous strips carries within it some of the questionable qualities of the money to be made in the City; a notion that there is something simultaneously seductive and dangerous at work here.

It is also particularly striking that from street level the strata build up an increasing overhang as they ascend the elevation so that the top storey has a deep, dark cap. It allows the building to appear breezy and glassy at its lower levels—where the streets are dense and relatively unlit—and shaded, with a dark, brooding presence on its upper levels. Just through the subtle manipulation of shadow EPA have created a building that seems to grow denser as it rises, though it in fact does nothing of the sort; it is merely an effect of a graded cantilever. The effect is most noticeable at the corner where the sharp curve appears to flare outwards as it rises. That same corner also allows the building to negotiate the awkward moment between the dense street and the former stock exchange tower, which never created a comfortable place.

ground floor plan

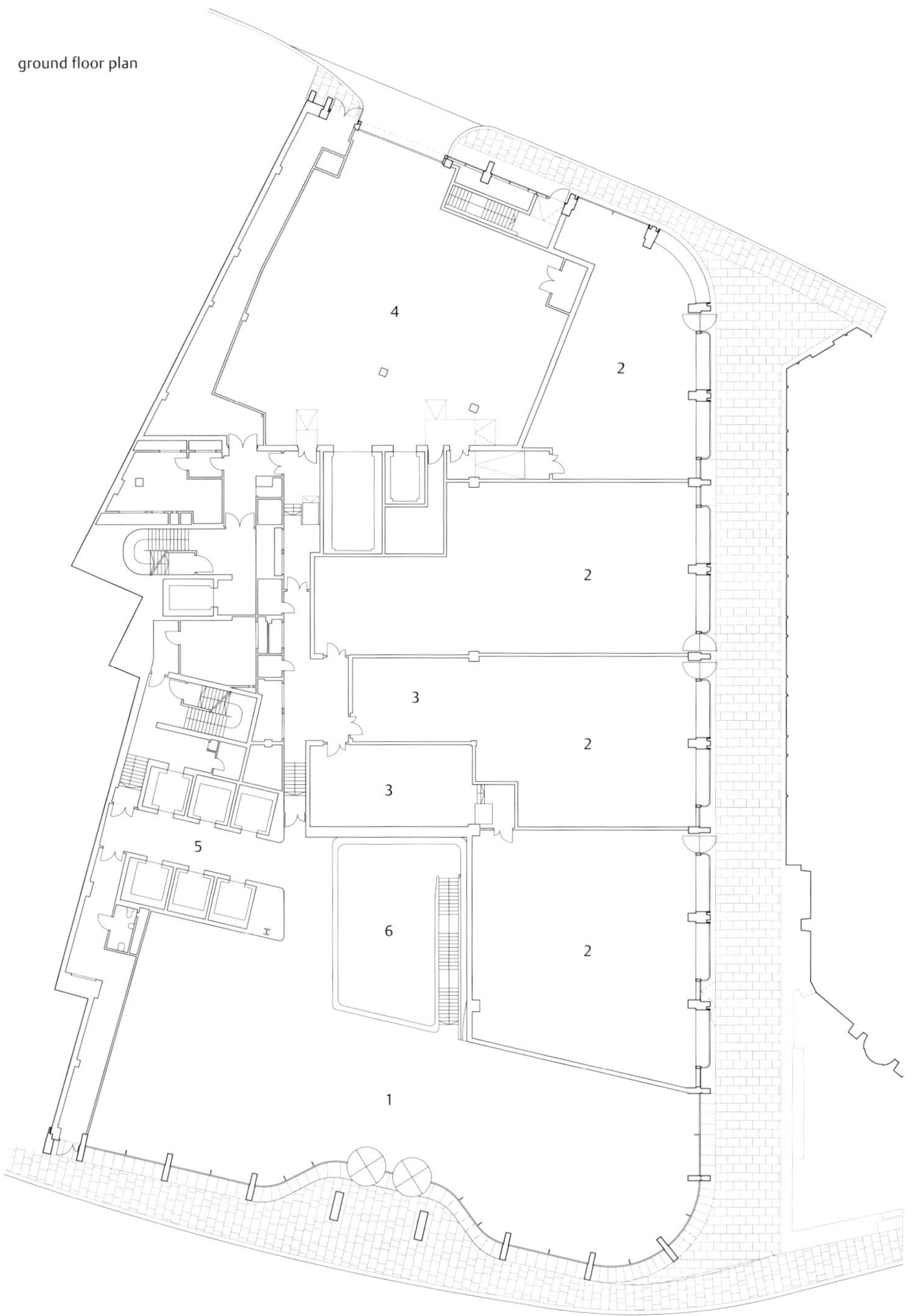

typical floor plan

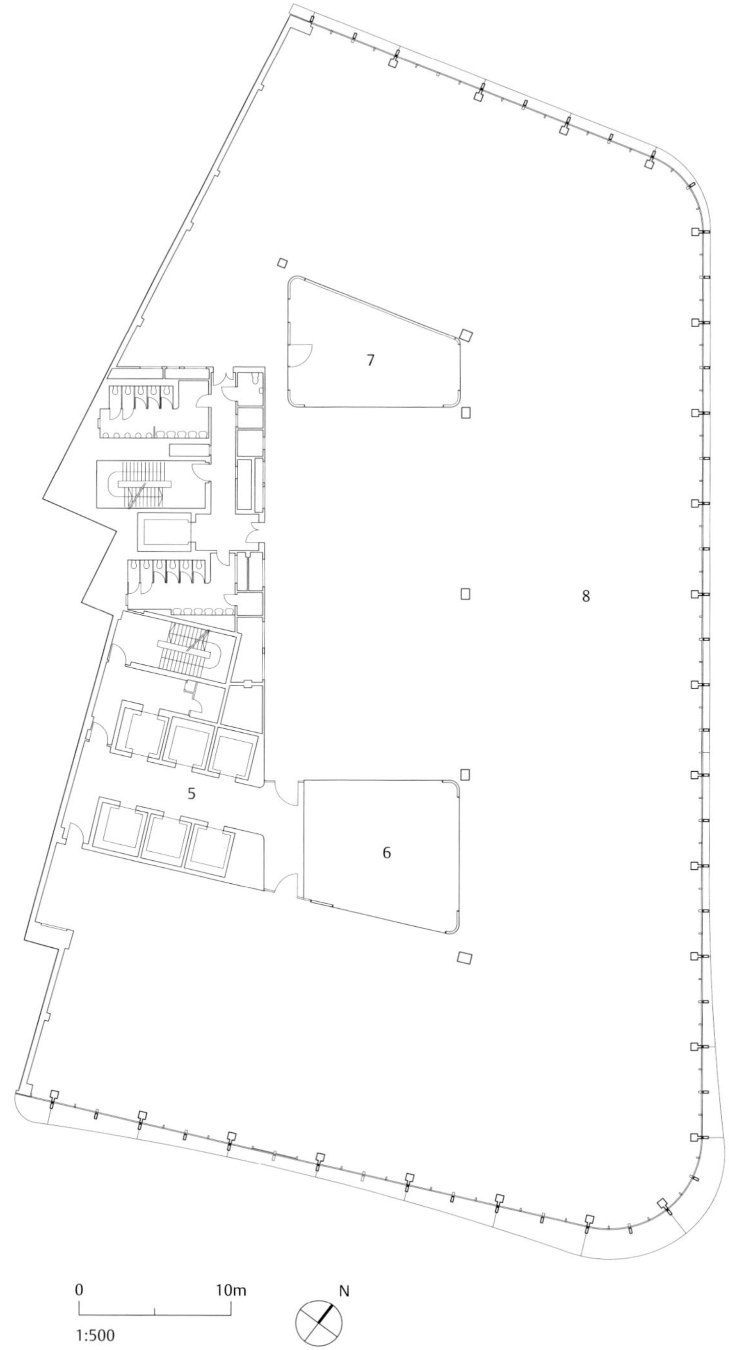

As with any office building the plan reflects the resolution of the *a)* urban context with the requirements of *b)* the optimum flexibility in the typical office floor plan and *c)* the resolution of complexity and efficiency of the core design.

The generous reception space (1) and top-lit atrium (6) fronting Threadneedle Street and the loading bay (4) to the north accessed from Throgmorton Street sandwich the retail and restaurant units that animate the new alley in the City, which inclines to the north. Fire escapes from the offices above run from the central core to the north and south.

1. reception / lobby
2. retail unit
3. retail store
4. loading bay
5. lift lobby
6. south atrium
7. north atrium
8. office

right: Initial elevation study made at scale 1:50.
Pencil, coloured crayon on cartridge paper.

The intention to use a dark lustrous finish to the metalwork; the relative weighting of parts; as developed, the horizontal solar shelves oscillate between a minimum of 0.75m and a maximum of 2.1m in depth; and the sciagraphy of the non-orthogonal solar scheme shelves are all established in this study.

Cutaway section of the façade as built, illustrating the layering of elements. The cantilever of the solar shelves is at a maximum of 2.1m, varying in radius and sweep to emphasise the corner of Threadneedle Street and cutting back to signify the entrance at the centre of the façade. The depth of cantilever was calibrated to the orientation of the building. The shelves are fabricated in 6m-long sections and additional solar shelves are set at 3m centres.

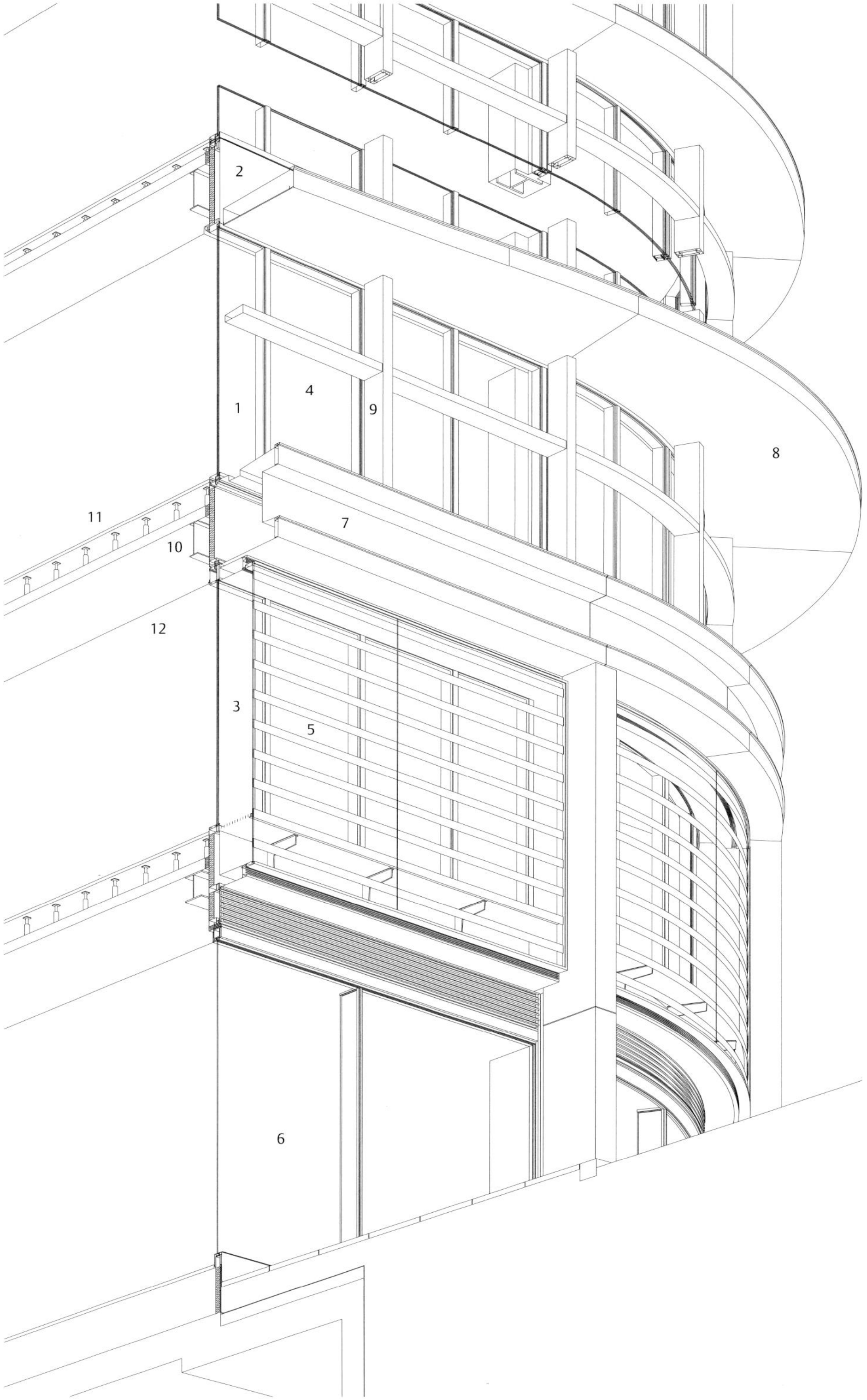

perspectival section

1. unitised 6m-wide, storey-height cladding system with full-height doubl-glazed units and insulated flat spandrel panels
2. PVDF liquid-applied external finish
3. unitised 3m-wide, storey-height double façade cladding system to first floor with full-height inner double-glazed units, vented maintenance cavity and outer laminated dichroic glass screen
4. 36mm double-glazed units: 10mm clear float glass outer pane with neutral coating, 16mm cavity, 10mm laminated inner pane
5. 22mm clear low-iron triple-laminated curved and flat units: 8mm low-iron float glass outer pane 6mm butt-jointed dichroic glass strips to the centre pane with PVB interlayer, 8mm low-iron float glass inner pane
6. 16mm clear low-iron laminated glazing with structural glass fins to 4m-high reception
7. fabricated metal cornice with integral gutter
8. fabricated cantilevering sun shelves of varying span, with rubber buffer strip to leading edge to provide protection from BMU (building maintenance unit)
9. fabricated external metal light shelf and mullions with flush sli-jointed fascia to conceal unitised system joints
10. 406 x 140mm UB perimeter edge beam with intumescent coating
11. raised access floor on composite steel structural deck
12. suspended metal plank ceiling with plasterboard margin, incorporating folded metal blind box

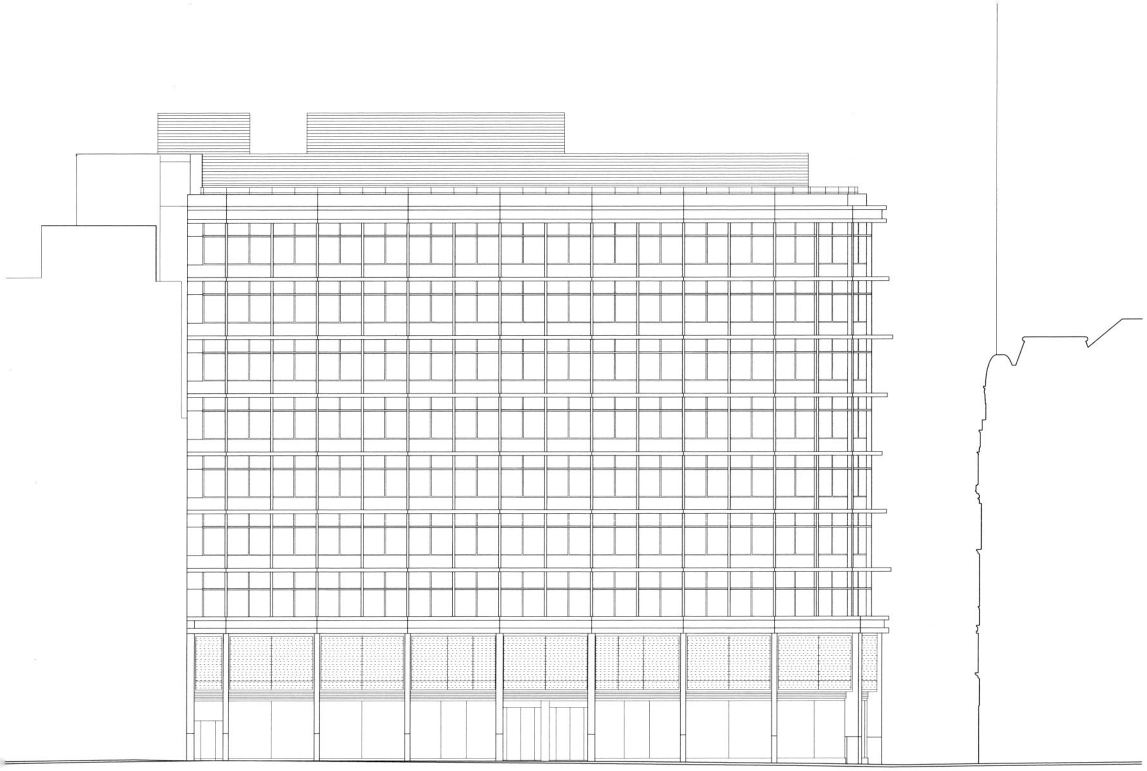

left: Threadneedle Street elevation. The double-height base at 6m centres with the dichroic veil to the first floor is capped by a clearly defined lintel. Above the body of the building is a balance of elements, as illustrated opposite.

below: Elevation to the new alley. With a width of 5.5m, it is typical of tertiary city connections. The inclining ground creates a series of finely crafted stepping vitrines and towards Throgmorton Street allows mezzanine levels within the units. The façade retains the woven order along its oscillation in depth.

The architectural language of radiused corners allows the building to 'peel back' to the smaller scale of Throgmorton Street, creating terraces to the offices at the upper levels.

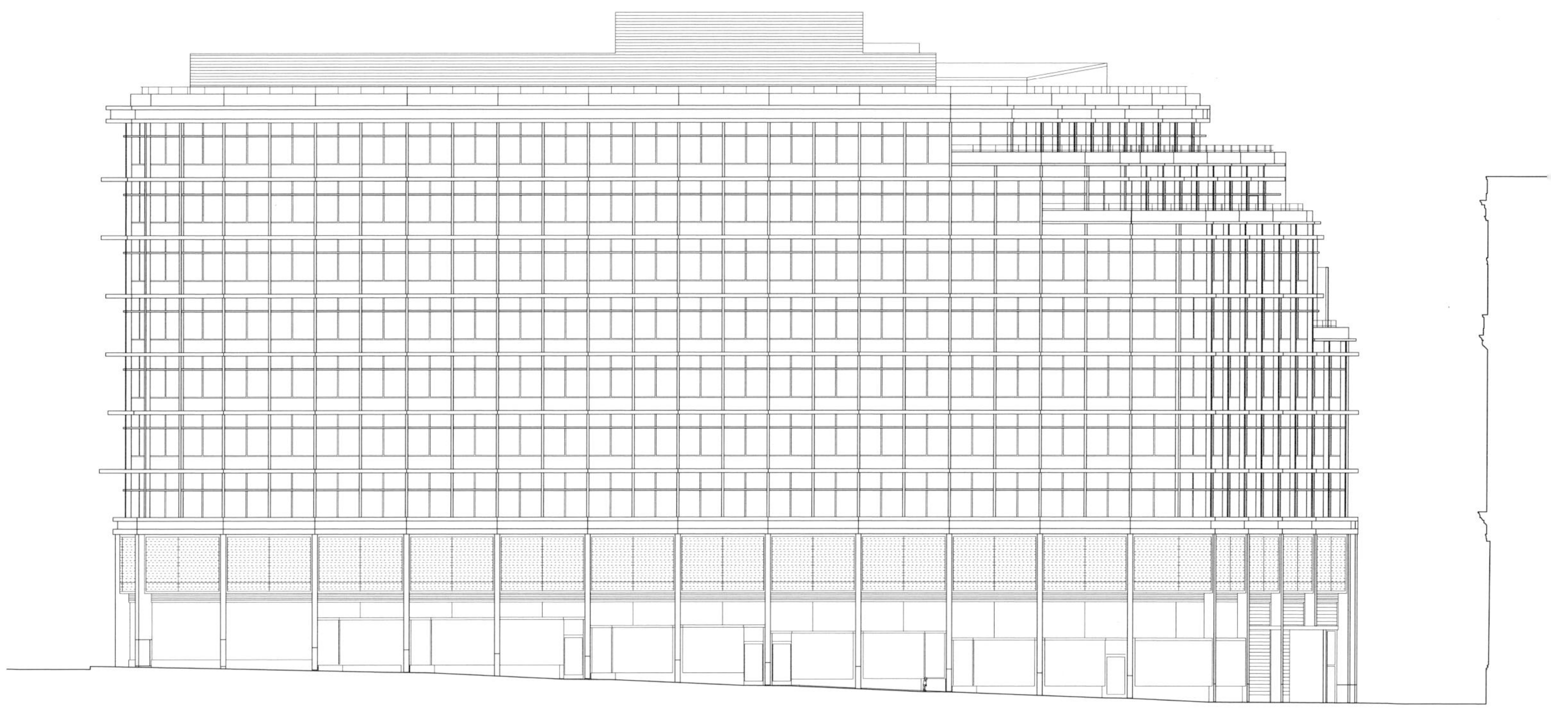

0 10m

1:500

View from Threadneedle Street looking east to the contrasting vertical ribbing of Tower 42, the former National Westminster Bank headquarters.

View from Throgmorton Street to Threadneedle Street, the new alley and the stepping vitrines, next to which are the shop and restaurant entrances.

In a way, this building creates an intriguing dialogue with Parry's building at 30 Finsbury Square. Both buildings play with shadow and with the layer of architecture which interposes between the private and the public, the interior and the street. But if at Finsbury Square Parry was concerned to create an architecture of solidity through the construction of a structural stone façade—a building which responds to the Edwardian stone pomposity of the square whilst reducing the rigid rigour of the traditional façade through the adoption of a complex and irregular pattern of stone uprights, at Threadneedle Street he has dematerialised the façade by introducing a subtle three-dimensional curve into the *brise-soleils*, giving the impression of a delicate concavity which calls into question the exact nature of the plan. The interior itself is spacious and almost luminous. The huge floorplates are aimed squarely at a City clientele, but the extraordinary lightness and transparency inside is in stark contrast to the rich darkness of the elevations. The lobby in particular is dazzling in its whiteness—the white polished floor and the white shell-encased stair appear like a reference to the heavenly escalator in Powell & Pressburger's *A Matter of Life and Death*. Here the moving stair is used as a high-tech symbol of ascent to a place that is both paradise but that one might not want to arrive at—quite yet.

The Modernist intent of the darkly, delicately curving façade, is perhaps a nod not only to Mendelsohn but also to a more local interpretation, Joseph Pemberton's elegantly curving Peter Jones in Sloane Square. And also, of course, we shouldn't forget Norman Foster's Willis Faber & Dumas Building in Ipswich, which is slightly at odds with Threadneedle Street's more solid and robust ground floor expression of deep, stone fin-like columns and trabeation, but is, in its way, nevertheless related.

The building's base finds a traditional manner in which to address the street and, as it curves around the corner, reveals a street of luxurious shop windows and a buzzing brasserie. To deal with the transition between the retail base and the offices above Parry creates a double-height order of trabeation and introduces a mezzanine level of dichroic glass which winds in and out of the columns, creating a scooped-out central section which draws visitors in through the revolving doors. The rather classical base seems to bond the building to the earth, acting as a counter to the ubiquitous commercial language of pseudo-transparency which surrounds it. Few contemporary buildings in the city deal better with the difficult shift from shopfront to glazed commercial, from pavement to elevation.

far left: At ground level, the horizontal interior is perceived from the outside almost as a dark mass, gradually opening up to the controlled brightness of the light within. The transition to the street alongside the oscillating façade is suddenly pacified into a different gradation of luminosity that lightens even the visual weight of the vertical piers. Large circles of light at ceiling level grant a dynamic to the depth of the space.

left: The vertical tension of the horizontality of each level unfolds a stacking punctuated by the wood revetement topping the vertical cut through the core of the building.

opposite: This vertical cut becomes an opening to the sky, illuminating the enveloping nature of the floors, and generating an urban interior.

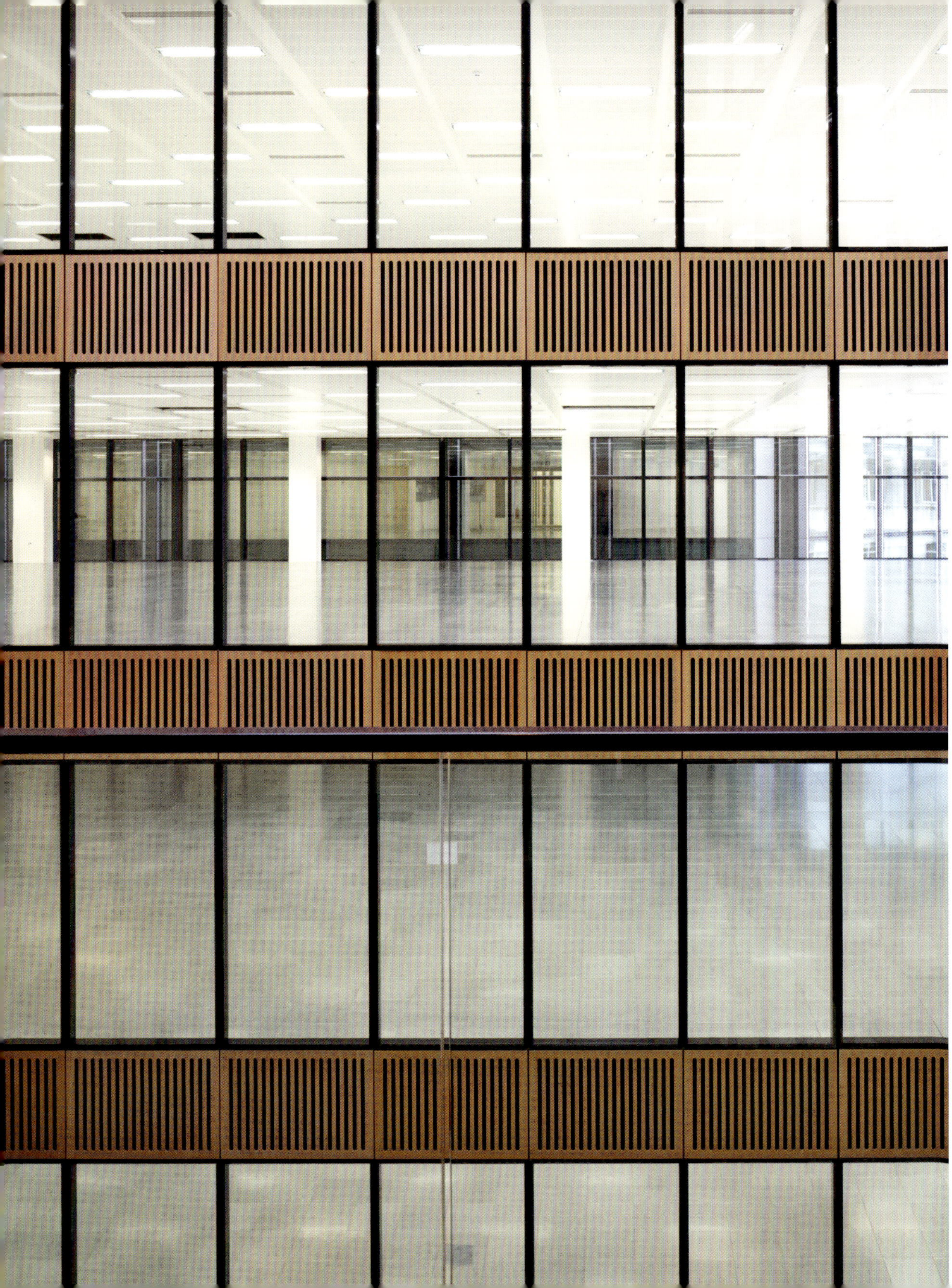

left: From across the vertical opening, each floor continues visually into the depth of another, also bringing to light the stacked topography of each level as a succession of identity and difference extending to the horizon.

right: Descending to the lower ground floor, the lobby above appears enveloped by the light mass of the building.

Holburne Museum

Situated as a culminating point of Great Pulteney Street, the museum and its collection represent a part of the city memory, and the availability of the museum for public events makes it an integral part of city life. The most important element in the scheme is the mediating role of the extension that links the museum with the garden.

1780s

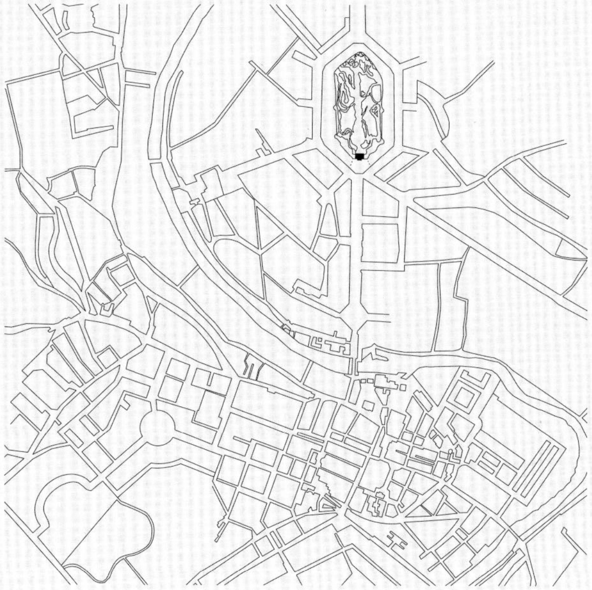

1801

1841

The Holburne Museum generated a deal of controversy which oddly exceeded the scale and intent of this modest extension to a famous bit of Bath fabric. To some extent that controversy was driven by an innate conservatism—a traditionally English objection to the architectural language of modernity— but I think we could also say that it was driven by a misunderstanding of the intent. EPA's concern in extending the Holburne Museum was as much about dealing with the way this Janus-faced building addressed the most extraordinary of gardens.

Originally built as the Sydney Hotel by Charles Harcourt Masters in 1795, the building was originally conceived as a 'casino', effectively little more than a grand point of entry to Bath's pleasure gardens. These gardens were a sylvan vision of a classical landscape of leisure, a fittingly fantastical termination to a perfectly planned Georgian city. Situated between city and country the building stood as a gateway, a place of transformation from *rus* to *urbs*. Visitors would have entered through arches at its base and passed through sets of gauze curtains decorated with the image of Apollo playing on his lyre, to emerge into the gardens beneath a terrace upon which musicians would have played. It was an ethereal entry to a charmed landscape of Georgian decadence, a magical point of movement in which the stress of the city could be shed for the titillating pleasure of dining and the romance of the gardens.

Eric Parry Architects' project for the extension was intended as a vague echo of that sense of ethereality—of the magical lightness of a point of transformation. The Bath conservationists might have wanted a heavy stone façade for the rear to match its front, but that idea was based on a misapprehension—that the front and the rear of the building were doing the same thing. In fact the front of the building was concerned with addressing the city and the long vista down Great Pulteney Street (which was never completed thanks to the financial crisis of the 1790s) whilst the back was about abandon. In this way the addition addresses these two different situations, with a rear extension of glass and shimmering ceramic which brings the colours of the sky and the landscape into the very expression of the façade.

The pleasure garden was a phenomenon of its time, embodying a romantic view of the landscape and a sense of decadent possibilities. The Victorian response to this landscape of leisure was to drive Isambard Kingdom Brunel's railway right through it. There could barely be a better illustration of the characters of two contrasting yet adjacent eras. The gardens and their casino went out of business and the building was reworked first to accommodate a school and subsequently to house the eccentrically extensive collections of Sir William Holburne (1793–1874).

2011

0 100m 500m N

1:20,000

historical location plans
(left to right):

Plan of Bath in the 1780s, showing the extent of Charles Harcourt Masters' 1795 plan for Sydney Gardens, recreated from *A New and Accurate Plan of the City of Bath to the Present Year 1798* (A. Taylor and W. Meyler, 1798).

Plan of Bath in 1801, including Charles Harcourt Masters' urban grid as built, as well as the Sydney Hotel; recreated from George Philip Manners, *A New and Correct Plan of the City of Bath* (1817).

Plan of Bath in 1841, showing the railtrack newly introduced by IK Brunel and crossing Sydney Gardens; based on George Philip Manners, *A New and Correct Plan of the City of Bath* (1841).

Plan of Bath based on the Ordnance Survey map of 2011, including the extension of the Holburne Museum.

far right: View of the Holburne Museum main façade from Great Pulteney Street.

Holburne had served in the navy at the Battle of Trafalgar (at the age of 11) and had subsequently amassed a diverse collection of stuff, from the finest of fine art, to exotic ceramics. The architectural works were executed by Sir Reginald Blomfield in a not particularly sensitive Edwardian outburst of classical bombast. The gardens were cut out of the house, the final link severed.

What Eric Parry Architects' design attempts to do is to reorientate the building towards the gardens, to revivify the rear and to evoke that umbilical link between architecture and landscape which is not only emblematic of the original gardens but, in many ways, of Bath itself; a beautiful architectural set-piece seen against a background of carefully constructed nature.

In this way the ground floor becomes what it once was—a space of passage and transformation from the urbane landscape of the city and the corridor of the street to the romantic landscape of a garden resurrected as a place of leisure. The passage is domestic in scale, with the stairwell and lobby a kind of portal. In place of the gauze curtain that once delineated the threshold between built space and constructed landscape, EPA have built a rear extension of delicate glass striated with vertical bands of ceramic. The idea was to reinforce the notion of a continuous journey opening up to the gardens.

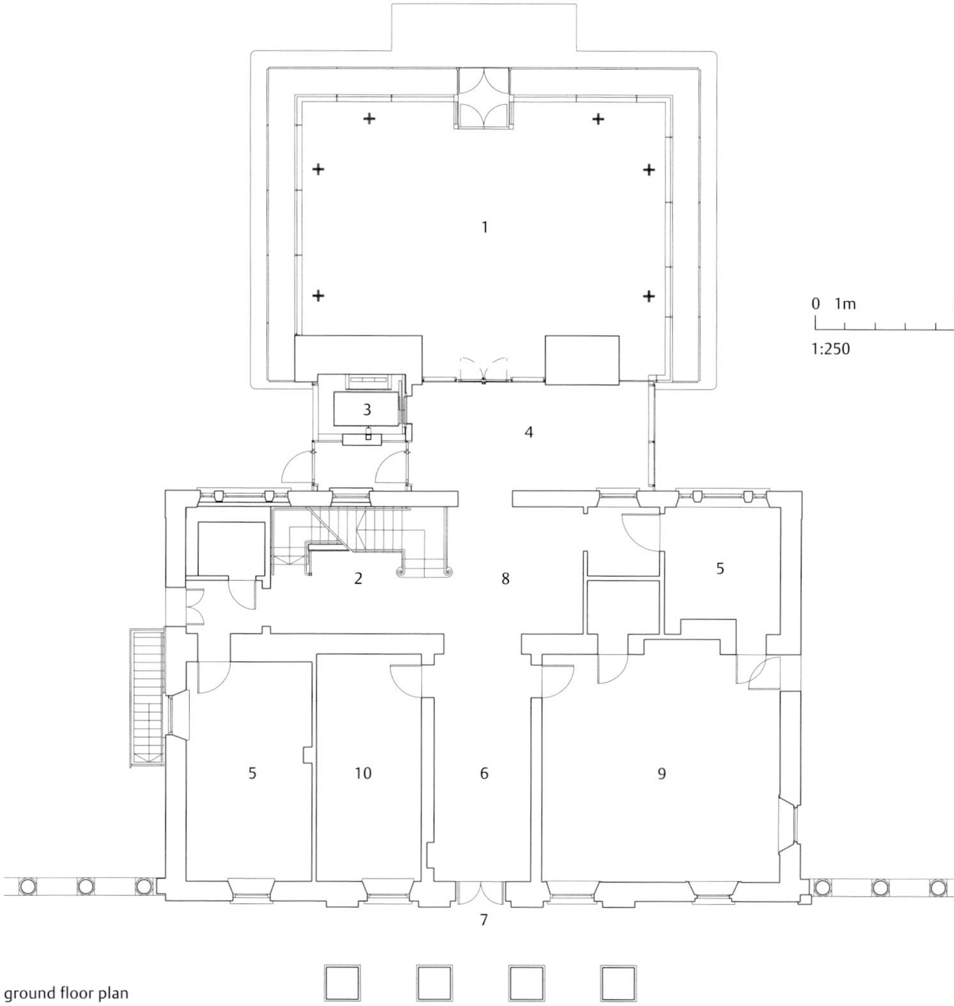

0 1m 5m

1:250

N

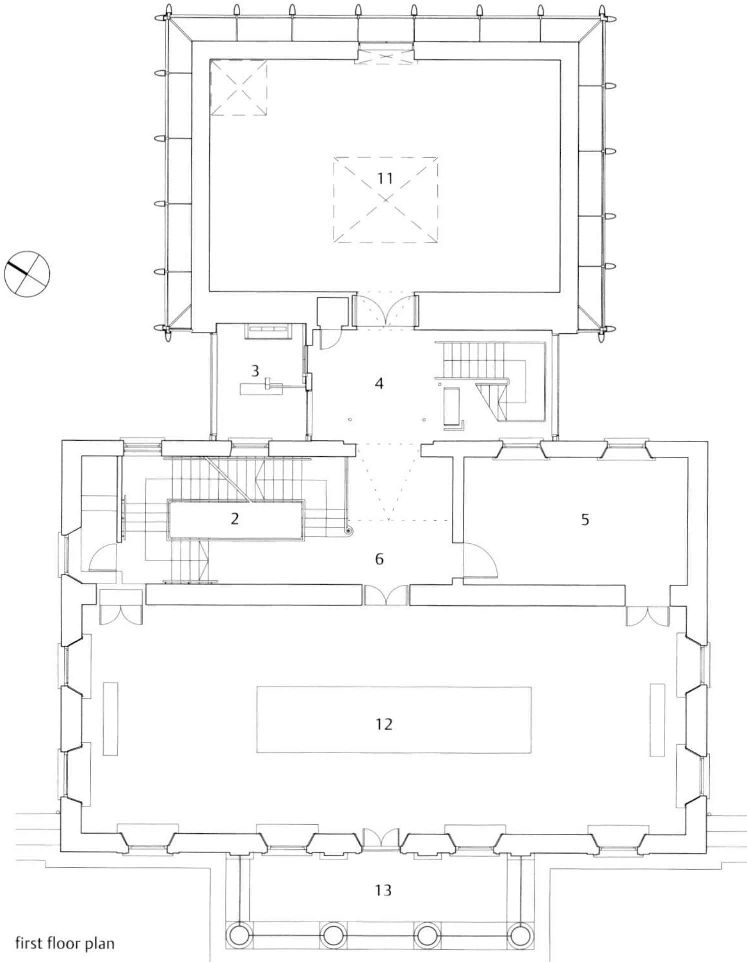

ground floor plan

first floor plan

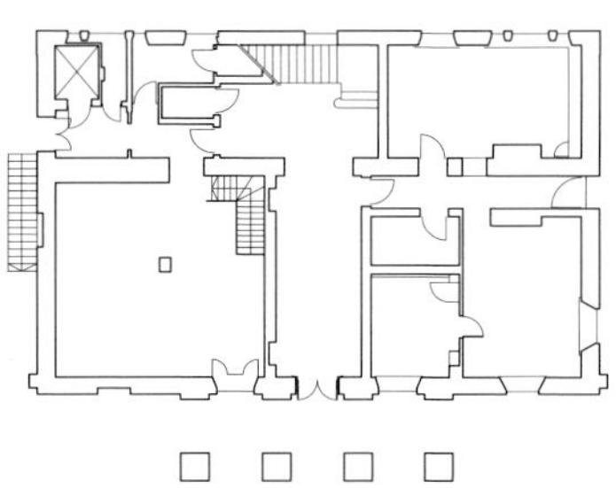

pre-existing ground floor plan

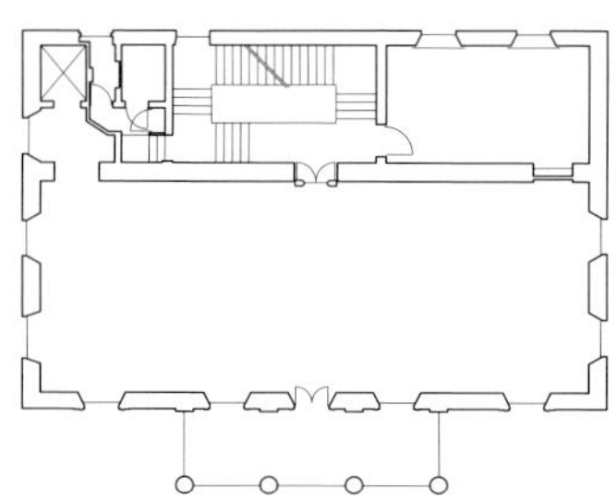

pre-existing first floor plan

0 10m

1:500

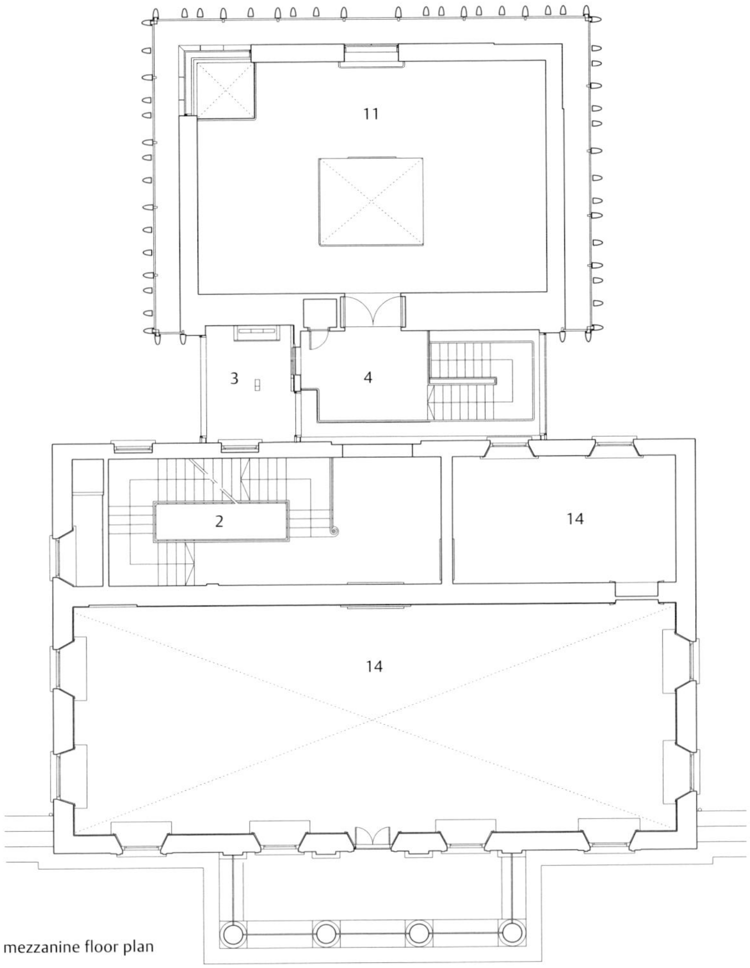

mezzanine floor plan

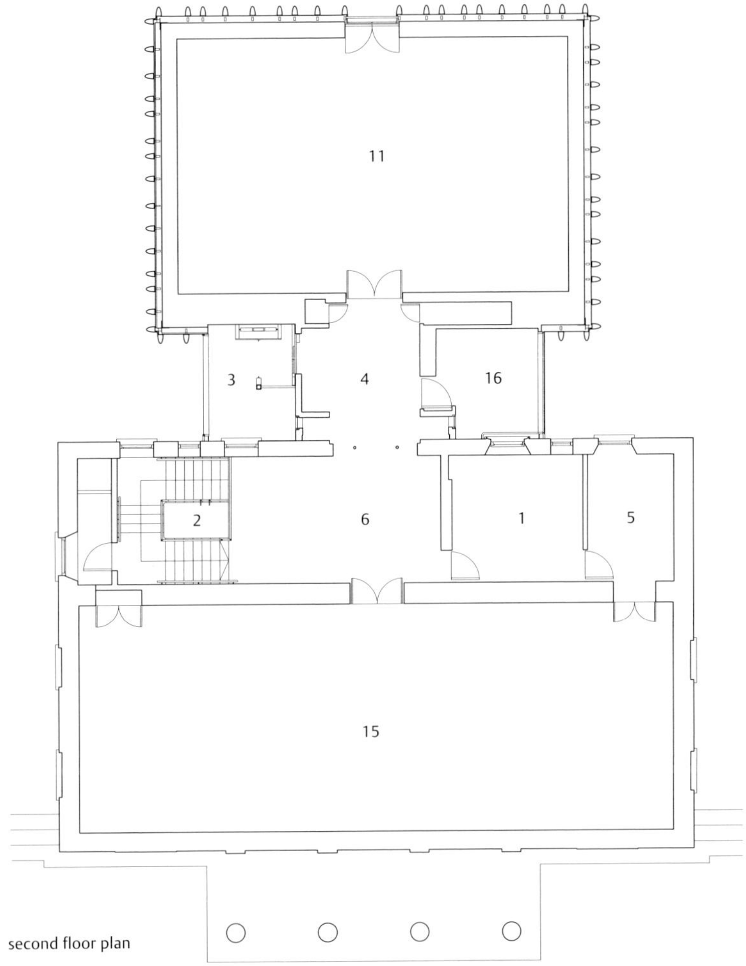

second floor plan

1. café
2. stairwell
3. lift
4. link lobby
5. office
6. hall
7. entrance
8. reception hall
9. education room
10. shop
11. gallery
12. ballroom gallery
13. balcony
14. void
15. picture gallery
16. education room

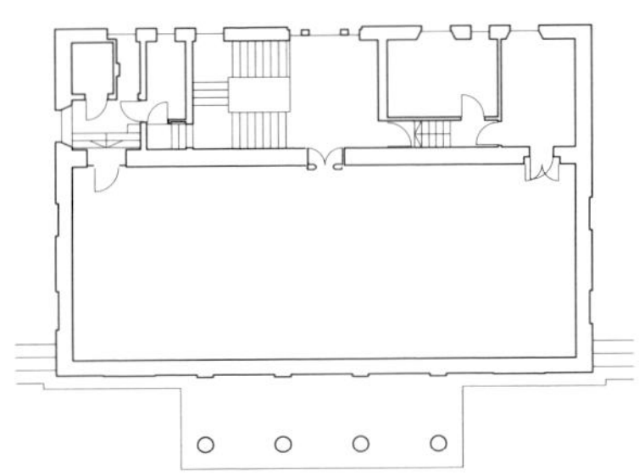

pre-existing second floor plan

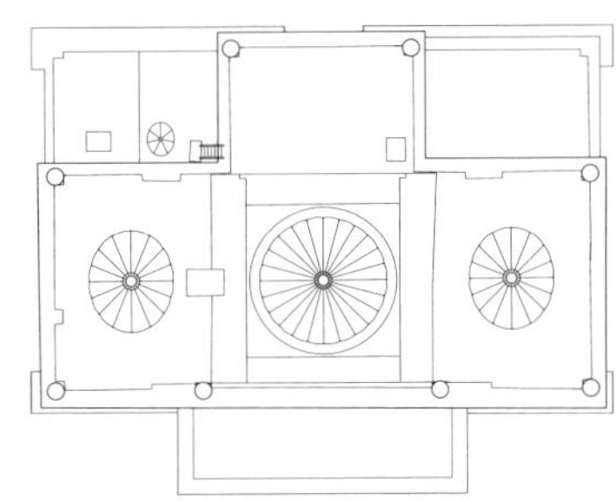

pre-existing roof plan

Contemporary illustration by John Nixon, dated from 1801, of the garden façade. The sinuous line of the busy supper boxes anticipates the theatricality of the semi-enclosed space, frequently used for fireworks and acrobatic displays. Music filled the air, provided from the covered terrace above the central entrance, the outer edge of which was furnished with a draped gauze with the ghostly outline of Apollo and lyre, to heighten the sense of transition from the classical setting of the street to the satiric nature of the garden. In the middle distance, a swing-boat in action can be seen, one of a series of elaborately disposed garden events, typical of the eighteenth-century pleasure garden.

Parry was adamant that the new rear extension had to express through its construction the nature of the building as a permeable screen at ground level, above which the galleries (requiring more protection from light and a more solid wall) could be expressed as treasure boxes containing a weight of culture. The conservation lobby meanwhile was keen to see a stone-built or clad extension, and Parry's resistance to the idea is, in a way, critical, as his refusal to give in illustrates his attachment to the notion of the transparency of the ground floor and the ridiculousness of attempting to crown a glass wall with a stone façade in which the structural logic would have been entirely lacking. In a way, the rear elevation (which Parry himself refers to as 'mannerist') becomes a light but still formally tripartite riposte to the portico of the front elevation. There is an interesting parallel here with the Pallant House Gallery in Chichester. Designed by Colin St John Wilson and Long & Kentish, this too was a fearsomely debated building and, also like the Holburne, an extension to a loved local landmark—in this case a Queen Anne house. The parallel is not so much in the coincidence of opposition and circumstance as in the expression of the elevation. Pallant House is characterised by a series of incised slots filled with the rusty coloured ceramic used elsewhere as a cladding. To me it always looked a little as if the building were shedding rusty, brick-coloured tears. Parry, with the glass façade at the Holburne, has done the inverse: used ceramic strips as fins, convex instead of concave. In the Holburne's elevation the ceramic fins become more frequent as the elevation climbs, which allows the wall to appear to become denser as it rises. The ceramic is a seductive green colour, flecked and mottled with blue to create a tone which blends with the greenery surrounding the structure. It is both unusual and beautiful, a layer of crafted, coloured modernity which acts as a screen. The rear of the ground floor is given over to a café, an echo of the supper boxes of the pleasure gardens and of the gauze between inside and out.

The main gallery is at first-floor level, the original ballroom, which spans the width of the building and opens out to the portico at the front of the house. The rear extension appears as a treasure box, a cabinet of curiosity referring to the origins of the museum as an archetype. With objects stuffed into vitrines, suspended from the ceilings and on brackets on the walls, there is much here to remind us of Sir John Soane's House in Lincoln's Inn Fields, with its combination of domesticity and eclectic collecting (most noticeably in the double-height space at its centre). The fact that the new extension is only around half of the footprint of the original structure ensures that the domestic scale is very consciously maintained and, even though the extension is characterised by its glass façade from the outside, from within it appears contained and enclosed behind a second stone façade.

opposite, top: Elevation study of volumes and inversions; stone gathering weight to the rusticated base ceramic mass rising, and the re-establishment of a radical difference of character, between town and garden.

opposite, below: The earliest sketch of the architectural concept for the extension. A tripartite-order, upper-level ceramic wall to the top-lit picture gallery; middle section recessed double-height 'container' for the permanent Holburne Collection with ceramic wall panels and external glaze veil stiffened by ceramic fins; at lower level 'a glazed garden room' for sculpture; structure placed off the corners, and indication of reflective pool.

Great Pulteney Street elevation

northwestern elevation

Great Pulteney Street elevation:
The pre-existing elevation facing and culminating the urban axis of Great Pulteney Street is the more immediately recognisable face of the Holburne, flanked by the porticoes giving access to the pleasure gardens.

Sydney Gardens elevation:
To the question raised by the pre-existing façade overlooking Sydney Gardens, we have responded with a modern intervention, allowing for a visual and chromatic dialogue to take place with the green nature of the gardens themselves by bringing the new volume containing important parts of the exhibition to the pleasure garden, almost in anticipation of the spaces and the nature of the museum pieces kept within.

northwest elevation:
Punctuated by the quasi-domestic rhythm of the pre-existing façade of true and false windows, the interstitial passage to the pleasure gardens is opened up to the visual continuity and transparency on the ground floor level, looking over the space of the café and esplanade.

southwest elevation:
From the urbanity of Great Pulteney Street (to the left of the elevation) to the pleasure landscape of Sydney Gardens (to the right of the elevation) a gradual continuity is established across the ground floor as a visual axis traversing the building. At the level of the *piano nobile* or first floor, a similar visual axis is observed from the balcony view of the street and across the building to the framed view of Sydney Gardens in the new building.

pre-existing Sydney Gardens elevation

1:500

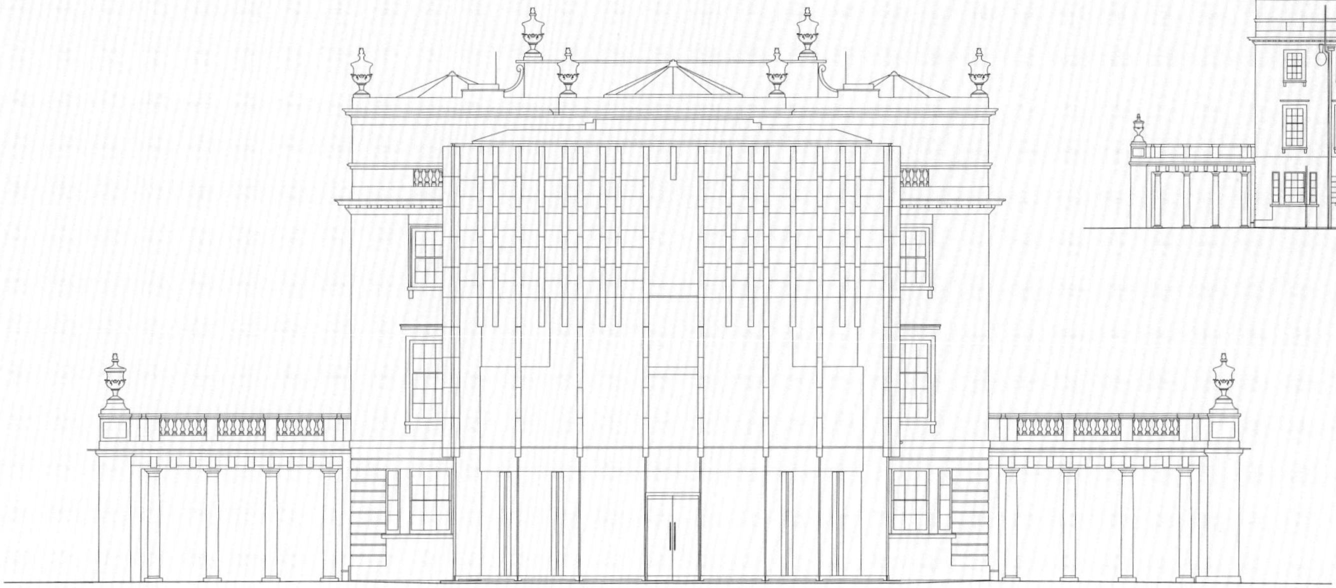

Sydney Gardens elevation

southeast elevation

opposite left: To reconnect the town to the garden, it was necessary to reposition Blomfield's stair and reuse the inadequate lift, which meant removing the internal elements of the three-storied rear volume.

left: Detail of the corner.

right: The structural response by Richard Heath, of Momentum, was to create stiff floorplates that step outwards. The first floorplate is propped by the cruciform posts (designed to reduce transversal impact) and the walls of the double-height chamfer above are designed to prop the floor slab of the top lit gallery above, the central section of which is held by four diagonal corner struts. The whole is given rotational stiffness by the concrete wall that supports the liftwell.

The permanent display, first floor and mezzanine of the new extension, setbacks, double-height openings and lightwell all contribute to the spaciousness of the interior.

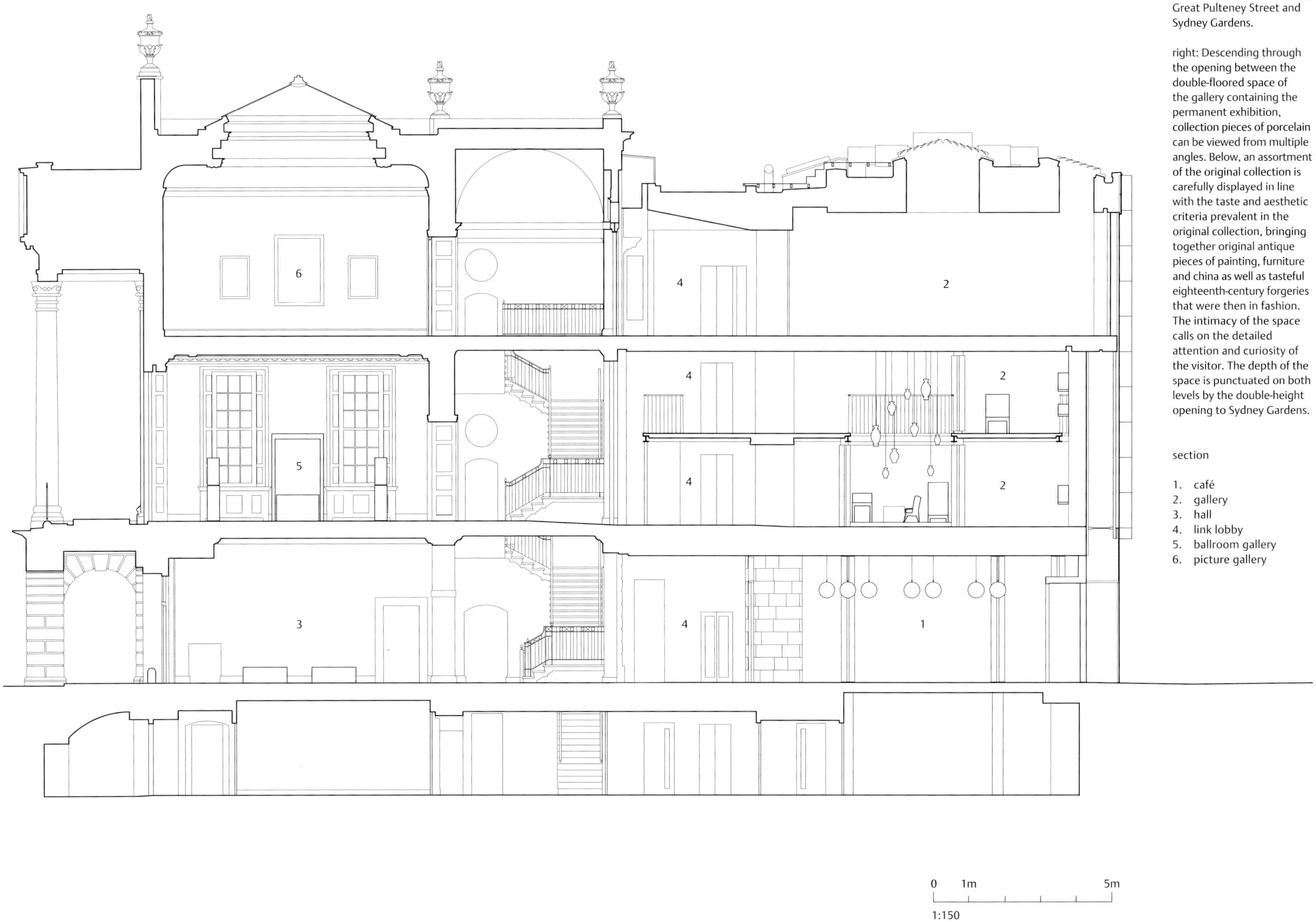

left: The longitudinal section enables potential views across the full length of the interior, visually connecting Great Pulteney Street and Sydney Gardens.

right: Descending through the opening between the double-floored space of the gallery containing the permanent exhibition, collection pieces of porcelain can be viewed from multiple angles. Below, an assortment of the original collection is carefully displayed in line with the taste and aesthetic criteria prevalent in the original collection, bringing together original antique pieces of painting, furniture and china as well as tasteful eighteenth-century forgeries that were then in fashion. The intimacy of the space calls on the detailed attention and curiosity of the visitor. The depth of the space is punctuated on both levels by the double-height opening to Sydney Gardens.

section

1. café
2. gallery
3. hall
4. link lobby
5. ballroom gallery
6. picture gallery

On the upper floor of the new building there is another new gallery space for temporary exhibitions. The adaptability and changing nature of the gallery space is accentuated by the difference in light from above—from the brightness of the temporary exhibition (on the right) Peter Blake: A Museum for Myself (May–September 2011) to the darker concentration on individual sculptural pieces in the exhibition (on the left) Presence: The Art of Portrait Sculpture (May–September 2012), curated by Alexander Sturgis.

left: Blomfield's fine purpose-designed top-lit gallery was plagued by compromises: air quality, lighting and an array of radiators that make hanging very difficult. The largest Gainsborough pictures needed to be deframed to take them out of the gallery. Closely controlled environmental air-conditioning has been carefully integrated into the original ceiling plasterwork, the main doors glazed and widened and the whole reserviced, relined and redecorated.

right: View of the first-floor ballroom. Metaphor's diningware display forms the single central display, replacing a turgid set of older cases; cabinets of ceramic and silverware form the wall displays, with pedestals for some of the finest intimate sculptures in the collection.

The galleries continue on the second floor with a new top-lit space for temporary exhibitions which balances Blomfield's very successful lantern-lit gallery at the front of the building. The section (front to back) reveals this symmetry; the top-floor, top-lit galleries counterbalancing each other as the rear elevation with its ceramic elements balances the portico at the front. But the section also underlines the nature of the route through the building. The main entrance to the museum is unusual in that it is not beneath the portico but instead through the arches of the heavily rusticated base. This originally created the maximum contrast between the grotto-like solidity of the base and the lightness of the gauze at the rear. Parry has recreated and extended that effect in the creation of a rear café wall which is completely glazed, and by clearly maintaining the relationship to the garden.

Eric Parry Architects' revivification of the Holburne Museum reconstitutes its pivotal position as a bridge between city and garden, and between a cityscape of carefully constructed urbanity and equally carefully created landscape.

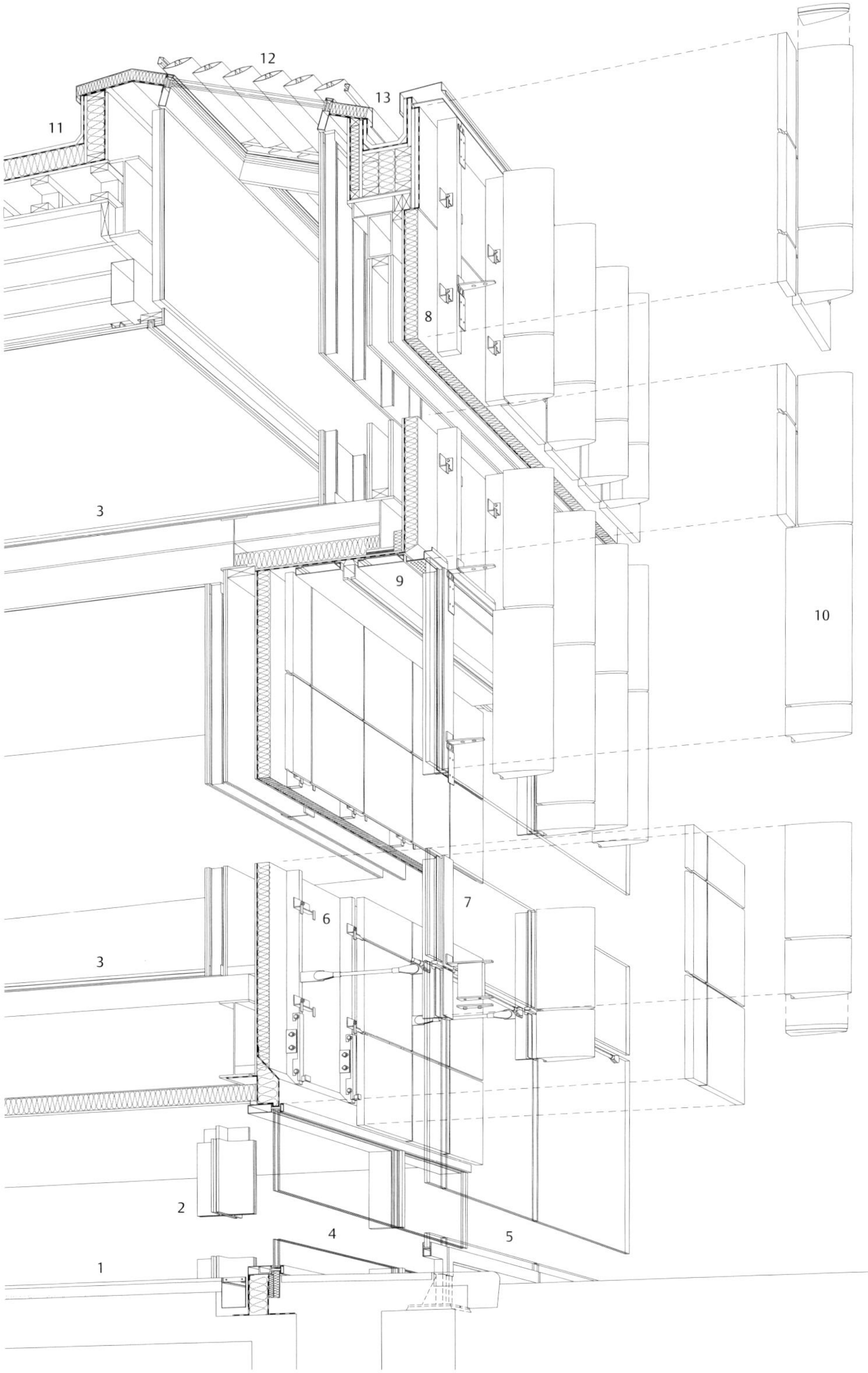

left: Perspectival section of the façade of the extension, displaying the steel and concrete structure, sustainable thermal insulation and revetement materials. The section is topped by an adjustable skylight enabling the thermal balance of the interior. The outer layers of the façade are clad in ceramic fins designed and manufactured expressly for the Holburne Museum.

right (top to bottom): The careful and detailed attention placed on the design and manufacture of the external fins is perhaps best reflected in this sequence of images, showing the primary role of handcraft in producing each element of the façade, alongside the most advanced ceramic technology available.

far right: The ceramic revetement on superimposed glass applied to the façade ensure optimal thermal stability. The careful chromatic balance of the ceramics, and the transparency and reflection of the glass, mirror the arboreal landscape of Sydney Gardens as a continuous dialogue of transparency and reflection, of building and landscape.

perspectival section

1. riven slate floor finish on semi-dry mortar bed
2. cruciform columns formed from curved mild-steel plates with intumescent paint finish
3. 18mm-thick end-grain natural oak timber floor with oil / wax finish
4. 3600mm-high x 41.5mm-thick low-iron laminated double-glazed curtain wall with low-e coating; 150mm curtain wall T-section glazing frames with 50mm satin anodised aluminium cappings
5. 4225mm-high x 31.5mm-thick laminated low-iron glazed rainscreen; open joints with satin stainless steel support rail
6. 80 x 50 x 3mm aluminium RHS with stainless-steel support brackets to ceramic panels; 50mm-thick ceramic cladding panels with lapped joints and 2-coat glaze
7. 5015mm-high x 25.5mm-thick laminated low iron glazed rainscreen sitting on stainless-steel glazing supports welded to vertical T-section; T-section restrained via 12mm-diameter rods tied back to first-floor edgebeam
8. 50mm-thick ceramic cladding panels with lapped joints with 2-coat glaze; RHS with stainless-steel support brackets to support ceramic panels
9. polyester powder-coated aluminium soffit with 80% high-gloss finish
10. 1000mm-high x 180 x 290 ceramic fin with 2-coat glaze; supported on stainless-steel base plate and restrained at the top
11. asphalt roof
12. rooflight with low-iron double-glazed unit and low-e coating and UV interlayer; PPC aluminium louvres
13. zinc gutter to roof perimeter

left: Interstitial space of one of the lobbies linking the old building (now restored) to the new gallery exhibition spaces. From above, natural light pierces through the space marking the transition and resolving the different transpositions, from stone to metal and painted stuccoed walls, with the change in flooring demarcating the difference.

above: The original stone arch where each stone is cut utilising a classical tradition of stereotomy. The arch leans on the bespoke metal structure reminiscent of the early use of metal in the Romantic classicism of late eighteenth- and early nineteenth-century architecture, a reference to the so-called 'serliana' or Palladian arch motif, appearing also on the pre-existing Sydney Gardens elevation.

right: Autumnal view of the new building mirroring the colours, textures and qualities of the Sydney Gardens landscape. The visual texture of ceramic fins of the outside shell of the building reflects the quality of much of the ceramic and porcelain within.

Iringan Hijau

left: View from the apartment adjacent to the northeast communal core, looking westwards towards Kuala Lumpur's Golden Triangle district. The Petronas Twin Towers, for a brief period the tallest in the world, mark the colonial-era racecourse, which is now the focus of downtown city development.

right: The communal pavilion overlooking to the right the swimming pool below and with the gardens to the apartment living rooms behind. Porous walls for ventilation and roofs for shading against sun or tropical rain transform the constraints of the building elements in temperate climates.

The tropical climate can lend itself to the articulation of a particular kind of Modernist design; the open, fluid spaces; the contiguous nature of interior and exterior space; the screens and louvers which allow flows of air, light and the illusion of continuous space; the broad balconies, courtyards and shady spaces. The fierce heat of the sun may militate against the big picture windows that have become the lingua franca of the International Style revival, and that defines contemporary architecture. Yet, in a way, the more complex and nuanced motifs and techniques needed for the tropics actually make for a far more interesting architecture.

Iringan Hijau is EPA's second apartment block in Kuala Lumpur—the first was the Damai Suria block—and it exemplifies this intricate, luxuriously tropical Modernism. In other ways, however, the architects' approach bears many surprising similarities to the kind of work they undertake in London. If we take St Martin-in-the-Fields for example, which might appear to be everything Iringan Hijau is not—a palimpsest of ancient archaeologies, a dense historic context, a northern climate, a disparate mix of uses—you might think the two buildings would need radically different approaches. Yet, in fact, the approach reveals many of the same concerns, passions and interests. Most notable is the sectional design. Just as they did at St Martin's, the architects create a vertical landscape through which the building is made clear. It begins not at ground level but at a basement arrival level. Many apartment buildings begin at the garage and it is always difficult to understand quite why the car park is treated with such architectural contempt—at best indifference. The intrusion of the raw concrete structure and the exposed services, low ceilings and utilitarian fittings which characterise parking design seems to indicate an impingement of the real values of construction on building, as if this were the real default condition of contemporary construction and everything else is a cosmetic application. It sets the building up as a lie. What the architects have done at Iringan Hijau is to create a condition of ambiguity at the lower level. The slender trees which sprout from the lower level create a landscape of light and shadow, a layered, almost stage-set theatrical perspective of subtle shading and filtering through delicate canopies of leaves, a subterranean landscape which links all the blocks. In section they work perfectly in parallel with the structure, their roots coinciding with foundations, their canopies with the apartments, and they emerge through a layer of grid in the courtyard.

The plan of the block is in a kind of squared figure-of-eight joined at a knuckle. One block is expressed as an L-shape, the other as two blocks framing a courtyard, but each creates a communal landscape in between. In response to the climate the interstitial spaces are left

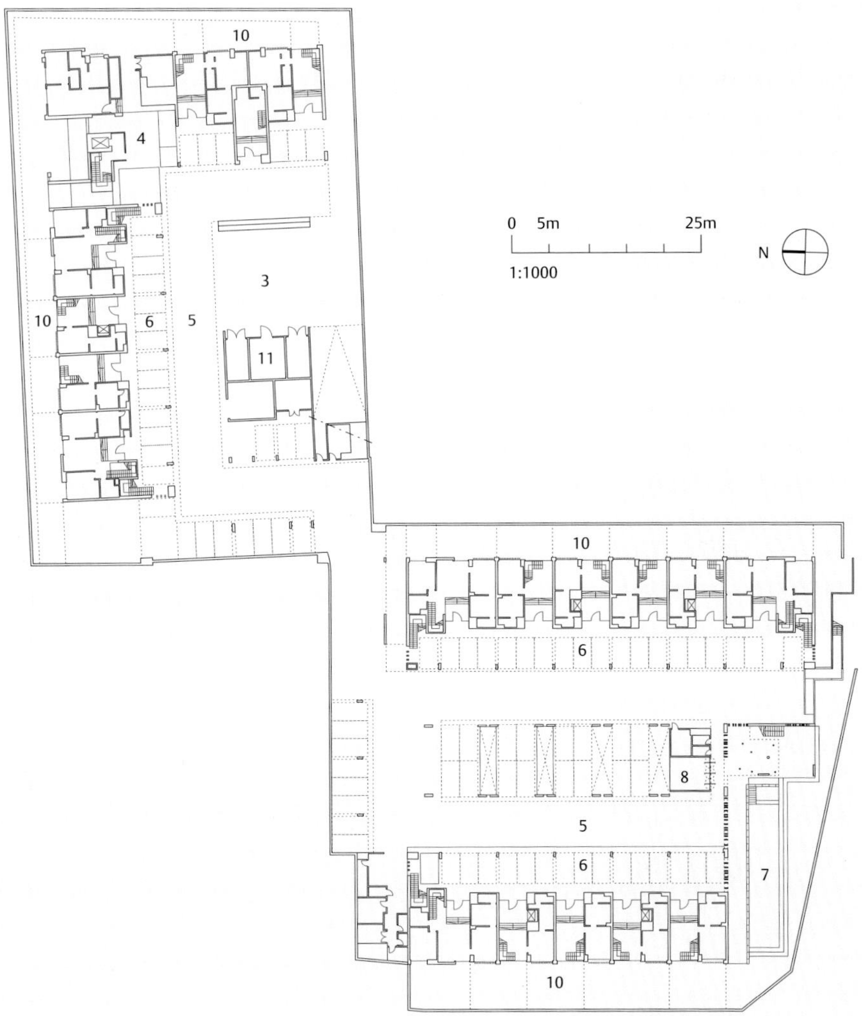

lower ground floor plan

typical floor plan

far left: Lower ground floor plan, showing the lower ground parking area, which is illuminated by light openings from the garden level above. These openings provide a connection to the exterior and conversely transform the lower ground into a semi-exterior space from which trees spring up, emerging at ground level above.

left: Ground floor plan, displaying the footprints of the Swiss Ambassador's residence (to the northwest) and a neighbouring apartment building (to the southeast). The building plan indicates the residential distribution and type of housing around central landscaped courts. To the southwest the slit openings on the garden pavement demarcate the entrance of light to the lower ground parking below.

right: Typical floor plan, with the footprints of the surrounding suburban setting. The plan cuts through our intervention, showing the dynamic of the interior spaces that results in the oscillating depth of the façades and different gradations of light and shade. The landscaped areas also display the volume of the treetops, accumulating the foliage from trees planted at ground floor level with that of trees rising all the way through from the lower ground floor parking.

1. entrance to residential complex with pergola canopy
2. garden over car park
3. lower court; entrance to car parking at lower ground level; fire brigade access and water wall
4. water wall; northeast core
5. car park circulation
6. parking at entrances to apartments
7. swimming pool
8. changing at poolside
9. communal pavilion overlooking gardens to the north and pool to the west
10. private gardens at apartment entry level
11. utility room and transformer room
12. typical living room at garden level
13. Swiss Ambassador's residence
14. neighbouring apartment building
15. smaller bedrooms facing the perimeter
16. family rooms and main bedrooms face the garden interior
17. tree canopies of the open tree wells to the lower ground level

ground floor plan

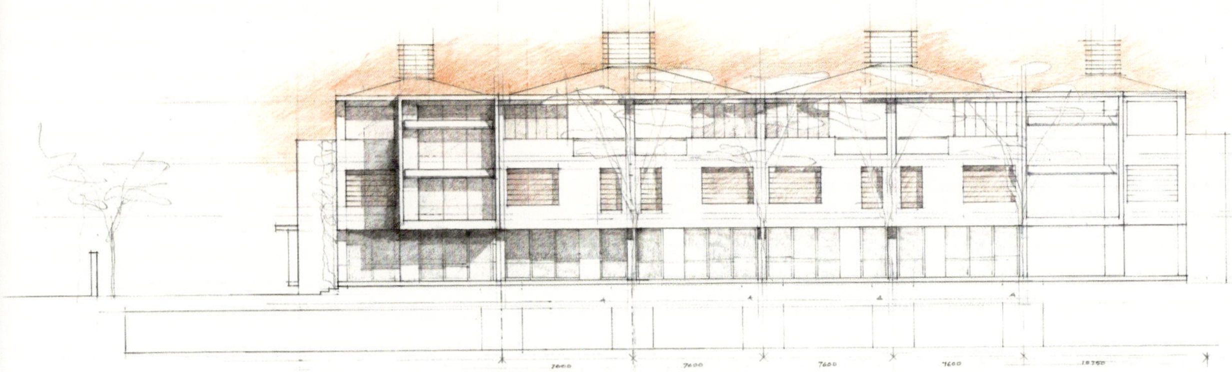

open with only a canopy above. Thus the stairs become a critical part of the development, sculptural spaces expressed in concrete, which differentiates them from the white rendered elevations of the more private areas. The landings jut out into the space between buildings, places to stop and chat, which gives the stairs a feeling of generosity and a sense of being a genuinely communal space contained not within walls but between concrete fins which keep them exposed, naturally lit and open to ventilation.

The elevations themselves meanwhile become an exercise in experimenting with the depth of the façade, which becomes elastic in the way it moderates between exterior and interior, between landscape, city and room. Glass-fronted balconies push into the communal realm and allow long-distance views to the centre of the city and the dramatic skyline centred on the Petronas Towers, whilst large sections of louvered façade shade deep reveals. The whole structure is capped by an overhanging eave separated by a shadow gap, which appears to make it float above the elevation but which also actually conceals the nature of the roof as an ensemble of shallow pitches culminating in a series of ventilation shafts appearing as chimneys. The luxurious nature of the development has also allowed the architects to concentrate on the detail in the architecture, right down to a language of ironmongery developed for the building and which creates an elegant introduction to each apartment and a sense of common language from landscape through to door handle and apartment numbers.

above: Initial study showing the section of the lower ground car parking with communal garden above, penetrated by tree planting to create shade and privacy to the apartment living rooms at ground level. The twin-level garden is expressed in the double-storey in-situ concrete wall construction, above which the brick walls are rendered and painted. The stacks provide ventilation and light to the centre of the upper floors.

right: View of the apartment entrance and car parking level looking southwards towards the swimming pool, across the four tree wells with light from the garden level above.

section XX'

section YY

0 10m
1:500

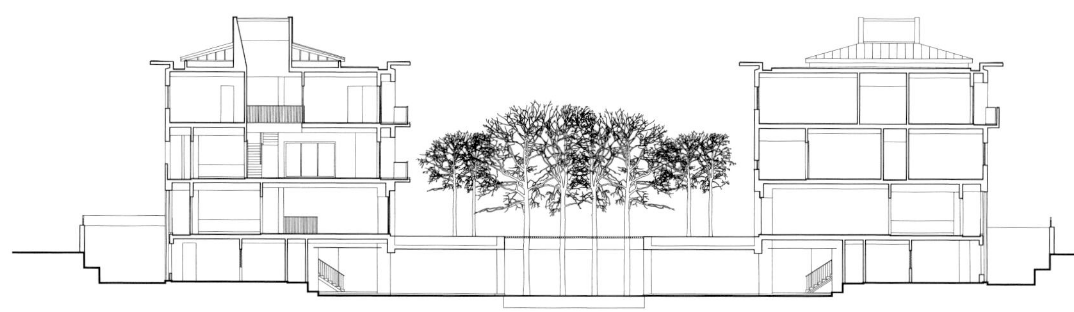

section ZZ'

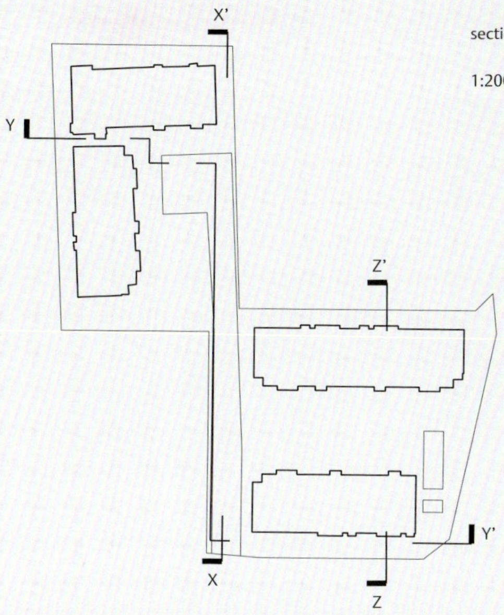

sections diagram

1:2000

The curious butterfly plan is the result of the parcels developed as single bungalow and house plots for colonial administrative staff. Our client, as with Damai Suria (see *Volume 1*), acquired two plots and our challenge was to draw them together.

The entrance axis running from east to west and then passing back beneath itself to connect both parcels at a lower ground level was the first uniting idea. The other was to produce a pair of shared landscape-centred spaces whilst using the perimeter setback, determined by regulation, to create private gardens at the lower ground level.

Section XX', the central circulation spine running from the western entrance under a pergola, slopes down to the vehicular court and rivulet water wall.

Section YY', taken at the perimeter, shows the double-height in-situ concrete base to the southern terrace, with intimate private gardens and the smaller scale of fenestration to the perimeter. The southern terrace illustrates the generous recessed terraces to the inner garden elevations.

Section ZZ', cut east–west through the southern terraces, illustrating the tree wells at the centre, with entrances at the lower level, rising to living spaces facing the upper garden level. The porosity of the section as it ascends towards the lightwells creates generous double-height spaces which, allied to the generous floor-to-ceiling heights, enables the spaces to be naturally ventilated.

The northeast core stair with projecting landings giving lateral views under the cover of the building roof.

left: Undercroft of the garden pavilion at lower ground level with childrens' pool at centre, and the edge of the 20m lap pool to the right.

right: Typical garden elevation. In-situ concrete downstand beam and piers at 7.6m centres; recessed entrance door and side panels; sliding doors to living room; double-height verandah to upper levels with *brise-soleils*.

Palladio Exhibition

This was the first major exhibition of Palladio's work in over 30 years and included around 200 exhibits. Parry refers to the first room as a place of fragments and ruins, of the sky and of the inspiration of a Rome that was buried in the dark earth beneath the modern city and which so inspired Palladio.

left: Preliminary study for the exhibition. The upper part of the wall features a reinterpretation of Marten van Heemskerck's *View of Rome* (1550), with a cornice fragment from the Temple of Venus Genetrix (to the right of the wall). The purpose of the exhibition was to bring together the original drawings, the vast majority of which are held by the RIBA, with the models, many built firstly for the Franco Albini designed exhibition of 1971 held in Palladio's Basilica in Vicenza and continued subsequently by the Centro Internazionale di Studi di Architettura Andrea Palladio, Vicenza. These drawings and models were augmented by a wonderful supportive group of paintings, documents and artefacts. The exhibition design challenge was how to reconcile the intimate scale of the drawings with the Royal Academy's monumental exhibition rooms. The sketch shows the intention to contain the framed drawings within a continuous horizon, to create a scenographic scale to the gallery walls behind and as a background to characterise the periods of Palladio's life that the exhibition focuses on. The floor space of the rooms was occupied by tables upon which, like a feast, the models stand. Due to their recent construction, the models had not yet acquired a value that meant they would have to be encased to be exhibited.

There is an extraordinary continuity of Palladian influence in London, so much so that Palladio, who spent all his career in and around Venice and the Veneto, could probably be said to be the most influential architect in the city's history. Much of this is down to one man, Richard Boyle—or Lord Burlington (1694–1753). Though not an architect himself, Burlington became patron to some of the great names of his day: Colen Campbell, Henry Flitcroft and William Kent. The latter's Chiswick House is one of the finest reinterpretations of Palladio's Villa Capra 'La Rotonda'. Burlington famously bought Palladio's drawings and brought them to London where they have remained an inspiration to architects, but his own home, Burlington House—now home to the Royal Academy—has proved an equally enduring and generous influence on the city's structure. Gibbs, architect of St Martin-in-the-Fields, was responsible for the columnated façade and was then replaced as architect by Campbell in 1718. So it was apposite that Parry, who had only recently been made an Academician and had been working on Gibbs's famous church, should design the Palladio exhibition held in 2010 and that the exhibition itself, celebrating the 500th anniversary of Palladio's birth, should be held here.

This was the first major exhibition of Palladio's work in over 30 years and included around 200 exhibits. Parry refers to the first room as a place of fragments and ruins, of the sky and of the inspiration of a Rome that was buried in the dark earth beneath the modern city and which so inspired Palladio. It was painted in a sky blue and was dominated by a large portrait of the architect and by a chunky model of Palladio's basilica for Vicenza—a building which somehow looks far more monumental at the reduced scale of the model than it does at full urban size. The issue of scale is addressed again in the fragments of drawings blown up on the walls that contrast with the actual drawings displayed and the books and manuscripts which appear as exhibits in cases.

The second room explores the move to Venice, the palaces and churches, the luxury of a city confident in its own beauty, if a little anxious about its declining power. The colour changes from powder blue to a deep Venetian red to indicate the transformation, the shift in scale and status. This room revolves around the model of San Giorgio Maggiore, a room of mature architecture, of the Villa Barbaro with its Veronese frescoes and San Giorgio with its dark Tintorettos,

right: Plan and sections through the different rooms of the exhibition at the Royal Academy.

key exhibits and themes

Gallery 1. Introduction and early years

1. El Greco, portrait of Andrea Palladio
   Titian, portrait of Giulio Romano
2. The Basilica and the Palazzo
   Chiericati in Vicenza
3. Palladio and Rome
4. Pallazzi Thiene and Porto

Gallery 2. Venice

5. Villa Barbaro, Maser
6. Church of the Redentore, Venice
7. Villas Chiericati and Malcontenta
8. Monastery of the Carità, Venice

Gallery 3. Later years and influence

9. The Rialto bridge
   project and gardens
10. Villa Rotonda,
    Loggia del Capitaniato
    and Tempietto Barbaro
11. Mediterranean dialogues:
    Palladio and Sinan

Gallery 4.

12. Drawing instruments, building
    the project, studies of military
    formations, printing
13. Influence
14. The books
15. An eternal contemporary

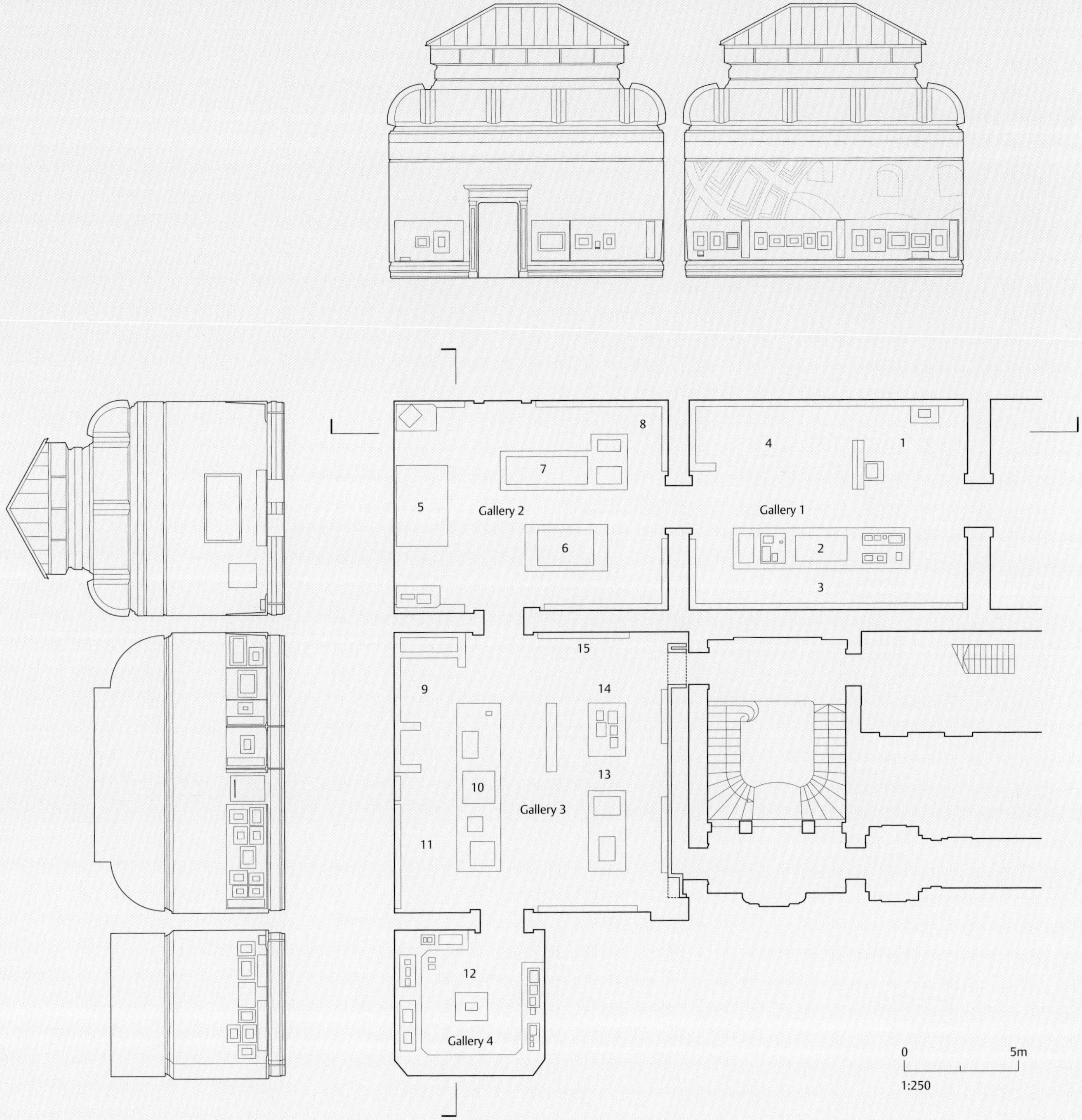

left: The axial view into the second gallery terminated on the inclined model of the Villa Barbaro (1550–1558), which allowed a view of the Nymphaeum cut into and retaining the hillside behind the villa. Hung above the model is Veronese's *Susanna and the Elders* (1585–1588) echoing the painter's wall paintings in the villa of 1559–1562. To the left of centre is Veronese's portrait of Daniele Barbaro of 1565–1570 with books reflecting the sitter's translation of Vitruvius, itself illustrated by Palladio.

right: The second gallery concentrated on Palladio's Venetian commissions. The models were placed on simple tables with chamfered edges to receive text, and supported by inflected panels, both for stability and to reduce their prominence. Framed drawings and more intimate pictures were contained within the horizon of the wall panels. The scale of real architecture was alluded to by the sciagraphic rendering of the gallery walls, based on the full-size drums of the engaged columns of Il Redentore, painted in a deep Venetian red. The cutaway model of this church is at the centre of the image. The two doorways give a view left back into the first gallery and right to the third gallery.

HARRY & CAROL DJANOGLY GALLERY

the High Renaissance incarnate. Parry refers to the models as sitting like "a feast on the table in the centre". Their complexity and beauty as objects is striking, an expression of how the architect has historically been mediated more through drawings and models than through the experience of the buildings themselves.

The third room is the darkest and the densest, a display of the late works, the most influential of all: the Villa Rotonda, and the extraordinary drama of the intense internality of the Teatro Olimpico, the oldest enclosed theatre still surviving. The walls were slate grey and a huge frieze from a blown-up sketch creates a theatrical end wall in negative, appearing as a triumphal arch, an architectural finale. Its formal grandeur is counterbalanced by the tools of the architectural everyday, the compasses and manuals of the physical reality of construction. Parry calls it a room about "the world of thinking, drawing and recording".

The journey is one from lightness to dark, from the exterior to the interior, from a dream of a classical past of idealised perfection to the midst of the darker visions of Mannerism. It is a journey into the mind of an architect with powerful bonds to both antiquity and modernity.

far left: The role of the room sequence in situating the museological structure of the exhibits. The background wall displays a reinterpretation of Vincenzo Scamozzi's proscenium and urban reference stage-set built for Palladio's Teatro Olimpico in Vicenza.

above: Early reinterpretative sketch for the proscenium wall.

opposite: View of the scale re-creation of the interior of the proscenium structure in reference to the urbanity of Scamozzi's stage set, where the confluence of 'streets' concentrates on the stage. In this reinterpretation the centre of Palladio's original amphitheatre becomes one of the rooms in the RA exhibition as experienced by the public.

Sebastian + Barquet

The art world can be cruelly fickle. So much so that this fine gallery, tucked discreetly into a Mayfair mews, lasted only a couple of years. The gallery's inaugural exhibition, New Hope, was curated by Parry and featured a fine collection of the kind of post-war American design that is not often seen in London.

The art world can be cruelly fickle. So much so that this fine gallery, tucked discreetly into a Mayfair mews, lasted only a couple of years. The New York gallery (based in Chelsea) specialises in post-war design and furniture and attempted to set up store in London. But it succumbed to the strange situation that London, whilst being one of the world's few real design capitals, a place where design is taught and generated perhaps more dynamically than anywhere, has never managed to develop a real marketplace for its products. New York and Paris remain effortlessly superior as places for the sale of design. Sebastian + Barquet's efforts to change all that seemed to augur well. The Mayfair location, the fine gallery space, the excellent roster of designer names, yet the gallery fell victim to the recession into which it opened in 2008. It is a real shame, because not only was the gallery a fine place to see the kind of design that often doesn't get much of a showing in London, the gallery was itself a smart intervention into the narrow brick-built mews which is so characteristic of the city. The shopfront was entirely rebuilt using a kind of French immediate post-war aesthetic—long, narrow glazed sections and a door with round viewing holes which evoked Jean Prouvé's industrialised and prefabricated, easy-to-assemble housing designs. The door featured a faceted pull handle introducing the only horizontal element in the elevation.

left: Location plan, showing the mews and full length of the allotments in Bruton Place.

right: Elevation; rehabilitation of the façade, where the design of the ironmongery work included the use of a Z-handle, which was extensive to the interior.

opposite: View of the ground floor exhibition room, with full-height glass windows, and natural light, modulated by artificial lighting where required by the pieces on display.

The interior was sparse, bright and executed in the kind of semi-industrial robustness which has become familiar from the gallery's original Chelsea milieu. The walls and downstand steel beams were painted white, the doorframes were expressed through a simple shadow gap, the lighting was simple spots and the floor was a rich slate-grey concrete, all reflecting the tough surfaces and finishes that would originally have employed in the space's use as a garage. A smaller gallery at the rear intimated a larger space, gave a sense of continuity deeper into the block and added complexity to the still relatively small accommodation.

The gallery continued upstairs where concrete floors gave way to parquet and timber doors to steel sections and glass, each highlighted by the bespoke faceted lever handle on a long, slim backplate which shared the language of the front door. The gallery's inaugural exhibition, New Hope, was curated by Parry and featured a fine collection of the kind of post-war American design that is also not often seen in London. After the gallery's demise in 2009 it was taken over by a shoe shop. The elevation has remained relatively intact (although the gallery removed the bespoke handles), though its industrial rawness has inevitably given way to a fluffier view of consumption.

far left: Early sketch, which was part of a sequence of studies for the interior and the pieces on display. The interior is treated as a container or vessel, punctuated by the presence of the furniture.

left: The concentration of the interior around each of the pieces lends them a dimension of domesticity, anticipating the actual domestic scale at play in the experience of acquiring furniture. The use of natural, zenithal light also contributes to punctuating the flow of the interior.

right: First floor and ground floor have been cleared to produce a fluent circulation space for the display connected by a stair, emphasising the identity and difference between each floor and bringing further into focus each of the exhibits.

1. gallery entrance
2. staff entrance
3. gallery 1
4. gallery 2
5. administration office

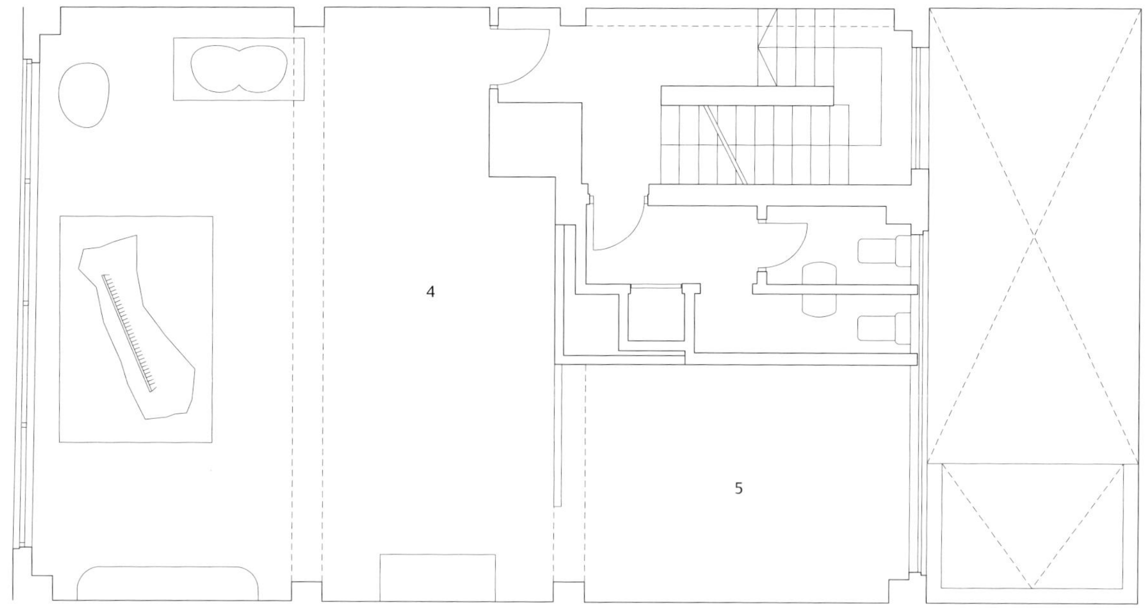

first floor

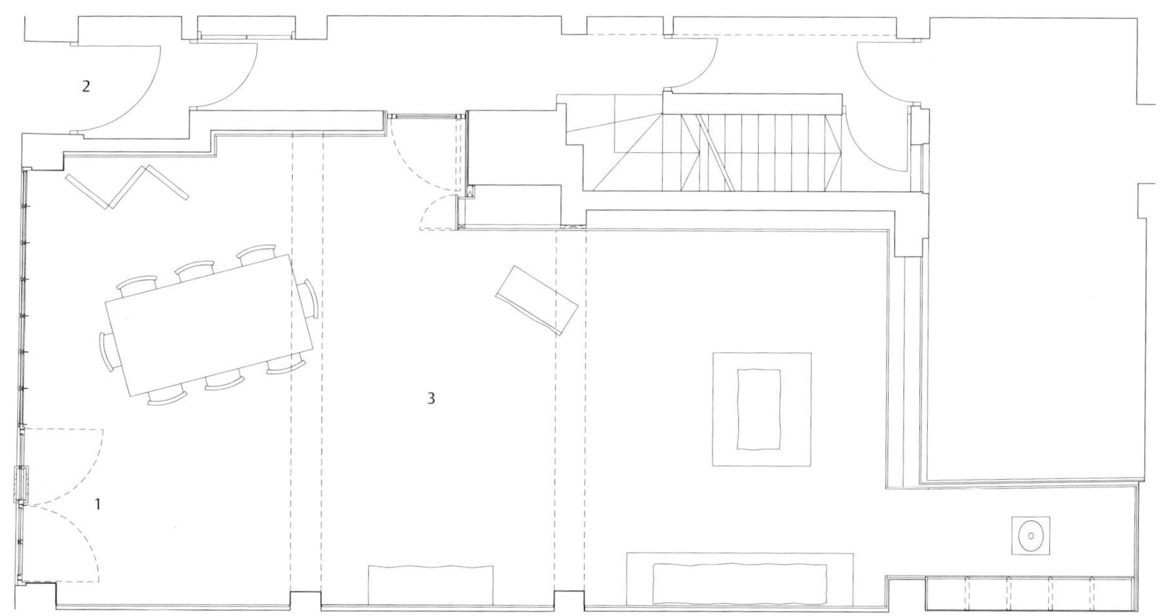

ground floor

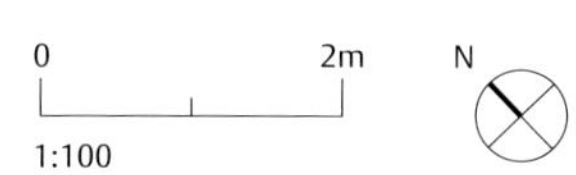

left: Detail of the furniture on display on the ground floor. The careful study of colour and lighting contributes to the viewing conditions of each piece. The choice of a dark tone for the floor emerged from our early studies for the interior. This pavement establishes a transition from the street level to the interiority of the display.

right: On the first floor the choice of wood for the floor underlines the interior display in dialogue with the different varieties of wooden furniture. A full-height veil for the windows now comes in place of the full-height windows of the ground floor below.

Eric Parry Designs

There is a sense now that some notion of craft, of the involvement of the maker and the craftsperson, brings an extra dimension to a product which gives it an aura of authenticity in an arena of mass-produced consumables which are globally distributed. Eric Parry Designs is an attempt to harness the work that goes into designing, prototyping, developing and manufacturing products for a specific arena and capture that effort to make available designs of enduring appeal.

There are a few architects who have created successful products—one thinks of Mart Stam, Mies van der Rohe and Marcel Breuer and their wonderful chairs, perhaps Le Corbusier's lounger or Max Bill's watches and clocks—but actually, if you think hard, it is remarkable, considering the bespoke nature of much architecture, how few enduring products by architects there have been. There is, it seems, a fundamental difference between what was known in the Modernist era as the industrial designer and the architect. I've suggested that there is occasionally a confusion about scale. Architects tend to work at a macro scale and, when designing products, often treat their designs as miniature buildings or icons. They become too self-conscious and begin to sacrifice function for form—as indeed did most of those original Modernists cited earlier, whose furniture is mostly successful for its enduring aesthetic rather than its comfort.

The other issue facing architects is an inevitable desire to design something for a particular situation; a bespoke piece which might struggle to have a life outside the specific place it was originally conceived for. Intriguingly, the Modernist notion of an International Style, or a universality which aimed precisely to strip away difference and specificity, has worked in their favour and is the reason that many of those early Modernist and mid-century pieces have survived so well. There was a desire for mass production—or at least for the appearance of mass production—which has made these products both universally applicable as well as easily reproducible and, as a corollary, easy to rip off.

There is a sense now that some notion of craft, of the involvement of the maker and the craftsperson, brings an extra dimension to a product which gives it an aura of authenticity in an arena of mass-produced consumables which are globally distributed. The material, the handcraft, the idea of making, as evidenced in Richard Sennett's book *The Craftsman*, has taken on a renewed impetus and an ethical dimension. Eric Parry Designs is an attempt to harness the work that goes into designing, prototyping, developing and manufacturing products for a specific arena and capture that effort to make available designs of enduring appeal.

I can bring myself into the story momentarily at this point, as one of Parry's products was one that I was involved in in my other capacity as a manufacturer. My company, izé, helped develop the Z-handle, originally for the Iringan Hijau housing scheme in Kuala Lumpur.

The Z-lever was designed so that the flat horizontal surface resolves itself through a series of angled planes into the vertical surface of the long backplate. It is a very different proposition than a standard lever which grows centrally from a circular rose, instead attempting to reconcile through a kind of process of folding, the horizontal and the vertical surfaces and, consequently, the connection with the architecture. The fitting of the top surface of the lever flush with the top of the backplate makes this a truly resolved piece of design, a rare example of the conscious integration of the projecting lever with the surface of the door. But it is also rather surprising.

above (left and right): Samples of bespoke fabric for EPA projects. Textiles are given careful specialised attention in their contribution to the overall architectural design.

opposite left: Vigilia bench, detail of structure, playing on the tensile forces at work in the stability of the bench itself.

opposite right: Vigilia bench, detail of woodwork and fabric, bringing to a positive contrast the different visual qualities and textures of materials.

left: Interior of the Dick Sheppard Chapel, St Martin–in-the-Fields. The space of the chapel is mediated by the sequence of vertical fins, filtering the lateral light coming from the cloistered space surrounding the light well. Inside the chapel this filtering quality is taken further by the use of lateral screens hanging in between the fins, and partly separating the prayer space from the outside. The lightness of Vigilia benches furnishing the interior of the chapel allows a swift transformation of the space for different religious services.

above: Detail of the new Euville stone altarpiece extracted from a fossile-rich quarry in France, where Dick Sheppard spent time during the First World War as army chaplain, and in memory of his personal support to returning soldiers suffering from severe shell-shock.

right: The lateral light coming to the interior through the fins is balanced by a discreet opening, giving way to zenithal light and illuminating the space of the altar, which at this point contrasted with a Gerhard Richter tapestry that was on loan to the Parish.

The faceted design is not particularly related to the specifics of the housing project; rather it is a kind of abstract idea about what a door handle should do, how it should resolve itself through the transition, and the result has a kind of origami delicacy, an abstracted elegance in which any extraneous moves are stripped away to leave an essence. The range of handles is designed as a suite with three different sizes of lever as well as a thumb-turn with a similarly faceted design and a top surface parallel with the floor. The long, rectangular backplate gives the suite of handles a slightly Central European feel, but it also allows the full variety of combinations of lock cylinder, turn, indicator and so on to be accommodated on a single backplate. The levers were also used on the Sebastian + Barquet shop in Mayfair where a long, waist-height pull handle was also developed which emphasised the horizontal surface that gives the range its identity.

The Vigilia bench was also developed for a specific building but similarly finds a universal application. Conceived originally for the Dick Sheppard Chapel at St Martin-in-the-Fields, the bench aimed to fill a gap in the curiously empty space of ecclesiastical furniture—but then also to address a need for simple furniture in the environment beyond, from domestic to commercial.

Its elegant design refers both to a Shaker tradition of crafts and the sleek lines of mid-century Modernism. It's a deceptively simple design, deliberately unassuming but in the subtlety of its details it reveals a sophisticated form. The turned elements which support the backrest are defined by a gentle swell in the middle which reflects the form of the legs appearing almost as bobbins. Slender bracing stretches between legs and seat and comes together to make an X-brace at the end, faintly evoking the designs of Charles and Ray Eames. The construction is made manifest in a bent metal junction which bridges seat and legs. A simple horsehair-stuffed seat-pad with a striated grey weave forms the top. Some versions have slots hung from beneath the seats for hymn or prayer books.

The Sanctuary bench designed for the same chapel is a strikingly different design. Here chunky timber legs are comb-jointed into one another where they continue around to form the side of the seat, back and fold in on themselves to create an arm. This question-mark profile is emphasised by a rear leg which is set back from the sides so that all four legs are visible in elevation. The same horsehair-stuffed pads make both seat and backrest cushion. Both items speak quietly of the setting for which they were designed, the chapel.

above, left: Clergy benches designed for the sanctuary at St Martin-in-the-Fields, London. The substantial ends are made of a composite of laminated sections of smoked oak with horsehair upholstery and designed to sit on either side of the travertine altar.

right: The Z-handle was designed to overcome the usual accumulation of parts—handle, backplate, escutcheon—by creating a continuous flow of surface from horizontal to vertical. It is resolved as a form when not in use, and the vertical plate absorbs locks and thumb-turns. Made of cast metal, the designer's preferred finish was nickel.

Glutz
CE

left: Interior view of the Four Seasons Hotel Spa reception featuring a bespoke reception desk.

right: Three-dimensional print of the reception desk used in the Spa.

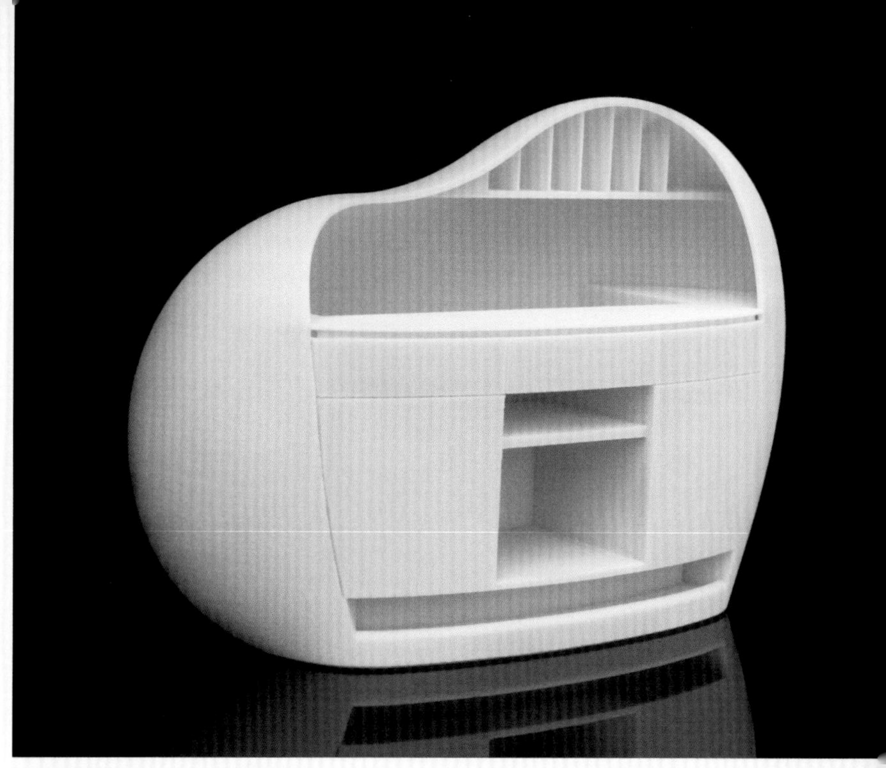

They are quiet and dignified, there are no structural acrobatics or sculptural flourishes, and both consequently embody a slightly Puritan aesthetic which chimes with the chapel but also with a Particular tradition of Modernism. This chapel's relationship with those it serves is unusual. The whole complex is very much about a kind of openness and the provision of a feeling of comfort, domesticity and embrace for those whom home is a deeply unsettling and absent idea. The furniture is required to tread a fine and difficult line between the ecclesiastical, the domestic, the robust and the contemporary. It gives an idea of a natural, domestic ease without sacrificing its purity or its lightness.

The handles and the benches might have been developed for a specific context but it was always in the mind of the designers that these might have an existence of their own beyond the immediate building. Other designs for furniture remain more firmly fixed to their context. The extremely function-specific desks at the Four Seasons Spa are intended to create a softer, more organic and more ergonomic setting for the Spa's manicurists and their customers. First the reception desk greets visitors with a form seemingly inspired by a river-washed pebble, the back of which reveals all the complex functions and connectivity of an office desk without confronting visitors with an array of technology. Formed in a thin sheet of structural solid surface the desk is slightly translucent, exuding light. The manicure desks themselves are less bulbous, rather forming themselves into an ergonomic workstation accommodating both customer and manicurist in comfort. A large cylindrical storage unit forms the base of the piece, apparently lifted slightly off the floor to create a shadow gap and reduce its ostensible mass. The table itself is an attenuated comma, a form that lends itself to the staff being able to comfortably reach the guests' hands in an outstretched position without anyone having to strain. Even the table's surface is gently heated with internal filaments to improve the experience.

These smooth forms are all about touch, about the experience of hands on surfaces and, in a way, all these items are about the physical, corporeal engagement with the building. We tend not to physically engage with buildings beyond having our feet on the floor. Door handles, perhaps handrails, a light switch and the furniture constitute our interface with architecture, and through their design an architect can modulate the experience of the building in subtle, surprising and affecting ways. That is what these designs do; they manipulate the experience of space and then extend architecture into the realm of production.

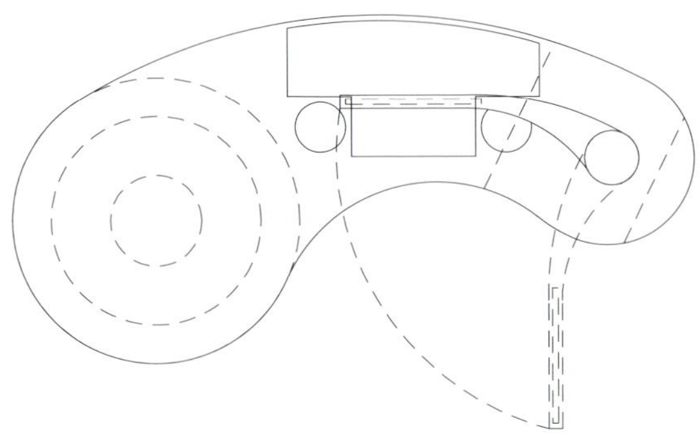

1:25

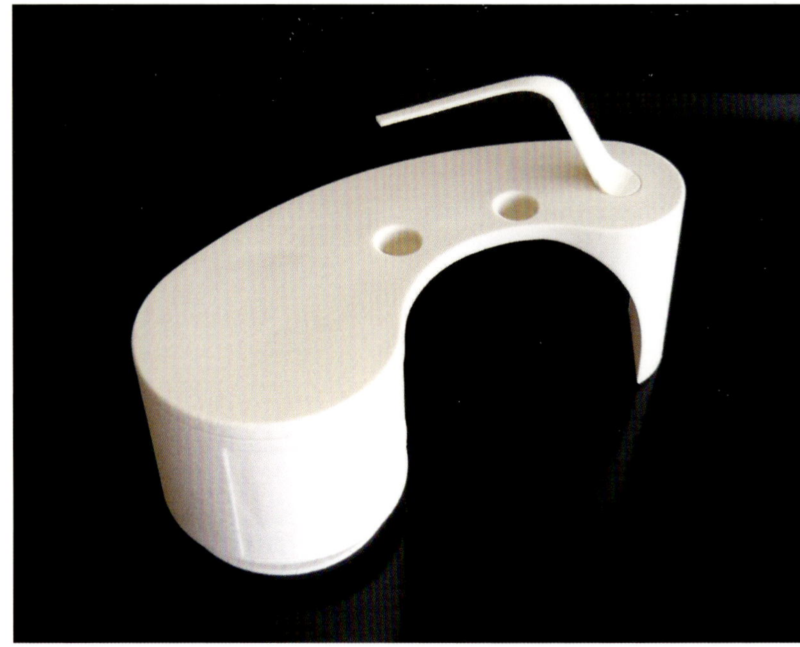

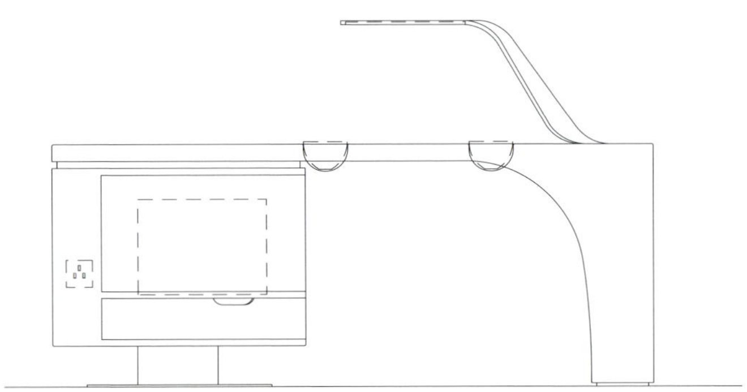

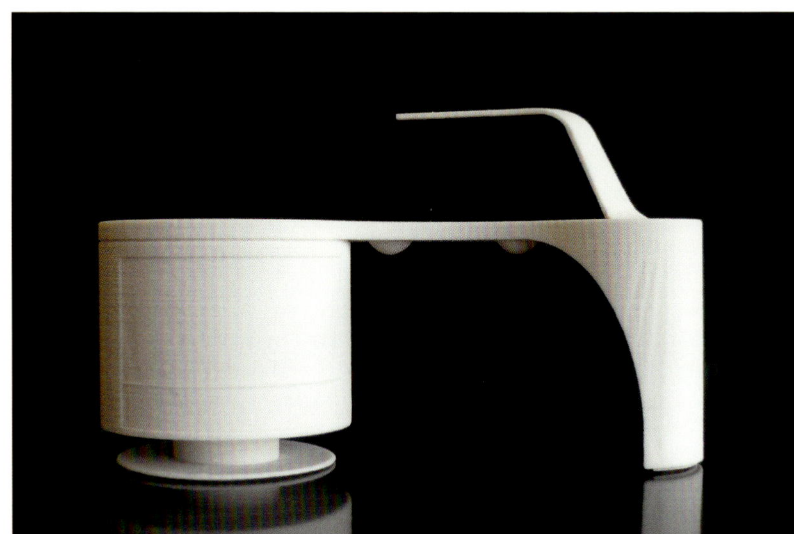

far left (top and bottom): Elevation and plan of the bespoke manicure desk used in the Four Seasons Hotel Spa.

left (top and bottom): Three-dimensional print at scale 1:10 as part of the model studies carried out for the design of the manicure desk used in the Spa. The curvature of the desktop is ergonomically designed to accommodate both the requirements of the hand treatment and the comfort of the client, facing a panoramic view of Hyde Park.

right: Internal view of the Four Seasons Hotel Spa featuring one of the bespoke manicure desks.

One Eagle Place, Piccadilly

One Eagle Place, Piccadilly, is the Crown Estate's first major project in its extensive St James's portfolio. The new Piccadilly façade in ceramic utilises the sculptural and cast qualities of clay and polychromatic glazes. Renowned sculptor Richard Deacon was invited to undertake the commission to the cornice which grows out of the body of the building, creating a memorable dialogue between architecture and art. To Jermyn Street a new building and façade of stone is augmented by a vigorous stone sculpture by Stephen Cox at the corner with Eagle Place, mediating between street and sky.

1. Piccadilly
2. Regent Street
3. Jermyn Street
4. Haymarket
5. Eagle Place

0 5m 25m N

1:1000

left: Location plan, showing the extent of our intervention in the urban block on the corner of Piccadilly and Regent Street and its more immediate surroundings. The urban block now includes two of our projects: One Eagle Place, which looks over Piccadilly and Eagle Place, and also our residential project for 15 and 20 Jermyn Street, which looks over Jermyn Street and Regent Street.

The couple of blocks between Piccadilly Circus and St James's Church is not a particularly long stretch yet it needs to deal with a transition from the messy imperial Edwardian bombast around the Circus itself to the restrained brick of Wren, whilst at the same time accommodating the pivot between the very particular worlds of St James's and Mayfair to either side. It is a remarkable run of buildings, arguably the most interesting in the city. First there is the frenetic visual mess of Piccadilly Circus, its buildings clad in LED hoardings which exist at a level brighter than any architecture could possibly hope to match, sucking the spare light out of an otherwise grey and grim selection of buildings and shops, which somehow consistently conspire to fail to live up to the prominence of the site. It is one of London's most recognisable yet simultaneously most anodyne spaces, an urban doppelganger of New York's Times Square which exists on a spurious touristy reputation of neon and memory yet which has succumbed to corporate global ubiquity. It is ill-defined precisely because of its centrality, its position as a pivot and a junction which stymies its own potential for becoming a self-sufficient place.

There is also the inflated British Baroque built in Nash's more delicate footprints; clown shoes over dandified breeches. There are Reginald Blomfield's attempts to create an architecture of a scale appropriate to London's imperial power and reach and his followers' underpowered attempts to keep up. There is Norman Shaw's massive Piccadilly Hotel with its odd, overscaled Mannerist upper-storey colonnade, but there is also the wonderful Air Street, a dark and brooding Piranesian alley beneath massive arches and overbearing columns. There is the exuberant Arts and Crafts flounce of Cordings, as close as London ever got to the organicism and lightness of Art Nouveau. Then there is the old Simpson's (now Waterstones), a stand-out piece of urbane Modernism with Joseph Emberton's concave curving shop window, which sucks the flâneur deep into the sphere of consumption without ever leaving the pavement. And then there is the pastiche classical/Egyptian of Robert Adam's corner building, a reflection of the kind of slightly unfortunate architecture clients and planners seem to think Piccadilly ought to be populated with and a fair argument for façade retention. The southern side is then bounded by the self-assured expense and old money of Jermyn Street, and pierced by the narrow alleys which connect the distinct areas of tourist trail Piccadilly and London gentlemen's St James's. It is into this disparate, rich and distinctly London context that EPA's One Eagle Place is placed. It is a series of interventions which has much work to do. That work is based around a single block which stands at the corner of Piccadilly and Lower Regent Street, and which turns the corners back into Jermyn Street and back round again into One Eagle Place. The actual corner of Piccadilly and Lower Regent Street is not part of the development, and there is also a short break in the Jermyn Street elevation which remains part of the original fabric.

right: View of the north-facing façade as it existed. The block bounded to the south by Jermyn Street, to the west by Eagle Place and to the east by Lower Regent Street, illustrates the unrealised ambition of the architects of the early twentieth century who conceived of Piccadilly as London's response to the rue de Rivoli in Paris. Richard Norman Shaw laid out the revisions to Nash's Circus in 1904–1905, Reginald Blomfield and his successor designed the grand and symmetrical façades and established the intended cornice height for Piccadilly. The block is made up of six buildings; the easternmost were outside our project boundary, as shown on the site plan. The three central and lower buildings are proposed for replacement as illustrated by the sketch on the opening page, whilst the foreground corner building will have its arched and corbelled detailing reinstated. This eclectic building of 1880 will be raised wholesale in order that the cornice aligns, as will the new floor heights, to the new adjoining façade.

Otherwise the scheme is a blend of new elevations and retained façades, a block that never seemed that big until you saw it demolished, when it seemed to leave an unsettlingly large gap in the fabric of the West End, like a blank in a row of gleaming teeth. The power of that gap to surprise shows quite how engrained this part of the city has become in our collective memories.

The key architectural move is a major new elevation on Piccadilly. Squeezed between two existing Edwardian façades of very different natures—one a restrained elevation which attempts to quieten down the bombast of the Blomfieldian corner to a more Georgian, almost proto-Deco dignity; the other, at the corner of Eagle Place, an explosion of Edwardian free style which manages to combine Scottish baronial, Rococo and Mannerist details with a kind of provincial Alhambra commercial exoticism. Parry's solution is a bold, terracotta-clad elevation which revisits some of the themes the practice has developed elsewhere in the West End but also introduces a huge double order to the central section of the façade, which gives it the gravitas to converse with Shaw's hotel and the scale of Blomfield et al. There is a memory of the building that stood here before, as if the ghost was allowed to be glimpsed in the new architecture. But there is also a continuity with the neighbours—the suppressed storey at first floor level which echoes the line of windows beneath the balconied storeys in the Blomfield façades, and in the continuation of a line through a cornice (with open attic storey above) which visually connects the elevation to the continuous balcony of its eastern neighbour and the eaves of the eclectic façade to the west.

On the early drawings this line is highlighted through heavy shading as a cornice of some significant mass. But it is only in the later drawings, and now, at the time of writing, on site, that its true striking nature is becoming apparent. This is a collaboration with the artist Richard Deacon, and the cornice is being developed as a polychromatic punctuation, an almost Constructivist composition of complex geometric forms which come together to create a rough quarter-round profile of extraordinary character. The elements are based on a series of fourteen prismatic forms so that the appearance is almost that of some great machine getting its cogs and parts lined up in order. The complexity of the cross-section makes this a contemporary equivalent of the deeply shadowed, profoundly symbolic language of mouldings and classical details—the dentils and brackets, triglyphs, ox heads and ovolos which went into modelling the traditional urban façade. It is a bold and ambitious crown which begins to drag some of the colour and vibrancy of Piccadilly Circus back down into the thoroughfare, but to integrate it into the architecture rather than leaving it to the applied and ephemeral language of advertising.

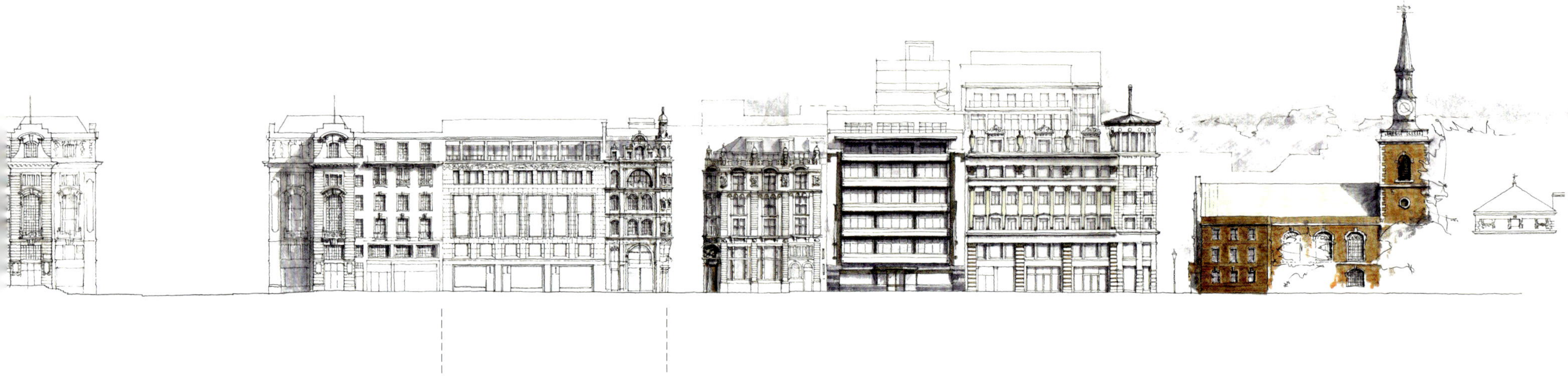

Colour reappears on the façade around the cheeks containing the double-order windows. These are characterised by oriel or bow windows (reminiscent of those used in nearby Bond Street) rising to half the height of the openings. These are contained within a row of bays, and the inside edges of these are splashed with what Parry refers to as a 'lipstick' red. They are speckled as the colour turns from creamy white to deep red and there is something Japanese about the colour, like a lacquered box with a sumptuous red interior or a ceramic bowl with a red lining. The effect is of a blush appearing in the middle of the building, a faint echo of the way the bright coloured lights on Piccadilly Circus reflect onto the surrounding architecture.

Turning round the corner into Eagle Place the tight, dark alley retains its historic proportions but bigger, brighter shopfronts might make it feel a little less constrictive whilst original cast-iron street furniture is retained and restored. Curious as it may sound, this was a favourite street of mine, precisely, perhaps, because it was little used, a simple shortcut between the broad, continental-scaled thoroughfare of Piccadilly and the domestic scale of Jermyn Street. Like the oddly dramatic Air Street which once connected Piccadilly and Regent Street to the dark, rather mysterious world of the rear of hotels with their endless array of services and smoking kitchen staff—but which has now been cleaned up into a bit more shopping. The retention of Eagle Place and its original scale is important, as it stitches the building into its fabric, creating that stop-start rhythm of grandeur and informality. The shops along Jermyn Street, traditionally the city's dandified man's realm, are all being returned, with the particular mix of bespoke crafts and top-end tailoring, so that the area's seemingly delicate but surprisingly robust commercial ecosystem is uninterrupted. The façade at the rear here is retained and behind it is a classic Continental model of urban mixed-use, retail, commercial and residential packed into an extraordinarily central site, one pretty much at the dead centre of the city. The apartments are, unusually for such a scheme, being interior designed by EPA and the feel is cool, modern, an antidote to the overstuffed luxury of most contemporary top-end development in which the purpose seems to be to demonstrate the expense of finishes and fittings and ultimately to justify an inflated price. Here, it seems, the location does most of the work, leaving the architects free to produce a framework for living without over-prescription.

left: Preliminary street elevation study illustrating the scale of the urban blocks facing Piccadilly and including the proposal for the central façade and the retained but raised corner building.

right: This pencil and crayon drawing from which detailed drawings for the ceramic façade to Piccadilly have been developed is notable for a number of points of principle:

– The vertical ordering; retail frontage at street level; offices to the 1st to 4th floors including the giant order to the 2nd and 3rd floors; the attic level supporting the proposed cornice; and in this version apartments behind the upper loggia;

– The depth of the façade of 900mm, illustrated in plan and section, allowing the returns to the openings to be read laterally in street views;

– The intended polychromy in the reveals of the 2nd and 3rd floor openings and the cornice earmarked at this stage for a collaboration with an artist to be chosen;

– The section shows the repetitive ceiling heights of the offices behind the articulation of the openings which respond to the classical ordering of the earlier façades;

– The six principal bays that respond to the street rather than the office grid; these reduce the three bays for the larger retail units below with the giant scrolled cill mediating the two scales. The attic level and the loggia create a field of five bays through which the cornice is woven;

– The use of horizontal repetition in response to the intended material of cast faience.

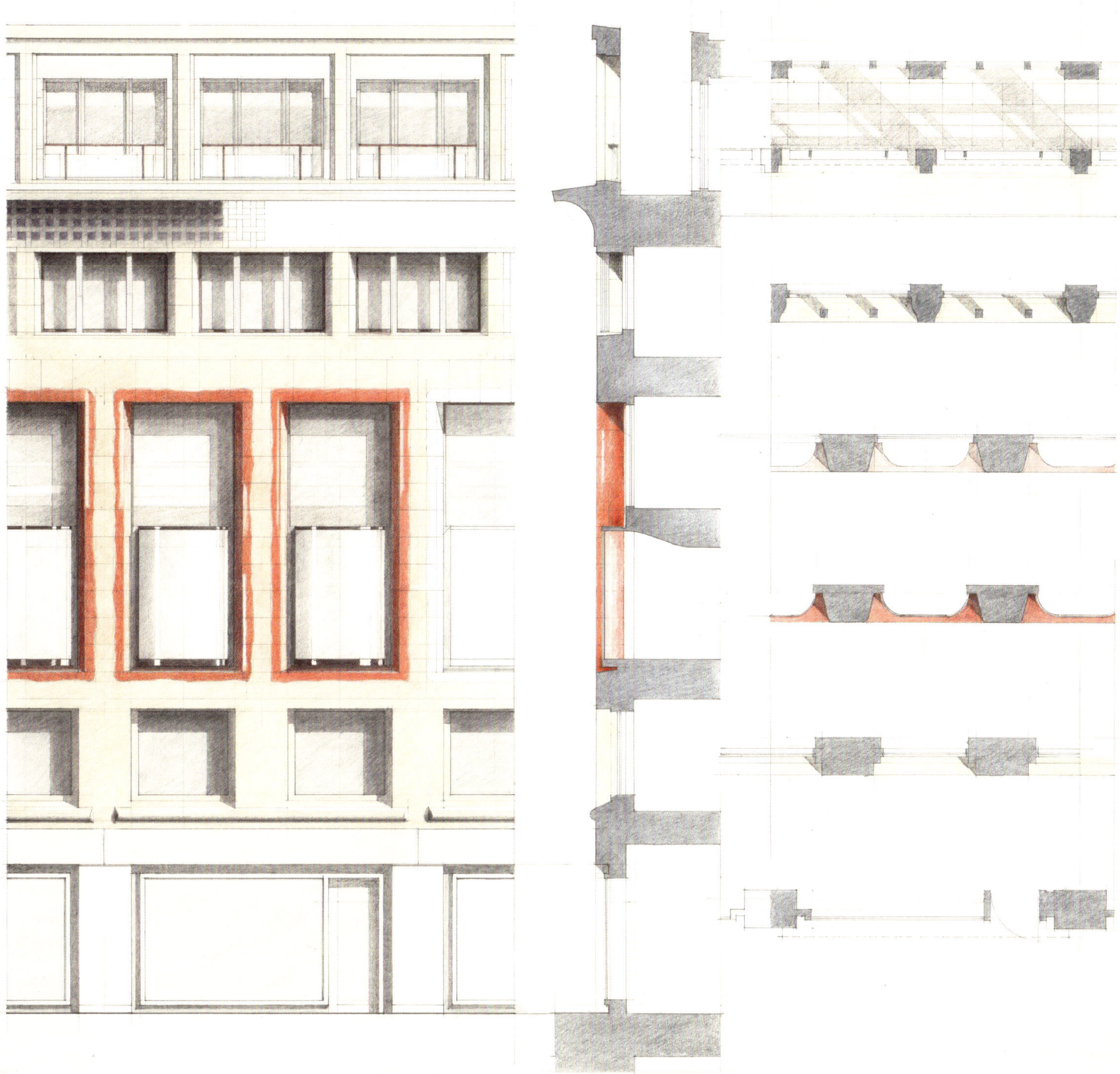

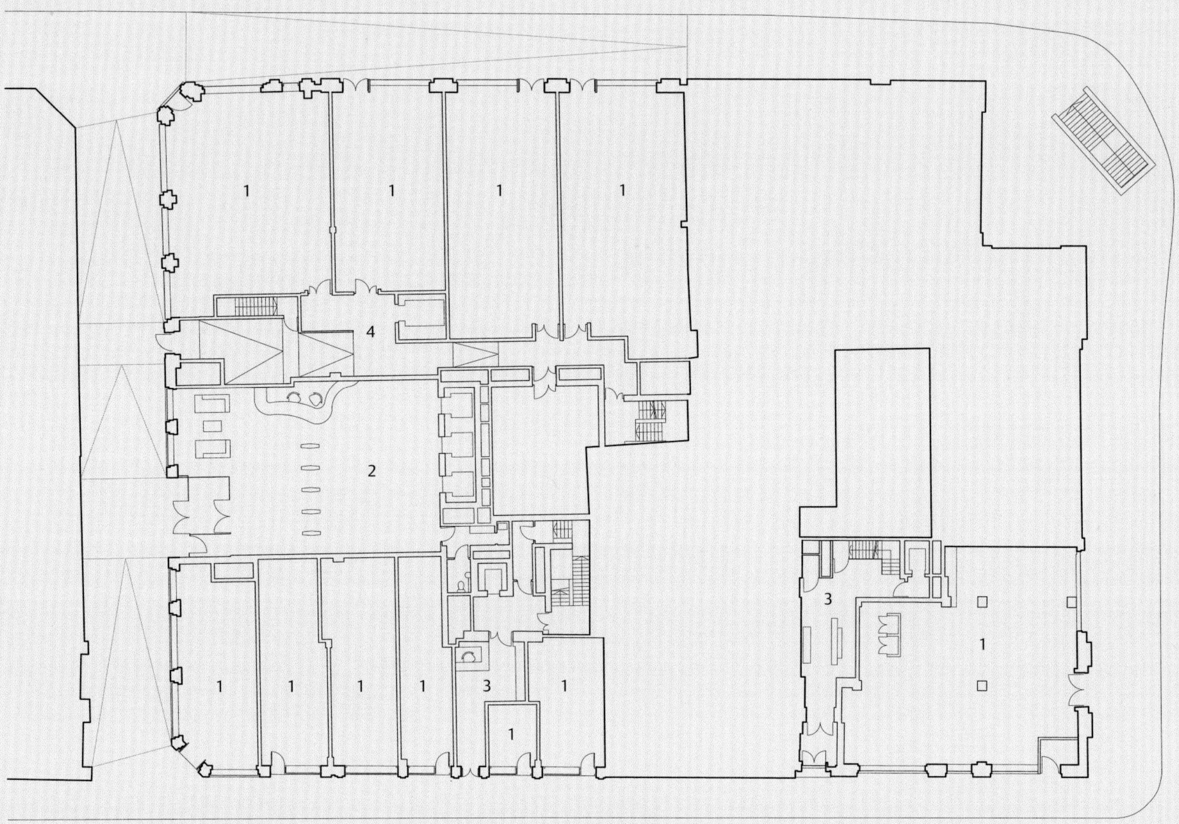

1. retail unit
2. office reception
3. residential lobby
4. service route

proposed ground floor plan

0 10m

1:500

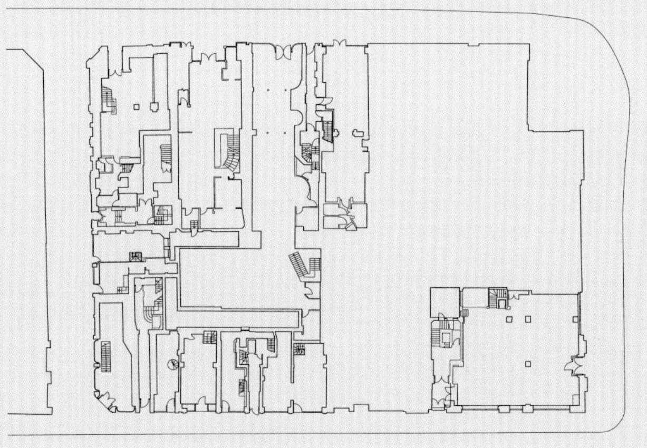

existing ground floor plan

0 20m

1:1000

opposite left: Proposed ground floor plan, illustrating the intensification of the public realm with retail space on Piccadilly and Jermyn Street, encircling the office entrance off Eagle Place.

opposite right: Existing ground floor plan, showing the warren of non-compliant stairs and spaces, and the decay of the block interior.

right: Proposed typical floor plan, showing the available interior office area for One Eagle Place taking up the entire west corner of the urban block and the respective services at the core of the block. The plan includes, on the east corner and to the southeast, our residential projects for 15 and 20 Jermyn Street respectively.

across the bottom of both pages: Richard Deacon's early colour studies for the cornice to our new Piccadilly façade of One Eagle Place.

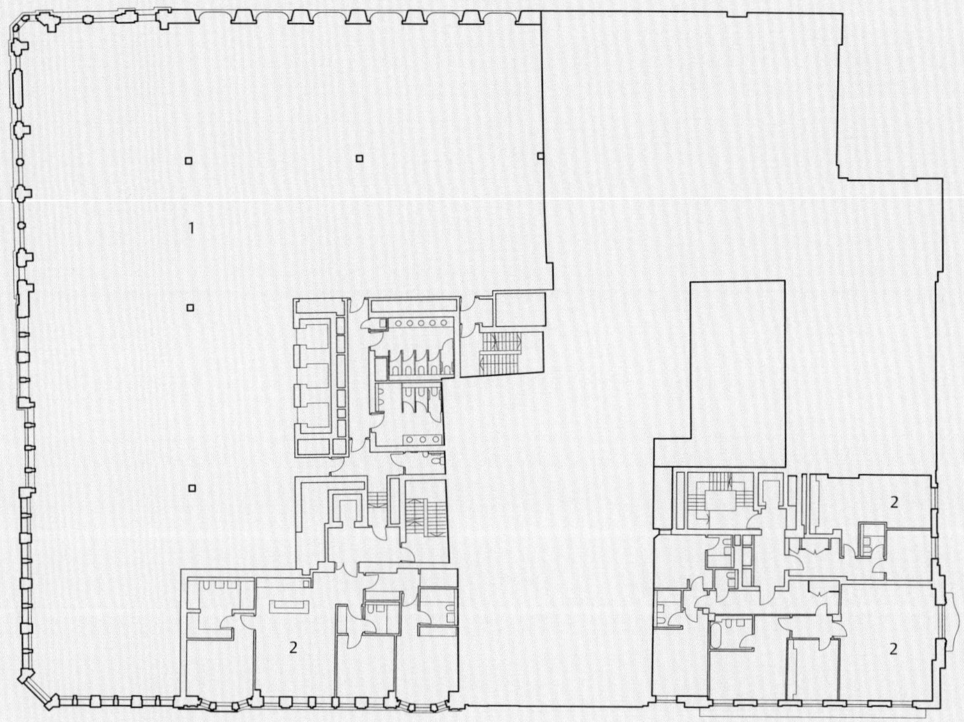

1. office
2. apartment

proposed typical floor plan

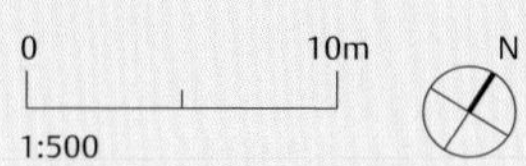

Piccadilly elevation

Jermyn Street elevation

top left: Urban block elevation to Piccadilly: the three retail units and six double-height aedicules, reflecting those of the early twentieth-century building to the east, mark the new ceramic façade; to the west is the elevated (by 1.7m) and rebuilt stone corner building matched by Alfred Waterhouse's bank building framing the opening to Eagle Place. The new horizons of base cornice, and the intermediate levels, take their cue from the ambition set by the earlier buildings.

bottom left: Urban block elevation to Jermyn Street. To the east (right) is the former bank building, the hall of which will be the shell of a retail use, whilst above 11 apartments are created. Behind the retained façade to the west (left) are at ground smaller retail units and four new lateral apartments. On the corner of Jermyn Street and Eagle Place a new elevation marks the new offices above and the top of the chamfered corner will house a sculpture by Stephen Cox.

top right: Urban block elevation of Eagle Place. Turning the corner from Piccadilly, the large retail unit strikes a horizon that, when combined with the fall of 1.5m, allow, the smaller retail units on Jermyn Street to incorporate a mezzanine office floor above, thus mediating the different characteristic scales of the two streets. The central section is marked by the entrance to the offices above.

bottom right: The urban block, Regent Street. Piccadilly Circus lies close to the north (right), the entrance to Jermyn Street to the south (left). The left flank will house the new apartments behind a carefully conserved and refenestrated façade.

Eagle Place elevation

Regent Street elevation

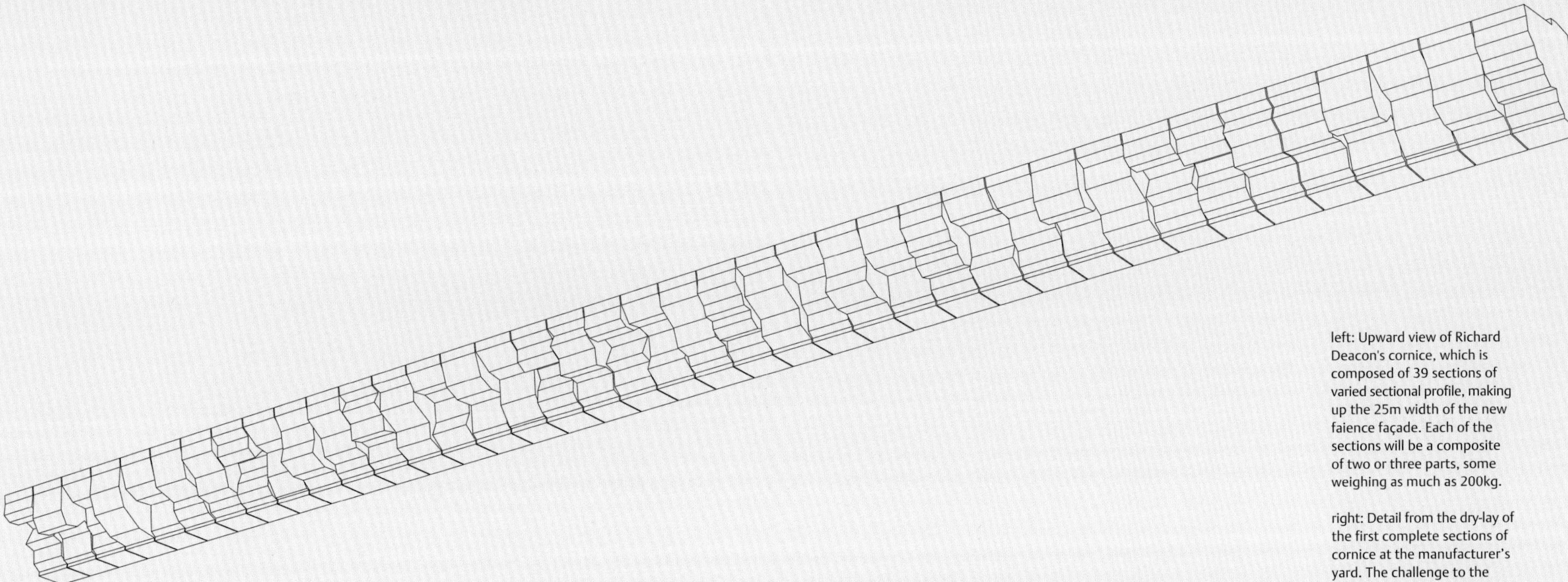

left: Upward view of Richard Deacon's cornice, which is composed of 39 sections of varied sectional profile, making up the 25m width of the new faience façade. Each of the sections will be a composite of two or three parts, some weighing as much as 200kg.

right: Detail from the dry-lay of the first complete sections of cornice at the manufacturer's yard. The challenge to the shortlist of artists approached for the commission was for a polychromatic cornice for this iconic London location, and the brilliance of Richard Deacon's sculpture belies the complex evolution of form and surface at this scale in the public realm.

The corner is marked by an artwork, an almost Renaissance cabouchon relief by Stephen Cox. The angled corner with its subtle decoration, a kind of draped stone effect, picks up the building opposite, an exercise in creamy Edwardian free style crowned by a small dome, and creates a little moment of relief along the narrow streetscape.

At the time of writing One Eagle Place is still under construction and it is difficult to assess the impact that such a substantial building might have. The colour of the cornice in particular will present a delicious challenge. It is also important to begin to see the project in the context of the Crown Estate's wholesale redevelopment and reimagining of the area. The scale of the intervention and its effect on the urban tissue needs to be seen as part of a major reappraisal of the streets radiating off Piccadilly Circus, including David Chipperfield's ambitious revivification of the Café Royal and Dixon Jones's pedestrianisation of Brewer Street and Sherwood Street and the replacing of the old Regent Palace Hotel. These schemes exhibit a kind of material and aesthetic ambition of clarity and coherence, as if all these architects were working within the same language and tradition and towards similar goals. The use of faience, of colour in glazed bricks, in a questioning of the pseudo-transparency of plate glass, in the primacy of the façade as a vertical extension the public space it contains and in the proportions and sub-divisions characteristic of the classical tradition are beginning to create coherence. It is arguably a moment which could not have occurred since the 1930s. With a few exceptions, Goldfinger, Emberton and a few others who have built well around here had difficulties in working around historical architectural traditions, whereas a few architects now seem able and willing to work within a tradition that refers to classical, Edwardian, modern and Modernist languages in a way which is deeply hopeful for the future of the centre of the city.

I think however that this will be seen in the future of the city as an important moment in the life of a street which has seemed to stagnate architecturally for decades; a new impetus in one of London's most extraordinary runs of buildings.

Projects Summary

Iringan Hijau

While our project for Damai Suria was under construction, Dawntree Properties commissioned a second scheme for a site nearby, still within the three-storey planning zone. Planning permission was granted, but the development was put on hold during the regional financial crisis. Resumed in 2002, work developed gradually into this final proposal, where the two different plots come to be conjoined. The design creates mixed-size apartments across the different buildings, which relate to one another through semi-enclosed garden areas and semi-interior communal spaces. In response to requirements for shade, privacy and protection from monsoon downpours that are typical of the region, the façades are equipped with sun-shading devices at varying spacings, framing views into landscape foliage, the city centre of Kuala Lumpur and the hills at Batu Caves.

C: Dawntree Properties Sdn Bhd
SE / M&E: Arup
QS: Davis Langdon Seah
LA: Ng Sek San
Local Architect: C'arch
A: EP, NJ* (1), LN* (2), RLL, GC, PC
Date: 1996–2009

Savile Row

At the heart of the historically sensitive Mayfair conservation area, the redevelopment of 23 Savile Row integrates much sought-after office space over large-scaled spaces, that I originally hoped would attract a gallery, and as chance would have it has become the headquarters of Hauser & Wirth, and therefore one of the epicentres of contemporary art worldwide. The self-supporting stonework was conceived as a sequence of punched openings within a stone wall, with each window opening flanked by pilasters supporting a profiled string course.

The building includes a significant new work of public art by distinguished American sculptor Joel Shapiro. He conceived a dynamic piece constructed of cast bronze, forming a dramatic but carefully integrated part of the main façade onto Savile Row.

C: Legal & General (prior to construction)
D2 Private
SE / M&E: Arup
QS: AYH Arcadis–Mott Green Wall
A: EP, RB, JS, RK, BH, MR, BD, GC, DC, ER, ZF, LN, FE, AVO, NH
Date: 2001–2009

St Martin-in-the-Fields

The site of St Martin-in-the-Fields is highly significant; a complex mix of buildings including the church, social care facilities, residential apartments, and the underground crypts and vaults. The architectural brief was to develop a masterplan that would unify the whole site, resolve spatial difficulties and create a series of uplifting spaces that are flexible enough to accommodate a range of activities now and in the future. Our response to the brief connects each of the different elements of the site, creating and framing a space to nurture and sustain the community. A new entrance pavilion provides access to a new foyer, and the crypt below is located at the western end of a widened Church Path linking St Martin's Place and Adelaide Street. The conservation works to the church, designed by James Gibbs, have removed later Victorian additions and returned the interior to its eighteenth-century glory, enhancing the architectural qualities of the original building while at the same time emphasising the church's continuing spiritual and social remit.

C: St Martin-in-the-Fields
SE: Alan Baxter & Associates
M&E: Max Fordham & Partners
QS: Gardiner & Theobald
A: EP, RK*, TL, CB, LN, SM, JPO, RC, NA, NL, SBU, FP, JDV, GC, OW, GH, BB, JO, LME, TO, AM, RLL
Date: 2002–2008

Holburne Museum

Following an invited competition, we were appointed architects to the Holburne Museum, and asked to compile and submit a Stage One Heritage Lottery Fund Application for the refurbishment of the museum itself. The proposal included the new extension onto Sydney Gardens that offers a café at ground level, as well as new gallery spaces on the upper floors, and a new archive research facility, ensuring the future of The Holburne Collection. With a strong base of local support in Bath, the proposal had as its main aim to enhance the historic building itself and its relationship to the Collection and the surrounding park. Servicing solutions, the sourcing of materials and the methods of construction were considered in relation to their environmental impact throughout all stages of design.

C: Trustees of the Holburne Museum of Art
SE: Momentum
M&E: Atelier 10
QS: Faithful & Gould
EPA Team: EP, RB* (1), CH* (2), CB, GP, GH, TO, RLL, JS
Date: 2002–2011

Four Seasons Hotel Spa

In 2005, we were appointed to create a new Spa and a rooftop extension. The Spa is situated with a double-storied rooftop pavilion on the existing building, an area previously occupied by a plant room. The 1,893m² space houses a gym, early arrivals facility and a new plant room in addition to the treatment rooms, pool and other areas associated with the spa. Stephen Cox has produced 15 memorably haptic pieces for the spa in Egyptian limestone and Indian granite.

C: Hisham Abdulrahman Jaffer
and Four Seasons Hotel Group
SE: AKT
M&E: Industrial Design Associates
QS: Gleeds
EPA Team: EP, RB, JO*, NJ, RC, SF, GC, AM, GH, JAS, MC
Date: 2004–2010

Threadneedle Street

The principle was to reconfigure the disjointed and publicly anti-social 1960s building into a clear urban block, creating a new city passage with shops and restaurants between Threadneedle and Throgmorton Streets. This part of the City of London within the Bank of England conservation area is characterised by finely articulated corners, most overtly Soane's at the Bank of England. These were the inspiration for the ordering of scale and urban negotiations between the complex of surrounding streets. We won the commission by competition in June 2004, and we were commissioned to design proposals for part of the redevelopment of the site of the former London Stock Exchange buildings at 60 Threadneedle Street. The sculptural qualities of the façade are created by the scale of units and a dark lustrous finish which responds to light and weather. The proposal for the new ten-storey office building, with a lower ground floor and basement, incorporates retail floor space on ground floor and part of the basement level on site of the old Market Hall Building.

SE: WSP Cantor Seinuk
M&E: Hilson Moran Partnership
QS: Davis Langdon
A: EP, NL* (1), MC* (2), RD, TO, CT, AVO, DM, JDV, GC, SBU, YK, BB, LM
Date: 2004–2009

New Bond Street

The redevelopment of 50 New Bond Street and 14 St George Street creates two high-quality office buildings within a highly restricted urban site, surrounded by listed buildings. New Bond Street has a new façade with a combination of curved bay windows and sculptural faience ribs. St George Street has an additional storey above the existing retained façade and a new façade to Maddox Street, with a combination of glass block and clear glass. The development includes a large retail unit to New Bond Street, and conversion of buildings on Maddox Street to residential use.

C: Scottish Widows plc
PM: Hanover Cube
SE: Ramboll UK
M&E: Hilson Moran Partnership
QS: Gardiner & Theobald
A: EP, NJ*(1), JS*(2), NH, JF, DL, MA, VR, NM, SBU, OW, KS
Date: 2004–2009

Belgravia Residence

Within the original nineteenth-century development of Belgravia, once commissioned by the Duke of Westminster, this private residential project required the interior refurbishment of the ground and lower ground floors of the existing Grade II listed building, as well as the partial demolition and reconstruction of the adjoining mews. A new, glazed structure provides the link between the main house and the mews. The envelope of the mews building is a new structure except for the upper half of the existing brick façade, which was retained in continuity with the policy of this conservation area. The interior finishes, apart from the fair-faced concrete, include large areas of hardwood timber wall panelling and built-in furniture. The stair is a major feature constructed of granite treads post-tensioned by steel stringers with curved glass sections of balustrades. Metal skylights have been installed in the new roof of the mews building, including the use of curved glass.

C: Private Client
SE: Michael Hadi Associates
M&E: Michael Popper Associates
QS: LG Consult Ltd
LA: Christopher Bradley Hole
A: EP, RC*, TSD, GC, CH, RLL, BB
Date: 2005–2010

Timothy Taylor Gallery, Carlos Place

This is the second gallery we have designed for Timothy Taylor, now in Carlos Place, Mayfair. The light and elegant intervention sits within the shell of a former bank building located just off Grosvenor Square in the Mayfair Conservation Area. The space is designed as a neutral backdrop to the art on display and can accommodate large-scale painting and sculpture. The total scheme occupies 615m^2, including viewing rooms, office space, painting storage, staff facilities and a workshop. Spread over ground and lower ground floors, the public and private areas are linked by a solid oak staircase.

C: Timothy Taylor Gallery
SE: Michael Hadi Associates
QS: LG Consult Ltd
A: EP, CH*, TSD
Date: 2006–2007

Pembridge Crescent Residence

30 Pembridge Crescent was a project located at the heart of Notting Hill. Our proposal was to rehabilitate two existing houses for a private residence, in keeping with a traditional approach to the façade and making use of contemporary building technology. An upper brick storey was to be reconstructed as well as the pre-existing timber coach house shuttering at ground floor level. Both the scale of the proposal and the choice of building materials were in consonance with those of the existing fabric. One of those elements was a shallow-pitch traditional slate roof which was retained in our design, while a screened glass link made the transition between the scale of the mews and that of the street.

C: IVC and Litvak Investor Corp
PM: The Millbridge Group Ltd
SE: Hoare Lea, Michael Hadi and Momentum
QS: Chelmer Site Investigations
LA: Kew Innovation Unit
A: EP, RD, BD, RLL, ZF, TP, HA
Date: 2006–2009

Lipton Residence II

In summer 2009 the approval for the reconstruction of this 1930s house, which we had already extensively remodelled (see *Volume 1*), was granted. Two immediate neighbours had already been rebuilt as neo-Georgian facsimiles, but ours was to be a contemporary version of the Regency villa. The commission was for a lifetime family home that would demonstrate sustainable construction and achieve Code for Sustainable Homes Level 4. The level access allowed a section and massing with three full floors above ground with an enlarged lower ground floor. The street elevation has a suppressed and heavily glazed ground floor with ten portrait-format windows to the bedrooms above. To the garden are the more expressive volumes of the principal rooms. The garden has been designed by Adriaan Geuze of West 8. The interiors were in collaboration with Chester Jones and developed the vocabulary of the original design, this time incorporating and articulating the reused elements. The landscaped garden, terraces and retained fish pool were completed with West 8.

C: Sir Stuart and Lady Ruth Lipton
SE: Arup
M&E: Arup
QS: Davis Langdon
LA: West 8 (Rotterdam)
Interior designer: Chester Jones Ltd
A: EP, RK, RD, DL, ZF, PC, RLL, MA, TS, BL
Date: 2007–2012

Rothschild competition, New Court

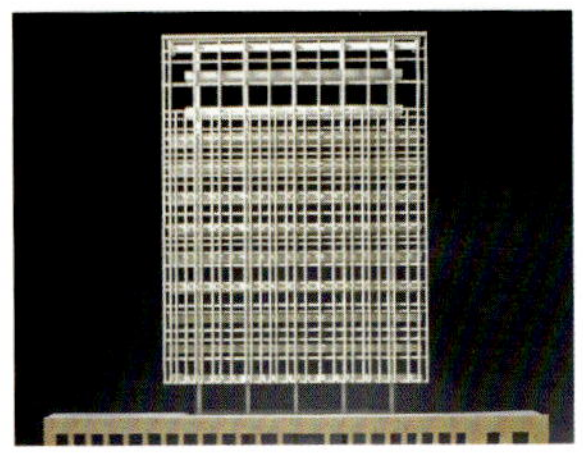

Our competition entry for the new Rothschild investment bank headquarters in London was located on King William Street, by St Swithin's Lane, a stone's throw from the Bank of England. Given the limited area and built constraints of the site, our project began to develop from earlier on as a dialogue between the different aspects of the brief. Our proposal was articulated along the lines of the semi-public spaces near the ground, acting as a stone basis for the more private office areas rising as a ceramic grid emerging from within the urban fabric of the pre-existing buildings.

C: NM Rothschild & Sons
Development Manager: Stanhope plc
A: EP, NJ, RK, NM, GC, TSD
Date: 2007

Wells Cathedral School

The school specialises in both vocal and instrumental music. The new recital hall and practice spaces will provide a much-needed physical heart to the school, set between the listed Cedars House and the listed landscape which surrounds the school's sports field. The gallery overlooking the performance space is at the level of the fields, and entry to the building is via a gentle ramp adjacent to an ancient yew hedge. The height of the hall required for acoustics is reflected in the floating structure raising the roof, and the walls are externally a juxtaposition of singular rusted metal panels and massive glazed panels. There are a number of smaller buildings and landscape included within the project.

C: Wells Cathedral School
PM & QS: Faithful+Gould
SE: Momentum Consulting Engineers
M&E: Buro Happold
LA: Land Use Consultants
A: EP, TL, PBA, CK
Date: 2007–2017

Sebastian + Barquet

We designed Sebastian + Barquet's first gallery in London, specialising in Modernist design from the time of the 1940s to the 1960s. Situated at the heart of Mayfair, the proposal included a new front to the gallery, and the refurbishment works made it possible for the new interior to include a versatile exhibition space as well as offices and a private viewing room. The gallery opened in October 2008 with New Hope, Sebastian + Barquet London's inaugural exhibition of American Modernist design, which was also curated by Eric Parry. Since its inception, the gallery has presented the public with a coherent programme of curated design exhibitions.

C: Sebastian + Barquet (London)
M&E: Johan Environmental Services
A: EP, CH, RC, RLL, ZF, GC
Date: 2008

One Eagle Place, Piccadilly

Our project for One Eagle Place, Piccadilly comprises the greater part of the urban block situated between Piccadilly and Piccadilly Circus to the north, and Jermyn Street and St James's to the south. The mixed-use site straddles two conservation areas (Regent Street and St James's). The design proposal is aimed at improving the condition, viability and sustainability of the existing buildings and façades, as well as responding to the contemporary demand for modern retail and office units.

C: The Crown Estate
Development Manager: Stanhope plc
SE: Waterman Partnership
M&E: Mecserve
QS: Gardiner & Theobald
A: EP, NJ, MC, AVO, CT, GP, JF, JH, LB, WA, JE, RC, ZF, CK, CLK, SE
Date: 2008–2013

Palladio Exhibition at the Royal Academy

We were appointed by the Royal Academy of Arts to design the exhibition devoted to the sixteenth-century master architect Andrea Palladio. Arguably the most significant exhibition of Palladio's work in more than 30 years, some 200 exhibits were displayed in a series of themed rooms conceived to appeal to both scholars and a wider audience. The design of the exhibition reflected the intimacy and immediacy of Palladio's own drawings and the completed projects through the display of contemporary models. A unique opportunity to share the vision of one of the most historically significant architects with the general public, the exhibition was organised by the Royal Academy in collaboration with the Centro Internazionale di Studi di Architettura Andrea Palladio and the Royal Institute of British Architects, marking the quincentenary of Palladio's birth.

C: Royal Academy of Arts
SE: Scott Wilson Engineers
A: EP, RLL
Date: 2008–2009

Mayang – Towers

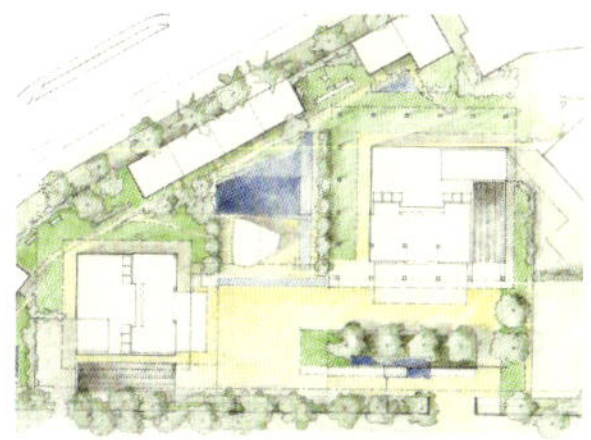

Located at the heart of Kuala Lumpur, in Malaysia, our design involves the construction of two high-rise residential buildings as part of the same project—the West Tower and the East Tower. Both towers have an oscillating width along their shafts, creating an array of floor areas. Our proposal includes an extensive car park forming the basis of the complex, which includes a series of townhouses on an elevated landscape. The interior concept design was also developed by us for both semi-public spaces, like the entrance lobbies to each tower, and the internal layout of each floor. The two-floor townhouses included in the building complex were also designed by us to include accommodation for a large family each, containing extensive internal areas, private landscaped areas and private swimming pool.

C: Bolton Properties Sdn Bhd
A: EP, NJ*, LN, TP
Date: 2008–2009

Olympic Village, London

As part of the 2012 London Olympics, we were commissioned with what was then Plot N10 of the athletes' village. This was meant to harbour the incoming Olympic athletes in the first instance, and later to be part of a mixed-market and affordable tenure residential development with some complementary retail use. Given the rigour of the masterplanning brief, our design response included the careful study of the façades, granting them with animation, depth and solidity, almost as a prolongation or space of transition to the domestic interior. This is especially the case of our treatment of the generous balconies, which is further enhanced by the strong colours of paintings by Eric Parry, offsetting the stolid nature of the buildings. The block encloses a large landscaped garden as a distributing space, whose light, green and treetops are in constant dialogue with the architecture.

C: John Sisk & Son and Lendlease
SE: Adams Kara Taylor
M&E: Haydon
LA: Applied Landscape Design, Kinnear Landscape Architects, Macfarlane Wilder and Vogt Landschaftsarchitekten AG
A: EP, NJ*, TL, LH, ARM, BD, CK, CLK, KS, PC
Date: 2008–2012

15 and 20 Jermyn Street, Piccadilly

As part of our project for One Eagle Place, we have designed two buildings of apartments on 15 and 20 Jermyn Street. Within the shell of a monumental 1920s office building at the corner of Lower Regent Street and Jermyn Street, we have created a mix of three-bedroom, two-bedroom and one-bedroom apartments that are fully furnished and decorated for the rental market. With a location overlooking Piccadilly Circus, the airy loft-like spaces of 15 Jermyn Street are a fresh arrival at the London scene. The interior design concept and the furniture fit out were fully developed by our office. In 20 Jermyn Street, we created behind a retained Edwardian residential façade, 5 lateral apartments for the sales market. The interior design concept was also fully developed by our office.

C: The Crown Estate
Development Manager: Stanhope Plc
SE: Waterman Partnership
M&E: Mecserve
QS: Gardiner & Theobald
A: EP, NJ, MC*, GP, JF, JH, LB, WA, RC, CK
Date: 2008–ongoing

Curzon Street Mayfair

This was an invited competition for a luxury residential development on a prominent site on Curzon Street, in Mayfair, that would offer unrivalled luxury homes of varying typologies to maximise the value of the investment. The concept of full concierge service was complemented by extensive private catering, spa and fitness as well as individual garaging and lift service. The design was streamlined as a classic Bugatti Type 57. Lateral apartments onto Curzon Street turned the corner to Bolton Street with their large windows framed in two-tone ceramic. On this tighter street individual entrances to townhouses and duplexes mirrored the rhythm of the surviving Georgian residences. Private gardens in the landscaped centre of the building are carefully screened from the neighbouring buildings.

C: Brockton Capital and Urban Solutions
Development Manager: Urban Solutions
A: EP, RK, LH, ZF, SF, WA, BL, CK
Date: 2009

Deutsche Schule, Madrid

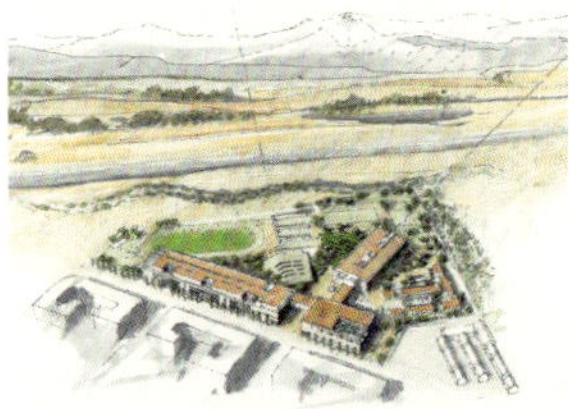

For the Deutsche Schule in Madrid, the concept was to embed the school into the hilly landscape and to open up the building complex to the views of the Hoyo de Manzanares mountain chain. Located at the end of the modern district of Montecarmelo, our design responded to the suburban block character of the site and introduced the use of natural stone, granting a timeless quality to our proposal. We also made use of the wide exterior for sporting activities and leisure spaces—visually anchored by the architecture of the school building complex with its centre in the Plaza (Forum). This is also where the main entrance is located, giving direct access to the school auditorium, the secondary school itself, and the primary school canteen. The auditorium has a 1000-seat capacity, providing the school not only with a useful facility, but also an added source of revenue, being equipped for concerts, theatre performances, conferences, lectures and video projections, with an adaptable stage for a potential 200-musician-strong orchestra, and a control room suitable to accommodate simultaneous translation for multilingual events.

C: Deutsche Schule Madrid
SE: Alan Baxter & Associates
LA: Latz und Partner
A: EP, RK, MC, RB, CT, DL, JF, ZF, CK
Date: 2009

House of European History, Brussels

Our aim was to create a new building embracing the pre-existing Art Deco Eastman building by Michel Polak, located in the historic setting of the Léopold Park in Brussels. We wished to take the internal meeting of the old and the new to create a stunning space of visual display, making the public areas of the museum immediately accessible to the visitor as a single perspective. Visually, this was not a simple case of opposing the new versus the old, but involved the complex reuse and transformation of the existing fabric, while fully preserving the architectonic quality of the Eastman building. Integral to our proposal was the cost-efficiency of both construction and building maintenance, by resorting to engineering solutions on the cutting edge of building technology.

C: European Parliament
SE: Alan Baxter & Associates
QS: Davis Langdon LLP
Exhibition designer: Metaphor
A: EP, NJ, CH, MC, WA
Date: 2009

Z-handle

Our design for the Z-handle was originally part of the project for Iringan Hijau, Kuala Lumpur, and later came to feature in other of our projects. The handles themselves were initially produced in dialogue with Edwin Heathcote's company izé. The purpose of the design was to resolve the transition from the horizontality of the handle, through a concatenation of surfaces, to the verticality of the backplate and the door. We have produced a range of Z-handles as variations of this design theme for different sizes and purposes, including long horizontal Z-levers used for the entrance doors in our renewal of Sebastian + Barquet, Mayfair, to be viewed as an intrinsic part of the design of the doors and the materiality of the façade.

Manufacturer: izé
A: EP, RLL
Date: 2009

26 Albemarle Street

26 Albemarle Street will house a handful of the most sought-after apartments in London. With a 25m frontage to the street opposite the Royal Institution, the building was built in 1905, probably for residential purposes, but used as offices until recently. The proposal includes the full retention of the historical street façade with only minor alterations, but the extension of the roof. The works to the rear façade are more substantial and take into account contemporary requirements such as the provision of outdoor spaces and the enlargement of window areas.

The interior design concept is fully developed by our office. Each apartment boasts a simple and sophisticated layout that provides a balance between entertaining space and the intimacy of domestic life. The roof will be extended to a mansard roof to create a duplex penthouse with large atelier windows to the street and landscaped terraces to the interior.

C: Albemarle Street Holdings
PM / QS: Jackson Coles
SE: Heyne Tillett Steel
M&E: Peter Deer and Associates
A: EP, RK, MC, SE, KS, LAF, WA, LB
Date: 2010–ongoing

Brighton College Music and Drama Schools

Brighton College is a collection of buildings set within a George Gilbert Scott designed campus on a tight city centre site. There are limited possibilities for expansion and the new performing arts hub we are designing relies on a detailed understanding of the intricacies of the existing buildings. We carried out a Heritage Assessment plan with a specialist conservation architect in order to demonstrate the enhanced setting the new buildings will provide. Recently, we were granted planning permission for two new buildings: the Music School, which will sit next to the Tim Ronalds' Performing Arts Centre completed in 2000; and the Drama School, that will provide a new theatre as well as back-of-house facilities and teaching rooms, and which will be located on a site currently occupied by the 1960s science building.

C: Brighton College
PM: Steve Patten
SE: Momentum
M&E: Skelly & Couch
QS: Academy Consulting Solutions and Subsight Surveys Ltd
A: EP, TL, CH, DL, CD, LV, CK, PBA
Date: 2009–ongoing

Elizabeth House, Waterloo

Following the joint developers' purchase we were invited to compete for this important Southbank building. Elizabeth House, York Road, Waterloo had planning consent for nearly 1 million square feet and it was envisaged the new planning application would be made for some 1.5 million square feet. The site is one of the most interesting in London as it will knit together Europe's largest cultural facilities and one of London's most active railway stations. The site is sensitive as it has views from Parliament and Parliament Square. Our proposal carefully considered the urban massing within these urban constraints and how the public spaces could link the redundant Eurostar terminus and the routes to the South Bank.

C: Chelsfield Partners LLP/London & Regional Properties
A: EP, RK, NJ, JO, AM
Date: 2010

Great Marlborough Street

We were approached directly by the client in spring 2012 to design proposals for a mixed-use development on a very restricted site straddling the southeast corner of Great Marlborough Street and Poland Street in Soho, London. The solution creates a campus of new and refurbished buildings around a new public courtyard, itself accessed by a public passageway through a high-quality façade to 54–57 Great Marlborough Street. This new building provides an office entrance, cafés and a courtyard restaurant at ground level with six floors of office above. Its façade is crafted from a weave of cast glass lenses, and vitreous enamel panels with granite piers. The campus is completed by two refurbished, remodelled and reclad buildings that also look onto the courtyard; a house on Poland Street and a 1960s concrete-frame building to the south, providing innovative modern offices accessed from the courtyard itself with three high-specification penthouse units accessed exclusively from Poland Street. The treatment of the Poland Street façades includes proposals for brick, abronze section and a riveted metallic section.

C: Henderson Global Investors
PM: ESPM Project Management
SE: WSP Group (WSP Cantor Seinuk)
QS: Rider Hunt
A: EP, JS, CT, LAF, MA, GSG, KS, TW
Date: 2010–ongoing

Msheireb Downtown Doha

We were commissioned to design three residential buildings in Phase 3 of Msheireb Properties' flagship project. Msheireb Downtown Doha is the world's first sustainable downtown regeneration project and will regenerate and preserve the historic heart of Doha. Providing high-quality apartments and communal facilities for families from the region and abroad, our designs build on the project masterplan and principles. Having collaborated with four other design architects the buildings define a new public realm in this new neighbourhood. Our façades and interiors respond to this new urban living, its scale, setting and the city's climate.

C: Gensler
SE: Buro Happold
M&E: Atelier Ten
QS: Gleeds
A: EP, RK, JO, LH, CB, PBA, SF, CK, CD, AM, JD, GS, JIS, LV, JW, TW, BL
Date: 2010–ongoing

Shell Centre, London

This competition entry for the Shell Centre was to be located in a centrally historic area of London, near the Houses of Parliament. Concerns with massing, urban rights of light and views, and the overall relationship of the project with the Thames, the London Eye and the forthcoming development of Elizabeth House, were crucial in view of the nature of the surrounding urban fabric and the existing listed buildings. In our proposal we were keenly aware of the Shell Centre's unique position to establish a new urban quarter, bringing a combination of workplace and living to the South Bank—being so close and well connected to the heart of political and cultural life in the City of Westminster and Lambeth. While our façade proposal reflected a classically modern approach to load-bearing Portland stone and glass, the volumes were topped by landscaped terraces with trees for shade, providing a space of leisure looking over the river to the iconic cityscape of Westminster.

C: Helical Bar plc
PM: GVA Second London Wall
SE: Waterman Group
QS: EC Harris LLP
A: EP, NJ, LH, AM
Date: 2010–2012

St John's, Waterloo

Our feasibility study proposed a re-ordering and extension of the Grade II church to improve accessibility and acoustics, and provide additional facilities for the community and arts organisations resident in the crypt. This comprised removal of 1980s extensions, the reinstatement of the first floor gallery lost in the Second World war, new stairs and lift, and phased excavation for a double-height rehearsal and performance space and a free-standing café in the re-landscaped garden.

C: The Parish of St John with St Andrew, Waterloo
SE: Alan Baxter
M&E: Skelly & Couch
QS: Academy Consulting
A: EP, TL, KS, PBA
Date: 2010

The Leathersellers' Hall

Initially a competition-winner for the interior design of the fit-out of the Leathersellers' Hall, the brief evolved into a building project. As part of the negotiations between the guild, as freeholders, and the developers of 100 Bishopsgate tower, a new proposal for their relocation into 5–7 St Helen's Place was agreed. The 1920s office's north façade onto the place is to be retained with new offices above the new Leathersellers' Hall. The reconstruction includes a new façade close to the historic St Helen's Church that will be seen from the new reception spaces. We will be completing the very specialist interior fit-out for the guild once the office building is completed by us in the summer 2015.

C: The Worshipful Company of Leathersellers / 100 Bishopsgate Partnership
SE: Price & Myers / RBG Group
ME: Chapman Bathhurst / Hilson Moran
QS: Gardiner & Theobald / Davis Langdon
PM: Gardiner Theobald / Brookfield Multiplex
A: EP, JO, RK, CH, RC, CPR, SN, SO, LAF, AM, RLL
Date: 2009–ongoing

Zitadelle Berlin, Spandau

The Spandau Zitadelle was built in the sixteenth century and is one of Germany's best-preserved Renaissance fortresses. Both the building complex and its individual buildings are listed. The competition included the redevelopment of the historic buildings for one exhibition of Berlin's monuments as well as a permanent exhibition on fortifications and military history, and also the architectural design of the exhibition. The brief encompassed approximately 4,900m^2. The Zitadelle has been enriched with new uses and meaningful connections, creating a charismatic place with a heightened experiential value. In our proposal the original appearance of the Zitadelle as a whole is to be strengthened, which requires intervening in those layers that were added at later stages. The overall positive experience for the visitor in steering through the Zitadelle was of great importance, and accordingly our proposal took the distinctive design of the entrances to the various museums as signs for the visitors.

C: City of Berlin
SE / M&E and Lighting Design: Arup
A: EP, MC, JO, JF, AM, WA
Graphic design: Peter Willberg
Date: 2010

Vicarage Gate House

Vicarage Gate House occupies a site, formerly a nursing home, in Kensington. Vicarage Gate House is at the junction of Vicarage Gate and Palace Garden Terrace. The site occupies a prominent corner position bordering the rear of Palace Green to the east, and St Mary Abbotts Churchyard to the south. The main entrance is from Vicarage Gate. The site has planning permission for the construction of 14 apartments and an underground car park with 14 spaces. The client brief was to develop generously proportioned apartments planned for ease of living that will attract a range of international purchasers. The building is to be constructed from good-quality materials with a high design content. Finishes will be a high quality for a speculative development.

C: Vicarage Gate Limited
PM: Northacre
SE: Conisbee
QS: Hampton
Interior designers: Forme Architecture
Building Service Engineer: Mecserve
A: EP, JO, ARM, BD, SF, AM, JW
Date: 2011–ongoing

White City Masterplan

Our masterplan proposes a mid-urban mixed-use development of residential, commercial and retail uses with the aim of breaking down the current isolation of the site by creating new vehicular and pedestrian linkages to the northern, southern and western boundaries. We propose two new key public spaces, an urban arrival square, which acts as a gateway into the site, and a central garden square which acts as the communal heart of the development. The aim is to create a neighbourhood in which all aspects of urban life and living can take place.

The development will have a variety of building heights throughout the site, within an average 8 to 11 storeys through the urban and garden squares, and a single taller 31-storey high block to the north of the site. Our public realm strategy is centred on creating a rich and varied sequence of spaces, and the proposal includes a basement where all car parking, bicycle parking, refuse and plant areas are located, allowing the ground floor to exist as an attractive garden landscape free from the compromise of servicing requirements.

C: Helical Bar plc
PM: Second London Wall
SE: WSP
M&E: WSP
QS: EC Harris LLP
LA: Grant Associates
A: EP, NJ, LH, JAS, AM, SO
Date: 2011–ongoing

King's Cross – Zone A

A competition proposal for Google to take the entire Zone A of the masterplan at King's Cross Central: Located between the new Boulevard and the western platforms of King's Cross Station, the proposal was to provide at least 730,000 square feet of offices. To respond to this scale the idea was for this to be considered the third shed alongside the two great railway stations. Our proposals allowed the building to be completed in phases and to allow subsequent flexible occupation. The architectural articulation within the prescribed massing emphasised the presence on Station Square and the north elevation's outlook over the Regent's Canal to Granary Square. The internal arrangement of a shared platform at first floor led to a variety of spaces for an organisation that has several worldwide campuses. Cycles penetrated the base and a stepped garden capped the roofline.

C: King's Cross Central Limited Partnership (KCCLP)
Development manager: Argent
A: EP, RK, JO, WA, BL, CD, SN, SG
Date: 2011

Accra North Site Masterplan, Ghana

This is a mixed-use project in Accra, on the banks of the Odaw River, only minutes away from the coast. Our proposal for the development includes a series of residential buildings with private gardens around an extensive central court—with arrival plaza, communal themed gardens, a leisure pool, terraces and walkways—over a 700-space car parking with direct access to each of the buildings above. The central garden will be taken up by three pavilions including leisure facilities for residents.

C: Trasacco Estates Development Company Ltd
SE: AKT Structural Engineering
LA: Grant Associates
A: EP, LH, RLL
Date: 2011

No. 1 Berkeley Street

Located in the heart of Piccadilly, just across from the Ritz, our proposal for the No. 1 Berkeley Street hotel included a variety of executive suites, guestrooms and suites, restaurant, café and bar. In our proposal, the ground floor establishes a gradual transition from the public area of the street to the semi-public reception and other amenities within. The upper floors are of domestic height in full consonance with the surrounding buildings. This is reflected on the structure of the façade, where the floors appear to continue the surrounding cityscape. The Piccadilly façade is divided into three sections following the rhythm of the surrounding buildings. The façade is centrally topped by a landscaped rooftop, mediating between building and sky.

C: Confidential
A: EP, WA
Date: 2011

120 Fenchurch Street

120 Fenchurch Street is a development at the scale of a city block. Following a transfer of ownership, a revised scheme from the 2007 approval was developed. It retains the three distinct sections: a permeable base with a new public passageway; a main body of 11 storeys of high-quality office space; and an upper setback with four office floors with a restaurant and a publicly accessible roof garden above. The specific geometry of the site informed the strong, faceted massing. The vertical ceramic fins provide depth and solar shading and some reflection into the streetscape. The upper fully glazed floors reflect the surrounding buildings and sky. The roof garden has a new topography of a gently folded floor, a water feature and green cubes which enclose the plant facilities below. Around the high-level 'Wisteria trees' a continuous perimeter walk gives vistas of the London skyline in all four directions. Inspired by the tradition of *camera obscura* an LED screen soffit at the centre of the pedestrian passageway will show imagery of the roof garden above.

C: Generali
SE: Arup
M&E: Waterman Group
QS: Gleeds
LA: Latz + Partners
PM: Core
A: EP, NJ, CT, RD, KS, CD
Date: 2011–ongoing

King's College School, Wimbledon, Masterplan

Our competition proposal for this independent school was a masterplan to address more than 11 individual proposals on the site. Our study sought to reinforce the character of the school's collegiate buildings around courtyards and the shared spaces that open onto its playing fields, whilst also addressing the shortcomings of the later buildings. The main entrance and teaching block are to be remodelled and extended with a new façade to unify the school's frontage to Wimbledon Common. A new structure surrounds the first quadrangle, providing accessible, covered links for students and visitors between the porters' office, dining hall, café and classroom stairs. Future specialist classroom blocks and sports spaces are proposed.

C: King's College School
A: EP, RK, TL, SN, JM, TR, SO
Dates: 2011

Hotel Suvretta House, St Moritz

We jointly won an invited competition for a masterplan to develop the Suvretta House estate in St Moritz with the Swiss practice Diener & Diener. It was a formidably good list of architects competing for the commission. The hotel, still in the founders' family ownership, was completed in 1912 and remains one of the most exclusive resorts in the world today, and the only hotel in the Engadine valley with its own access to the mountain slopes. The brief included the provision of a group of suites to be set in the beautiful wooded landscape; a new spa; arrival arrangement and a separate sports hotel, and a ski and mountaineering school. The process of permissions was achieved after lengthy consultations with the Canton and particularly sensitive neighbours. We hope that our vision will proceed to implementation.

C: Candrian Catering & Hotel Suvretta House
Joint architect with EPA: Diener & Diener Architekten, Basel
Planning Consultant: Planpartner AG
LA: Latz + Partner
A: EP, RK, LH, PC, ARM, BL, SF, AM, GH
Date: 2007–ongoing

Staff List

The order of initials reflects design responsibility; * marks project team leader. Where this was passed on between design (1) and construction (2) the * is followed by the respective figure.

References for Design Team:

C	Client
PM	Project Manager
SE	Structural Engineer
M&E	Mechanical Engineering Consultants
QS	Quantity Surveyor
LA	Landscape Architect
A	EPA Architects

EP Eric Parry

BA Hons (Newcastle),
MA (Cantab), MA (RCA), AADipl,
Hon DA (Bath), RIBA, RA
founded practice in 1983

RK Robert Kennett

MA (Cantab), DipArch (Cantab), RIBA
worked at EPA from 1989 to the present
appointed director in 1997

NJ Nick Jackson

BA Hons (Cantab), MA (Cantab),
DipArch (Cantab), RIBA
worked at EPA from 1990 to the present
appointed director in 1997

JO Julian Ogiwara

BA Hons (UEL), DipArch (UEL), RIBA
worked at EPA from 2000 to the present
appointed associate in 2007
appointed director in 2010

JS Justin Sayer

BA (Oxon), BSc (East London),
DipArch (UCL, DBA), RIBA
worked at EPA from 1996 to the present
appointed associate in 2003
appointed associate director in 2007

MC Merit Claussen

Textile designer, Architect RIBA
worked at EPA from 1999 to the present
appointed associate in 2007
appointed associate director in 2010

TL Tim Lynch

BA Hons (Newcastle),
DipArch (Mackintosh), RIBA
worked at EPA from 2004 to the present
appointed associate in 2007
appointed associate director in 2010

LH Lee Higson

BA Hons (Leeds),
DipArch (London Met), RIBA
worked at EPA from 2006 to the present
appointed associate in 2007
appointed associate director in 2010

RB Roz Barr

BA Hons, MA Design,
DipArch (UCL), RIBA
worked at EPA from 2000 to 2009
appointed associate in 2003
appointed associate director in 2007

CB Christopher Burton

MA Hons (Mackintosh),
DipArch (Mackintosh), ARB
worked at EPA from 2004 to the present
appointed associate in 2010

RC Ros Cohen

BA Hons (Cantab), MA (Cantab),
DipArch (UEL), Architect ARB
worked at EPA from 1998 to 2001
and 2003 to the present
appointed associate in 2010

RD Robert Dawson

BA Hons (Birmingham),
DipArch (Oxford Brookes), ARB
worked at EPA from 2006 to the present
appointed associate in 2010

CH Christine Humphreys

BSc distinction (McGill), BSc (Arch) (McGill),
PostGradDip Painting (CSSD), RIBA
worked at EPA from 2006 to the present
appointed associate in 2008

NL Nigel Lea

BA Hons, DipArch (Edinburgh)
worked at EPA from 1999 to 2007
appointed associate in 2003

LN Lisa Ngan

MA Hons (Edinburgh),
Dip Arch (Edinburgh), RIBA
worked at EPA from 1999 to 2010
appointed associate in 2003

TP Tanya Parkin

BSc Hons (QUB),
DipArch DipBRS (OBU), RIBA
worked at EPA from 2001 to the present
appointed associate in 2006

CT Claudia Tschunko

Dip.Ing.-Arch. (Stuttgart), Architect ARB
worked at EPA from 2007 to the present
appointed associate in 2010

Architects

AVO Alvaro Valdivia a l'Onions
ARM Anil Mistry
AM Aya Maeda
BB Ben Burley
BH Ben Hassell
BL Brenda Leonard
BD Brendan Durkin
CK Catharin Knuth
CLK Cecilie Kjeldsen
CH Christine Humphreys
CB Christopher Burton
CD Christopher Daniel
CT Claudia Tschunko
CPR Crispin Ryde
DL Damien Lee
DM Denitza Moreau
DC Douglas Carson
EH Eimear Hanratty
EF Eliot Foy
EP Eric Parry
ER Eva Ravnborg
FE Felipe Errazuriz
FP Freddie Phillipson
GH Gert Halbgebauer
GC Gonzalo Coello de Portugal
GSG Gordon Sung
GP Guy Parkinson
HA Hayley Anderson
JD James Davies
JPO Janna Posiadly
JE Jeff Essen
JF Jeremy Foster
JIS Jiehwoo Seung
JH Joanne Hemmings
JW John Weir
JSC Jonathan Schoening
JM Joseph McKay
JO Julian Ogiwara
JAS Julie Stewart
JDV Juliet Davis
JS Justin Sayer
KS Krystin Schwendel
LV Lan Van
LH Lee Higson
LB Lewis Benmore
LME Lina Meister
LN Lisa Ngan
LZ Lydia Zhou
LAF Lyn Ang Ferrari
MR Martin Reynolds
MC Merit Claussen
MA Mohammed Ageli
NA Nan Atichatpong
NM Neil Matthews
NH Nicholas Hornig
NJ Nick Jackson
NL Nigel Lea
OW Owen Watson
PBA Paul Barke-Asuni
PC Phil Clarke
RC Ros Cohen
RB Roz Barr
RD Robert Dawson
RK Robert Kennett
RLL Roo Lam Lau
SE Sarah Ellner
SO Sarah Oxley
SN Shabnam Noor
SBU Simon Buss
SF Sofia Ferreira
SM Susanna Miller
TP Tanya Parkin
TSD Tao Sule-DuFour
TR Thomas Roberts
TW Thomas Windley
TO Thorsten Overberg
TL Tim Lynch
VR Vania Ramos
WA William Aitken
YK Yamaç Korfali
ZF Ze'ev Feigis

Non-architectural staff

Anthony McGoldrick
Catherine Harrington
Chloé Robinson
Clare O'Regan
Elaine Labram
Emma Tracey
Gabriella Gullberg
Jake Bailey
Jacqui Barhouch
Jin Georgiou
Jonathan McCall
Julia Wedegaertner
Karen Cheung
Kira Aujila
Rachel Harding
Rebecca Megson
Rolandas Simkevicius
Sarah Benson
Sergio Garcia
Simon Hessler

Photo Credits

Cover: HB (detail)

4. JH

Introduction

9. ES
10. HB
13. MCR
14. TS
16. AP / WD
19. TS
23. EPA

St Martin-in-the-Fields

28. TS
32. TS (above)
32. GS (below)
33. TS
34. TS (left)
34. TS (right)
35. TS
36. TS
37. TS
38. GS
39. GS (left)
39. GS (right)
40. BLX
41. TS
42. TS (left)
43. MD

Savile Row

44. TS
47. Smoothe (left)
47. Smoothe (right)
49. AP / WD
52. TS
54. EPA (left)
54. EPA (right)
55. TS
56. TS
57. TS
58. TS (left)
58. TS (right)
59. TS

New Bond Street

60. TS
63. Smoothe (left)
63. Smoothe (right)
68. TS
70. EPA (top and middle)
70. GS (bottom)
71. TS
73. TS
74. TS (left)
74. PTC (right)
75. TS

Belgravia Residence

76. ES
81. AP / AI
83. ES
84. DL
85. ES
87. ES
88. DL
89. DL

Timothy Taylor Gallery

90. NK
92. EPA
93. NK
96. NK (left)
96. NK (right)
97. NK

Four Seasons Hotel Spa

98. ES
101. ES
103. ES
104. EPA (left)
104. ES (right)
105. ES
107. ES (left)
107. ES (right)
108. ES
110. ES (left)
110. ES (right)
111. ES

Threadneedle Street

112. TS
115. AP (left and right) / KD
116. TS
117. TS
122. TS
123. TS
124. TS (left and right)
125. TS
126. TS
127. TS

Holburne Museum

128. TS
131. HB
134. Trustees of the British Museum
138. GS (left)
138. GS (right)
139. GS
141. PR
142. PJS
143. CC
144. PR
145. PR
147. GS (top, middle and bottom left)
147. HB (right)
148. HB (left)
148. TS (right)
149. HB

Iringan Hijau

150. GS
152. NJ
153. GS
157. GS
159. GS
160. GS
161. GS
162. GS
163. GS

Palladio Exhibition

164. NK / SBM
168. NK / SBM
169. NK / SBM
170. NK / SBM
171. NK / SBM

Sebastian + Barquet

172. NK
175. NK
176. EPA
178. NK
179. NK

Eric Parry Design

180. XY
182. EPA (left and right)
183. XY (left and right)
184. NK (left and above)
185. NK
186. XY (left and right)
187. DL (left)
187. FC (right)
188. ES
189. EPA
190. EPA (above and below)
191. EPA

One Eagle Place

195. Smoothe
203. EPA

Back cover: Lisson Gallery

Photographers

Andrew Putler	AP
Benedict Luxmoore	BLX
Dirk Lindner	DL
Chris Cardwell	CC
Edmund Sumner	ES
Eric Parry Architects	EPA
Grant Smith	GS
Ferdy Carabott / izé	FC
Hélène Binet	HB
Jason Hawkes	JH
Mark Craemer	MCR
Mike Doherty	MD
Nick Jackson	NJ
Nick Kane	NK
Paul Riddle	PR
Peter Cook	PTC
Peter J. Stone	PJS
Timothy Soar	TS
Xavier Young	XY (for Gavin Ambrose)

Modelmakers

Andrew Ingham	AI
Kandor	KD
sbmodelmakers	SBM
Weird Dimensions	WD

Acknowledgements

Volume 3 opens with the completion of St Martin-in-the-Fields in 2008, which like the Holburne Museum took close to a decade from beginning to end. It closes with the promise of One Eagle Place in Piccadilly and the image of the polychromatic ceramic sections of Richard Deacon's cornice at a dry-lay in Darwen, Lancashire.

I am delighted that Edwin Heathcote accepted the offer of writing the critical text placing our work in a broader framework. As the *Financial Times* architectural correspondent and a prolific writer, he has that perspective. His introductory essay is an excellent reflection on our period of massive change to the social and physical make-up of London.

Our debt to Dalibor Vesely is great. He has written the introductory essay which situates the city beyond its purely physical manifestation. His inspirational thinking about the European city over a period of more than 40 years has been a cornerstone of our practice.

I have not previously expressed enough gratitude for the photographers' art, particularly Hélène Binet and Tim Soar. Nick Kane and Edmund Sumner have contributed fine images for some of the more intimate projects. Grant Smith has formed a very special photographic record for us of the progress of construction—so easily lost after the event.

I am particularly grateful for the dedication and patience that José de Paiva has contributed to the coordination of this volume, drawing together a multitude of fragments both of memory and physical matter.

Many members of the office have given time to the ordering of the specifications and drawings. Aya Maeda, Sarah Oxley, Jiehwoo Seung for projects; Tao Sule-DuFour for the plans of urban change—and there are others. Graham Bizley created the projective drawings of the construction of façades to understand better their layering. I am grateful to Emma Tracey for her archival care and contribution, and to Gabriella Gullberg, who was involved in the early stages of the endeavour.

Graphic design has been a shared endeavour between José de Paiva and Sergio Garcia and Russell Watson in our office, and particularly Laura Varžgalytė at Artifice.

The greatest privilege in the process of design and making architecture is the breadth of social engagement that flows from beginning to end. Each project carries many epic individual contributions and for example to see the master-mason Andre Vrona's gnarled hands stroking his by-now worn masonry at London Bridge or to share the pleasure of the craftsmen's skill in making the ceramic sections and the layered glazes for New Bond Street is a celebration of the complexity and teamwork that is needed to bring an idea to fruition. Likewise the act of opening a building is a reminder that architecture is a form of offering—a gift that is a cornerstone of community. Peter Blake's giant ribbon-cutting at the return of the remodelled Holburne Museum; the remarkable act of consecration of the renewed project at St Martin-in-the-Fields or the quiet decorum greeting the first guest to the rooftop Spa at the Four Seasons Hotel are all a part of a broader ritual of renewal in which we play a part amongst casts of hundreds.

Artifice Press Limited
298 Regents Park Road
London N3 2SZ

t. +44 (0) 20 8371 4000
office@artificeonline.com
www.artificeonline.com

First published in Great Britain in 2015.

2

All views expressed within this publication remain the authors' own and do not necessarily reflect those of the publisher.

Designed by Laura Varžgalytė.

British Library Cataloguing-in-Publication Data.
A CIP record for this book is available from the British Library.

ISBN 978 1 908967 03 9

Artifice Press is an environmentally responsible company. *Eric Parry Architects Volume 3* is printed on sustainably sourced paper.

Printed in Italy by Faenza Printing Industries S.p.A.

Artifice